Christian Mystery in the Secular Age

The Foundation and Task of Theology

Christian Mystery in the Secular Age

The Foundation and Task of Theology

By
John Thornhill, S.M.

Christian Classics, Inc.
Post Office Box 30
Westminster, Maryland 21157
1991

FIRST PUBLISHED 1991
© 1991 BY JOHN THORNHILL, S.M.

ISBN: 0 87061 182 8
LIBRARY OF CONGRESS CARD CATALOG NO.: 91-72128

PRINTED IN THE USA

To My Sister, Rita

Contents

FOREWORD

The purpose of this book is to introduce the intelligent believer to the vast and complex world of theology.

If theology is the interpretation of faith's response, made within the cultural framework available to the believer, it follows that every believer is, in some fashion, a theologian. No doubt most intelligent Christians recognize this. Unfortunately, they are often denied access to the basic resources they need by the fact that the specialized discussions of theological scholars take much for granted that the ordinary person needs to have explained. This text aims to explain these foundations, and in doing so to make the reader aware of the immense scope of theological inquiry.

Contemporary secularization provides our starting point. This context, it will be argued, should be seen in a positive light. It helps to clarify the nature of faith itself, and to uncover some of the ambiguities under which it has labored.

If theology is an interpretation of the response of faith to what God has done for the world in Christ, its essential characteristics, as we shall explain, are related to the nature of faith as a human response.

The pluralism of contemporary theology is one of its most baffling aspects. The great variety of approaches which are to be found in Christian theology down through the ages, and especially today, are not evidence of confusion, it will be argued, but may be interpreted as an expression of the endless richness of Christian truth. As existential concern has shifted its focus, the message of faith has spoken with a new realism to different moments of human awareness. The reader will be introduced to the history of theological endeavor, through the examination of selected texts of famous theologians and the approaches they have adopted.

PART ONE

Situating Christian Faith Today

CHAPTER ONE

Contemporary Secularization

The present work aims to introduce the reader to the world of theological inquiry. Christian theology is an interpretation of faith in God as he is revealed in Jesus Christ: faith rendering an account of itself in various human and cultural contexts. Our inquiry bases itself, therefore, as we shall see, upon the assumption that the essential characteristics of a wholesome theology are related to the nature of faith itself.

Contemporary believers within the Western tradition make the response of faith within a cultural context which is without historical precedent. From the dawn of history until our own era, religion (the lived expression of relationship to the divine through worship and service) has been taken for granted as absolutely basic to human existence and to the world-building processes of the cultural traditions which have united human communities. Historian Christopher Dawson describes the all-embracing consequences this assumption has had until the recent past:

> Religion is the key of history. We cannot understand the inner form of a society unless we understand its religion. We cannot understand its cultural achievements unless we understand the religious beliefs behind them. In all ages the first creative works of a culture are due to religious inspiration and dedicated to a religious end. The temples of the gods are the most enduring works of man. Religion stands at the threshold of all the great literatures of the

world. Philosophy is its offspring and is a child which
constantly returns to its parent.[1]

Today, however, there has emerged a cultural situation in which our contemporaries are no longer possessed by the assumption that the human project must be
grounded in a relationship with the divine. Even those
who unhesitatingly accept the truth of God's existence
are often perplexed as they seek to relate their life-project
in its day-to-day reality to the understanding of God they
have derived from institutionalized religion, and as a
consequence, institutionalized religion finds itself pushed
to the margin of life in the contemporary world. This cultural shift has come to be called secularization.[2]

It is clear that our approach to Christian faith and its
interpretation must be situated within this development.
Indeed, as we shall find, an understanding of this development can bring to light the ambiguities which have
sometimes been present in the religious response of
Christian believers.

The Emergence of the Sacralized Culture

The best way to achieve some understanding of contemporary secularization is to compare it with the situation which it has replaced. Prior to this contemporary
Western development, cultural projects, as we have said,
were grounded in the assumption that one could come to
terms with mundane reality in a satisfactory way only by
relating it to the transcendent "beyond" in which it ultimately has its being. Let us look more closely at the
function of religion in these cultures.

In the earliest human experience to which we have access, religious concern found expression through mythology and ritual. In its basic meaning, *myth* refers to an attempt, common to many cultures, to break out of the framework of time and history, to pierce the "beyond" and find the transcendent order which explains the enigmas of the human situation. Mythological lore found a practical expression in the rituals through which humans attempted to establish and maintain themselves within the divinely established order of things. The symbolism through which religious cultures have expressed themselves has been derived from the world of their experience. In fertile regions, such as the Mediterranean basin, for example, this symbolism was provided by the phenomenon of fertility; in the vast spaces of the continental interior, on the other hand, nomadic peoples looked to the sky for symbolism which could lead them to a meeting with the divine. It has been suggested that the gods of Greek mythology came, in the second millennium, B.C., from a fusion of the Nordic sky gods of invaders from the continental interior and the fertility gods of Mediterranean culture.[3]

Considering these developments, we may note two things which will prove significant in our later inquiry into the nature of secularization. In the first place, the interpretation they made of the human situation antedated philosophical reflection in the proper sense.[4] Secondly, these interpretations were the expression of an existential concern—that is, a concern for human well-being at the deepest level. Confronted by the limited and precarious nature of personal and mundane reality, these cultural traditions sought to satisfy humanity's deepest yearnings and needs by explaining this reality through reference to a sacred realm in which it was grounded. These two observations already point towards the conclusion that the reversal of this process—something essential to secularization—is to be explained, not through philosophical developments, but through cultural processes which are closer to the lives of ordinary men and women. In historical fact, philosophical developments are more often than not a reflection of cultural change rather than the causes of that change.

The Findings of Mircea Eliade

The findings of Mircea Eliade's immense study of religious institutions, in a vast range of cultures, and the symbols they have employed, allow us to fill in some of the details of this quest to establish a relationship between mundane reality and the divine beyond. *Hierophany* is the term used by Eliade to describe the mundane realities which are the symbolic vehicles of access to the divine transcendent.[5] Within a wide range of different religious traditions the same kinds of *hierophanies* emerge.

Sacred space is constituted when a particular location—a mountain height, a solemn grove, a place of worship—serves to give reality to all space by providing access to the divine order. Such sacred space holds at bay a "terror of chaos"; it is an expression of an "ontological thirst" to participate in the depths of being. In temples, religious cultures find a "centre of the world," a "source of absolute reality" which "ensures communication with the gods."[6]

Sacred time provides a similar hierophany. According to Eliade, there is "no warrant for interpreting periodic return to the sacred time of origin" described in the mythologies of these cultures as a rejection of the real world and an escape into dream and imagination. "On the contrary, it seems to us," he writes, "that, here again, we can discern the ontological obsession to which we have referred and which, moreover, can be considered an essential of the man of primitive and archaic societies." It implies a "return to the presence of the gods, to recover the strong, fresh, pure world that existed *in illo tempore*—that is, in the moment described by the mythologies."[7] In the judgment of Eliade, "myth is bound up with ontology; it speaks only of realities, of what really happened, of what was fully manifested."[8] Conforming to the pattern of the myths through the festival rituals is an imitation of the gods and brings authentic existence to those participating.[9]

In many of its aspects, nature provides a source of hierophanies for the religious culture. As a work of the gods, it is not chaos but cosmos, having a transparency which gives access to aspects of the sacred.[10] The sky gives rise to a powerful symbolism. So do life processes such as sexuality and fertility—a symbolism which is expressed in the mythologies of woman and the earth. Symbols such as mother earth, cosmic tree, the sun, the moon, the stars, water and animals of various kinds have a universality in widely separated religious cultures.[11] Eliade makes an observation concerning the sacredness of nature for religious cultural traditions which has implications for one seeking to understand the changing mores associated with the process of secularization. For those who have been formed in contemporary Western culture, sexuality and nutrition "are simply physiological acts"; for one nurtured in a sacralized culture, on the other hand, they serve as

> sacraments, ceremonies by means of which he communicated with the force which serves for Life itself.... This force and this life are simply expressions of ultimate reality, and such an elementary action...becomes a rite which will assist man to approach reality, to, as it were, wedge himself into *Being,* by setting himself free from merely automatic actions (without sense or meaning), from change, from the profane, from nothingness.[12]

For Eliade, therefore, the religious quest of the cultures we have been considering was not an effort to escape from the world of immediate experience into some alien sphere of make-believe, but an attempt to interpret the world of immediate experience in a manner which laid hold of its ultimate reality. It originated from and was animated by a most profound existential concern.[13]

Chenu's Interpretation

The French theologian M.-D. Chenu sums up the process which produced the situation described by Eliade:

> Religion as such emanates from man. Its aim is to satisfy the needs he experiences in his thought and in his actions, the full meaning of which he recognizes—although in a pre-reflexive way—by basing them on the lived acknowledgement of a divine Being. In referring them to God, he sacralizes these needs and hopes. For that reason, he surrounds them with "signs" and rites that withdraw these terrestrial realities from current usage, and also from the investigation of reason. These needs proliferate in great variety and differ according to time and place, person and environment. Among their manifestations various types can be distinguished which differ greatly in object as well as in the value of their sacralization.[14]

Chenu's summary recapitulates important elements which we have already come to appreciate through Eliade's analysis—the existential concern which motivates the religious project, its interpretative function, the symbolic currency through which it fulfills that interpretative function, and finally its pre-philosophical or "pre-reflexive" character, as existential concern seeks a wisdom which sheds light upon the enigma of human existence. Chenu also brings out the developmental aspect which is implicit in Eliade's descriptive findings. The religious cultures which emerge in particular traditions owe their essential features to human creativity, a creativity which has shaped the "lived acknowledgement of a divine Being" in such a way that it has been readily appropriated by those participating in the cultural tradition in question. In fact, a situation has been created in which it is impossible for individuals within that cultural tradition to share in its benefits without owning the interpretation of reality which is proposed. Chenu calls this process sacralization. Upon reflection, we may recognize that this process has been at work not only in so-called primitive cultures and archaic civilizations, but also within Christendom until the emergence of the secularization process in the present era.

The analysis which has just been made brings out, however, the ambiguities inherent in the process of sacralization. In the first place, those formed by a religious cultural tradition have often succumbed to the illusion that the symbolic hierophanies which their cultural development has brought into being are divinely established. Examples could be multiplied: the primitive is convinced that the spirits of the ancestors have called into being the annual cycles of festivity; the devotees of ancient Greek temples and their Hindu counterparts today have seen the ritual performed as laid down by the divinity; popular Christianity has invested sacred objects with more than a functional and representative value, and so forth.

Secondly, while membership in a sacralized religious tradition may give access to profound existential wisdom concerning the human situation, this wisdom, being pre-reflexive, is uncritical—indeed, as Chenu notes, it may well be strongly resistant to critical assessment.[15] In fact, it has often combined profound concerns and insights with what is distorted and grotesque, making it very vulnerable before the critical spirit of Western modernity.

Looking back, therefore, at the development of the cultural shift of secularization in the past century, and at its antecedents in the emergence of the spirit of modernity since the late Middle Ages, we may well judge that it was inevitable that some process of disillusionment should have taken place.

From Sacralization to Secularization

Today we are in a position to understand the disillusionment—if that is not too strong a term—which has taken place, and to assess its various aspects. August Comte's nineteenth-century attempt at such an assessment is well-known. Comte distinguished successive stages of human development: the first, a religious stage; the second, a philosophical or metaphysical stage; and the third, a scientific or technological stage. Those who are convinced of the enduring place of religion within the human project have often completely dismissed Comte's view. The Swiss Catholic theologian Hans Urs von Balthasar, however, has judged that it provides a valuable framework within which to understand the process of secularization.[16]

The world view typical of the first period, according to von Balthasar, "is characterized by a semi-religious relation of man to nature bearing magic, animistic and totemistic traits." In the second period—in which "the mind becomes conscious of itself in the great religions, and philosophy comes into existence"—although the naiveté of the first stage is essentially outgrown, its symbolism survives in subtle ways: "The cosmos will retain certain divine features, from classical Greece to the Areopagite, and down to the Renaissance and German classicism and romanticism." With the transition from the second to the third stage—from philosophy which considers nature to science which masters it—von Balthasar points out, a similar pattern of overlap may be observed:

> For in a period when the attitude to nature becomes increasingly technical we are neither able nor willing to give up the philosophical attitude to the world, though...the third, technical attitude is no longer compatible with the first, religio-magical one.

This development, von Balthasar notes, implies at once a gain and a loss: the simplicity with which the world was viewed gives way to a complicated, analytical view; the primary fact of nature is forgotten as things are made to "move in obedience to the call of the human mind"; as the intellectual project develops, "the whole world of animal instincts, by which sub-human life communicates with itself and its surroundings," is lost.

The consequences for sacralized cultures of the developments which von Balthasar has analyzed are not difficult to recognize. The principal characteristics of secularization emerge, it is clear, in Comte's third, or scientific, stage. The symbols which constituted powerful hierophanies in the first phase of cultural development become ineffective. As a consequence, von Balthasar notes,

> Modern man has had the frightful misfortune that God in nature has died for him. Where religion once flowered like a blooming meadow, there is nothing left now but only clay.[17]

If the immediate effect is devastating, von Balthasar judges that this may ultimately be assessed in positive terms: perhaps it had to come, "perhaps that religion was like the Pontine marshes that had to be drained."[18] He does not judge that those living within such a cultural situation are incapable of a religious world view and commitment. They will find, however, that the thought patterns and symbols inherited from previous ages no longer serve as they did. A new order of symbolism and self-expression must be found to replace that which has been undermined by the cultural developments which have taken place. In a not unrelated context, Paul Ricoeur has suggested that, in a "second naiveté," myth and symbol may well become a "dimension of modern thought" in the post-scientific era, if, losing their "explanatory pretensions," they reveal their "exploratory significance and its contribution to understanding."[19]

The German theologian Johannes B. Metz adopts a view very similar to that of von Balthasar. In evocative terms, he analyzes further the symbolic function assumed by a "divinized or numinized world" in religious traditions "up to the recent past."[20] To pre-scientific awareness, the totality of nature seemed absolutely superior to and larger than the human subject, unconquerable:

> This nature constantly rejected him and withdrew itself from him, as the ultimately untouchable, "vernal" mystery of his experience of the world. It was his "bosom" and "mother," in which he knew that he was held graciously, but also an "avenging goddess" who pursued him with her catastrophes and calmly destroyed what he had created. Thus the life of man in the world was dominated by the experience of a nature that, in the sovereignty of its reign, seemed to possess almost divine features. He saw himself as the image of this comprehensive cosmos of nature...as a "microcosm." It was ultimately also an excellent medium for his religious experience. Man's open ex-

posure to an uncontrollable nature gave to the face and processes of nature, in man's eyes, something of a tangible divine subjectivity.[21]

As Metz goes on to point out, this sacralized understanding of nature is inevitably modified in today's scientific age. Nature no longer seems to possess uncontrollable power and a "numinous radiance" through which God's presence and power seem to be refracted:

> Nature, formerly the one who embraced, has become the one who is attacked; it has lost its majesty and is becoming enslaved. Its laws are in our hands. We have, as it were, had a peep at its cards, and this has resulted in the disappearance of everything numinous...from our experience of the world.[22]

It will be recalled that we are considering secularization by way of prelude to a discussion of the Christian faith, which theology must interpret. Metz makes an observation which is important in this regard:

> This immediate divinity of the world, this religious, mystical veiling, the apotheosis of nature and a direct piety based on it, are not Christian but pagan.[23]

Once one has accepted this conclusion—and it seems beyond question—one is led to reflect critically upon the Christian past. Clearly, as Metz points out, the message of the gospel challenged Hellenistic understanding of this relationship between nature and the divinity, a view which was in grave danger of compromising the divine transcendence: "For the Greeks, the world had always had a numinous side; there was always a dark beginning of God himself; all their horizons merged into a twilight of the gods."[24] For them, God was a "world principle," a "cosmic reason and cosmic law," an "immanent regulating principle of the universe"—and, as a consequence, "the divine was itself an element of their picture of the world."[25]

But, closer to home—and this is in accord with the analysis of von Balthasar we have outlined—Metz judges that the sacralized view of nature played an important part in the life of the Christian community in later centuries:

> For a long time the classical view of the world persisted within the Western Christian world. Today it must be admitted that even the "classical" Middle Ages had a strong general quality of the pre-Christian world view about them, and were dominated by a straightforward "divinism" (Y. Congar).[26]

We may conclude with Metz that the cultural shift taking place in contemporary secularization challenges Christian believers to a more adequate appropriation of the essential significance of Christian faith.

We have spoken of the ambiguities arising from the process of sacralization. Metz puts his finger upon the most radical of these ambiguities: "This view never allowed the world to become wholly secular because it never let God become wholly divine."[27] On the one hand, because the transcendent was called upon to validate a meaning for the cosmos which allayed the human agent's existential fear of chaos, the divinity was compromised by being made to assume the form of a world-maintaining principle; on the other hand, the process of sacralization, interpreting nature as an immediate manifestation of the presence and power of God, invested it with a numinous radiance which prevented it from being appreciated for what it is in itself.

It was inevitable that such a view of mundane reality should come into conflict with the spirit of modernity, for it may be argued that the essential concern of modernity has been the vindication of the proper autonomy of the secular order. Tragically, the history of the emergence of modernity is, more often than not, a history of conflict with the Christian establishment, which saw the call for a proper autonomy for the secular order, to replace the sacralized culture of medieval Europe, as an attack upon essential Christian values.[28] We are now in a position to recognize that this was not the case: in fact, the Christian faith—which accepts as its basic principle that, through the incarnation, God has affirmed the inherent value of mundane reality—can acknowledge that "a genuinely Christian impulse is working itself out historically in this modern process of an increased secularization of the world."[29] Christian faith, as we shall see, is radically differentiated from the view of God which comes from the process of sacralization.[30]

An Existential Option
at the Heart of Western Culture

The cultural shift of secularization is one in which we all share. It touches the believer as well as the non-believer; it touches the man in the street as well as the philosopher and the academic. On April 8, 1966, *Time* magazine registered this fact with a cover theme: "Is God Dead?" Today, many feel dissatisfied with the traditionally accepted image of God. We can recognize that this image was shaped by the process of sacralization as much as by the message of the Christian gospel. It is not surprising that, as a consequence, some find it difficult to reach an understanding of God which has any relevance to their life project. Not a few of our contemporaries would argue that the very notion of God is inimical to the best interests of humanity, since it prevents people from assuming responsibility for the world and its future. In a small volume entitled *Honest to God,*[31] Anglican bishop and scripture scholar J.A.T. Robinson pondered these views sympathetically. Popular concerns were, once more, evidenced in the fact that this book became one of the most widely read religious books ever published.

Those who have studied the symptoms of the secularization process have concluded that this change in attitude is grounded in an *existential option* at the heart of contemporary Western culture. In the words of Jean Lacroix, "In the nineteenth century, atheism passed from an intellectual to an existential plane."[32] American theologian John Courtney Murray made a similar judgment as he concluded his study *The Problem of God*: "The problem of God today is not posited simply in the order of ideas and affirmation where the terms of the argument are essence and existence. Its plane of position is the historical-existential order."[33] If the process of sacralization had its origin in an existential concern which was basic to the culture of primitive humanity, the reversal of the process, through secularization, has had a similar motivation.

In retrospect, we may recognize that the nineteenth-century philosophers Karl Marx (†1883) and Friedrich Nietzsche (†1900) anticipated in a prophetic fashion the existential option towards which Western culture was moving. Dismissed by most in their own time as eccentric, their writings have been taken much more seriously in the twentieth century.

Nietzsche's Evangel of the Death of God

Against the background of the understanding which we have gained of what the secularization of our culture implies, Nietzsche's parable of the madman who appeared with a lantern in the marketplace looking for God shows how profoundly he had grasped the cultural shift which was taking place.[34] The parable describes a dramatic confrontation between the madman and the people in the marketplace. Because they no longer believe in God, they scoff at him and ask ironically where God could have gone to. "Where has God gone?" shouts the madman, turning on them. "I will tell you. We have slain him—you and I. We are his murderers." And he confronts them with the stupendous thing they have done in excluding any notion of God from their understanding of their world:

> But how did we do it? How could we drink up the sea? Who gave us the sponge to wipe out the whole horizon? What did we do when we unchained this earth from its sun?...Do we not now wander through an endless nothingness? Does empty space not breathe upon us? Is it not colder now? Is not night coming, and even more night? Must we not light lanterns at noon? God is dead. God stays dead. And we have slain him...

His hearers can only vaguely grasp the implications of his terrible proclamation, and they gaze at him in shocked silence. "I came too early," the madman declares. "It is not my time. The monstrous event is still on its way.... This deed is still further from men than the remotest stars—and yet they have done it."

The parable is made all the more poignant by the fact that its author—who clearly identified with the madman who came before his time—ended his days in an asylum for the insane. Nietzsche had diagnosed the essence of the problem emerging in Western culture: the God of the religious cultures of previous ages was dying, and this development called for a revolutionary transformation of the world view of the Western world. Pressing on, Nietzsche attempted to point out the way this transformation should be undertaken.[35] Schopenhauer's taking of "the godless existence" as a presupposition in the formulating of a life-philosophy for the new age pointed the way forward.[36] The coming philosopher, according to Nietzsche, must be

> a tripartite mixture of skeptic, critic and experimenter.... He must be prepared to take a radically new stance towards the world, himself and God. It is only through introducing a "dangerous perhaps" about the nature of things that the hold of God and a theistically grounded morality can be loosened and finally broken.[37]

As the parable of the death of God makes clear, Nietzsche recognized the terrible responsibilities which devolve upon the human agent, if—with the passing of sacralized cultures—the God who is the source of all norms and values is removed from our understanding of human existence. He confronted his contemporaries with the unsatisfactory nature of their situation: though they no longer accepted God, they failed to assume the responsibilities which this position thrust upon them. Anticipating the stance of today's atheistic existentialism, he saw concepts like law and value as no more than pragmatic tools employed by the will-to-power and aesthetic judgment of superior individuals, to establish meaning and purpose in the great sea of becoming in which humanity finds itself.[38]

The tragic flaw in Nietzsche's position lies, of course, in the fact that, as he seeks to define the existential option which must provide the basis of his *Lebensphilosophie,* he fails to consider the possibility that, if one understanding of God—that produced by the process of sacralization—could not survive in our culture, it does not follow that other understandings are not possible and necessary. The significance of Nietzsche in our present discussion, however, lies in the way in which he makes clear the existential option involved in the secularization process.

The "dangerous perhaps" contemplated by Nietzsche is like a two-edged sword. "Perhaps God does not exist!" If so, we find ourselves in a featureless, transient cosmos, devoid of all norms. Nietzsche cannot bear to live with this possibility; he must immediately set about overcoming such a chaos. We are in the presence of an existential fear of living in meaningless chaos similar to that which was at work, at an early stage of cultural development, in the process of sacralization. The cultural shift of secularization involves an existential option of this kind at the heart of Western culture as a whole.

Karl Marx's Rejection of God
in the Name of Human Responsibility

The work of Karl Marx helps us to understand more clearly the nature of this option. The sacralized view of the relationship between mundane reality and the divine had the disadvantage, as we have seen, that, on the one hand, it did not allow the world to become wholly secular, and, on the other, it did not allow God to be seen as having a divinity which truly transcended the world. Within a secular order which has claimed its proper autonomy, the question of human responsibility for that order becomes a paramount issue. Marx, like Nietzsche, perceived this. But if Nietzsche's suggestion as to how this responsibility is to be taken up came from an individualistic romanticism, the proposals of Marx were shaped by profound and original insights into sociological and historical reality.

The nature of Marx's atheism is open to discussion. His disengagement from commitment to a theistic position is far less traumatic than that of his colleague, Engels, and of Nietzsche after him, both of whom came from strongly religious backgrounds. For them this disengagement raised a painful personal issue; the family background of Marx, however, was not deeply religious. Marx's criticism of theistic ideologies which serve to validate class-interest were certainly not irrelevant to the sacralized understanding of social order which had prevailed in most cultural traditions. In an existential option similar to that which Nietzsche would make after him, Marx chose to see the assuming of full responsibility for human history as demanding the rejection of a theistic position in any form. Responsibility for history belongs, not to the God of class ideologies, but to human agents. For Marx, to opt for this latter position was to make one the enemy of the former.

The history of the twentieth century can leave no doubt that the option made by Marx anticipated a cultural mood which was to become widespread in our society. Those who, in the twentieth century, identified with Marx's interpretation of the human situation have changed the course of history. John Courtney Murray has summed up the program of the God-opposed cadre of Marx's Communist world revolution.[39] Its rejection of God is directed against the historical plight of humanity in the industrial age. If the God of traditional belief does not remove this evil, then the revolution must: "This is the purest and most passionate form of atheism, when man rejects God in the name of his own more God-like morality."[40] Though the outcome of the Marxist revolution makes this paradoxical, the Marxist is inspired by a vision of freedom. If humanity is responsible for the outcome of its history, "true freedom is the empowerment to alter nature, to transform man and society, to build a new world, to inaugurate a new history."[41] The idea of God as the all-powerful one is the ultimate enemy of freedom in the Marxist sense, because such a notion is the ultimate form of humanity's alienation, preventing us from owning our responsibility for history. If God is not, then the human agent is the *Pantokrator*.[42] Thus the Marxist sees the option for responsibility for history as involving an inevitable conflict with religion. From the Marxist point of view, religion cannot be considered a private affair: "Marx and his heirs...had the genius to see that religion, even in the form of private faith, is the most public of all public affairs,"[43] because upon it hinges our attitude to responsibility for human history.

The Marxist is convinced that "it is history, not God, that makes the nature of man."[44] It belongs to his Party, the focus of humanity's awakened responsibility for history, to lead the people into the promised land. The ideals of the Marxist revolutionary, Murray declares, make him "the *contrefaçon* of the Servant of Yahweh," who in the songs of the Isaian writings brings the Good News to the poor: "He is selfless...incorruptible by money or pleasure...committed to the asceticism of constant work...to hasten the consummation of the Revolution." If he seizes power, it is "only in order that he might thereby save the world." He will renounce this power and "even wills his own death" in order to bring the classless society into existence. "This event is invisible now, but he confidently sees it coming."[45] Concluding this description, Murray remarks that he has deliberately struck "a somewhat mystical note." He judges "that the God-opposed man of the Revolution is not fully understood unless the note of his mysticism is heard."[46]

The tragedy of contemporary Marxism and the immense impact it has had on the twentieth century lies in the fact that, while he had a valid criticism to make of the shortcomings of a sacralized social order,[47] Marx failed, like Nietzsche after him, to recognize that the passing of the sacralized understanding of God is not the discrediting of *all* understanding of God. Marx and his followers failed to contemplate the possibility that a more adequate understanding of the relationship between mundane reality and its creator may, in fact, call the human agent to a complete identification with Marxism's legitimate concerns.

In making this comment, we should recall that, in the judgment of the Second Vatican Council, believers must bear a large part of the blame for this inability of many of their contemporaries to recognize "the authentic face of God and religion."[48]

But there is another important lesson to be derived from the impact the revolutionary movement inspired by Marx has had upon the twentieth century. That impact must be attributed to the fact that it spoke to the deepest existential concerns of contemporary Western culture, filling the void left by the passing of the God of sacralization. For those whom it won to its cause, by closing off any outlet for these concerns in a meeting with the transcendent, it turned existential anguish into an explosive force which may still be far from spent. The fascination Marxism has had for the youthful idealism of countless young people throughout the world in the mid-twentieth century can help us to understand where the existential concerns of the contemporary world are to be found. Those who interpret the message of Christian faith in our times must show how this message speaks to these concerns.

Secularization and Concern for the Transcendent

It is not surprising that some observers of the cultural shift which we are considering have been tempted to conclude that through it humanity will outgrow religious concern. As historian Owen Chadwick has pointed out, secularization is "a subject infested with the doctrinaire."[49] E. Evans-Pritchard is extremely critical of the "theories put forward to account for primitive man's beliefs and for the origin and development of religion." Not only was much of what was proposed not backed up by the facts already available, but it appeared "contrary to common sense" and could be explained only by the climate of thought prevailing at the time, "a curious mixture of positivism, evolutionism, and the remains of a sentimental religiosity."[50] Concentration upon primitive religions made it impossible, in Evans-Pritchard's judgment, for the essential features of religion to be made clear: "For as the advances of science and technology have rendered magic redundant, religion has persisted, and its social role has become ever more embracing."[51]

If it is understandable that some of the pioneers of the study of comparative religion were led by the emerging phenomenon of secularization to anticipate the disappearance of religion, contemporary sociology is led to judge that their predictions are not being verified.[52] The sociological research of Andrew Greeley leads him to conclude that "there is in man a need for the sacred, a need for the transcendent, a need for something beyond himself that gives meaning and significance to his life." He is careful to qualify his conclusion in accordance with the inductive methodology he employs as a sociologist:

> What we can say is that most...in most times of history have acted as though there was need for the sacred in their lives, and that when the sacred is taken away from them it tends to turn up in very odd places.[53]

New Symbols

If the symbols provided by an earlier world view no longer provide an access to the transcendent, new symbols and ways of access must be found. In this regard, both von Balthasar and Metz, whose studies we have cited, point to the implications of the central place the human person has assumed in the world view of contemporary Western culture. They draw the conclusion that tomorrow's theism will find access to God through a deepened understanding of the mystery of being human.

According to von Balthasar, we must find "the sacrament of the brother/sister." We will suffocate, he declares, if, in the everlasting meeting with other persons which makes up our daily life, we meet nothing but a self-contained human existence:

> The adventure of losing self will not be worthwhile if I do not meet God in my brother, if no breath of infinity stirs in this love, if I cannot love my brother with a love that comes from a higher source than my finite capacity of loving.[54]

Metz contrasts the *hominized world* with the *divinized world* it has replaced. An authentic involvement in this world can prove a frontier experience which impels us to acknowledge that we will never fulfill our aspirations if we remain locked within the confines of mundane reality. He judges that such an experience may well constitute "the future of a genuine Christian experience of faith."[55] The experience of involvement in human history through the actualization of our freedom—something peculiarly new to contemporary humanity—may, Metz suggests, bring a similar realization. With this perspective, transcendence

> is what is still to come in history; it is the future of man. God is no longer merely "above" history, he is himself "in" it, in that he is constantly "in front of it" as its free, uncontrolled future.[56]

Berger's Signals of Transcendence

Taking up the issue in more concrete terms, sociologist Peter Berger points to the "prototypical human gestures" within human experience which constitute "signals of transcendence" for our contemporary culture.[57] The first of these which he discusses takes us back to an issue which has emerged more than once in our discussion: our propensity for order, which refuses to understand reality as chaotic, but sees it as constituted in a way which derives "from a divine order that supports and justifies all human attempts at ordering."[58]

Berger suggests that the play which takes us to the frontiers of our limited existence is another signal of transcendence. The human activity which we call play is "found in just about every sector of human culture." Essentially ordered towards joy, play is a breaking out of the confines of the mundane world of human seriousness, whether it is "the third round, the fourth act, the *allegro* movement, or the second kiss."[59] It has a profound kinship with religion, which it looks to as its "final vindication."[60]

Humanity's unconquerable hope for the future, through which we "overcome difficulties of the here and now," however daunting they may be, constitutes for Berger another signal of transcendence.[61] Like Metz, Berger points in this context to the work of Ernst Bloch, who—within a Marxist context—has led reflection upon this dimension of human existence in our time:

> In a world where man is surrounded by death on all sides, he continues to be a being who says "No!" to death—and through this "No!" is brought to faith in another world, the reality of which would validate his life as something other than illusion.[62]

Experiences of injustice awaken a similar response, demanding a justice which transcends the here and now. Within the context of our historical world, "our sense of what is humanly permissible is so fundamentally outraged" by what we see to be taking place that we refuse to accept that both offense and offender will not be called to account in a reckoning "of supernatural dimensions."[63]

Finally, Berger points to the humor which is essential to the life of every human community, in which our attention is directed to the

> one fundamental discrepancy from which other comic discrepancies are derived—the discrepancy between man and the universe.... The comic reflects the imprisonment of the human spirit in the world.[64]

Berger declares:

> By laughing at the imprisonment of the human spirit, humor implies that the imprisonment is not final but will be overcome.... Humor, like childhood and play, can be seen as an ultimately religious vindication of joy.[65]

Les Murray on the Sub-Theological Themes Present in Australian Culture

There are many points of contact between Berger's comments and the intuitive wisdom of poet Les Murray in his discussion of the place of religion in contemporary Australian culture, sometimes said to be one of the most secularized cultures in the world today.[66]

It is generally agreed, Murray notes, "that something like a religious dimension exists in every human being."[67] Though some in the Western world will still try to explain this away, their suggestions that something other than authentic religion—and indeed the religion inspired by Christian faith—can meet its needs are wearing thin:

> There is as yet no other vision abroad in our society which commands the same authority as ours does, the same sense of being the bottom line, the great reserve to be called on in times of real need.[68]

In comparison, Murray sees the themes of the political rallies which have been so influential in today's world as "necessary problem-solving stuff and little more." The "spiritual supermarket"—as Murray calls the dilettantism of the contemporary West's search for spiritual meaning—he sees as "fair-weather stuff, adjuncts to a prosperity which may now be vanishing." If "unbelief" once seemed "a daring and rather aristocratic gesture," today it no longer looks that way, nor serves as a form of rebellion and protest. The same may be said of "sexual indulgence, pornography, and the like." In a world of aging populations it will be difficult to sustain "the cult of unremitting youthfulness and physical beauty." Today, "liberal humanism" is fragmented by dissension, and its most dedicated followers "are often covertly uneasy at its lack of gentleness, its readiness to force the facts and its desolate this-worldliness"; they can offer no hope in the face of the "tragic complexity and strange intractability of the world"; "and often when people who subscribe to it relax for a moment, their eyes are seen to contain an almost desperate appeal: Prove us wrong, make us believe there is more to it than this, show us your God and that Grace you talk about." This situation contains a renewed challenge to those who are the bearers of the Good News of Christian faith:

> We are more widely judged on our own best terms than we think, and more insistently expected to be the keepers of the dimension of depth than we find comfortable.

Murray reflects upon some ways in which "Australians attempt to feed their concern for the transcendent, apart from the means of mediation offered by the Churches"—in other words, signals of transcendence—to be found in the midst of our secular culture and way of life. No doubt, readers from other cultural traditions will find parallels to these in their own situations. He points to the existential implication to be recognized in the *sacrifices* (he stresses the horrendous ambiguity of the concept) made in times of war and national crisis.[69] We have, he points out, created icons to which we give a reverence that implies a reaching out beyond the here and now: locations and sites, aboriginal things, etc. These give rise, he notes, to "anxious sub-theological debate."[70] Murray discusses the peculiar humor characteristic of Australians, a humor which gives rise to what he terms "clown-icons," derisive symbols which are "comparatively rare in other countries" and which display "far less fatigue and angry despair...less childishness" than derisive humor of other national traditions. This humor, which includes "traditions of working people's irony and fantastical peasant wit," relativizes the experience of life through an "ability to laugh at venerated things, and at awesome and deadly things."[71]

What Murray calls "the proletarian evolution" taking place in Australian culture, he sees as being comparable with the great revolutions of history and as having a capacity to provide a singular contribution to humanity in general, in its practical acceptance of the value of the person and its invitation to reflection upon the basis of that value.[72] Murray sees Australians as having a relationship to the land in which they live which has a remarkable potential for the generating of symbols open to a religious dimension. The fact that "nothing human has yet happened in Australia which stands out above the continent itself" means that our material surroundings inspire a peculiar sense of awe which we have just begun to explore. The strangeness of the land and its seasons, which it has taken so long to come to terms with, means that, "unlike North America," our story here cannot be "a vaster repeat performance of primeval Europe." He links this with one of his earlier themes:

> And it may be, in the end, that humour is the touchstone for the viability of any import here.... Australia really seems to be where God puts a sardonyx on the lips of Western man and teaches him to laugh wisely.[73]

Finally, Murray sees pre-theological stirrings in the spirit in which we participate in the mass ritual forms we share with our age: political rallies—for which, he notes, our spirit of proletarian evolution gives us a healthy distrust—and pop or rock concerts. These he interprets as animated by a ceremonial "secret," which promises release from the here and now through an

> exciting new perspective on things, which exalts...at least the fantasies of the lowly by substituting for their lonely imaginings something far more vivid and imminent, something they can take with them out into the dull world of bewilderment and dreary work, or deadly unemployment.[74]

Murray's intuitive wisdom and poetic gift make it possible for him to capture the pathos which from the beginning has attended humanity's religious project, and to contrast its limitations with the mystery of God's goodness which has broken into our world. The mass rituals of youth, the "fair-weather spiritual supermarket," and the fascination with the occult, "whose vogue has paralleled that of the rally very precisely," like the symbols of the sacralized cultures they have succeeded, can "only deliver what we think we want." As Murray astutely observes, such a project can never provide satisfactory sources of spiritual well-being, "since what humans imagine to be their salvation can't logically be anything greater than the human measure."[75] The transcendent mystery, however, towards which we are drawn, because it alone gives sense to our human existence, is by definition beyond all human measures.

Murray presses home his point: "'This world of appearances,' writes the Australian poet Robert Gray, 'is the Diamond.' True, perhaps—as a poet myself, I certainly think it is true—but it is not the Light." Neither our imagination nor our creative perception, nor the political commitment, the art, the drugs nor the other things to which we turn can provide a substitute for "the true otherness to which we are, as it were, keyed in the depth of our being." Without it, the human spirit knows a restlessness which can make it "capable of any enormity." It may change the world—but it remains the world:

> All you have done is to rearrange the pattern of joy and pain, bewilderment, disappointment and dominances. The hunger of the soul remains, even if we feed it on our very heart and mind and on the lives of millions of the innocent.[76]

Murray contrasts the pathos of humanity's religious quest and the tragedy of a suffocating world which has no access to the transcendent, with the gift of faith, making us alive to the mystery of God's goodness finding expression in our world in the life, cross and exaltation of Christ. If our religious project reaches out for what we think we want, God's Spirit

> gives us what we need, and doesn't necessarily heed our petitions. God may not even rescue us from cruel death when we implore Him to. Being God, He can see both sides of death, as we cannot.[77]

As Murray observes, this is not easy to bear, but it is the way which leads to life.

Thus our discussion confronts us with the radical novelty introduced into humanity's religious quest by Christian faith. We are ready, in the chapter which follows, to take up this question in which our whole understanding of the nature of theology must be grounded.

CHAPTER TWO

The Revolutionary Message of Judeo-Christian Faith

We concluded the previous chapter by pointing to the revolutionary nature of the Judeo-Christian faith when it is situated within the arena of humanity's religious strivings. The self-disclosure of God which culminated in the life, death and resurrection of Jesus of Nazareth has radically transformed the dialogic relationship between humanity and God. In humanity's religious quest, the medium which had given access to the transcendent had been provided by nature (the symbolic potentialities of the cosmos, the yearnings of the human heart); now the medium is a history in which God is recognized to be active among his people. This revolutionary development points the way beyond the ambiguities inherent in the religious project, and the distortions to which it has so easily succumbed. The nature of faith will be clarified if we consider in more detail the way in which these ambiguities are overcome.

The Impact of Christian Faith on Humanity's Dialogical Relationship with God

In the previous chapter we cited Chenu's description of the movement essential to religion—whereby it emanates from humanity and strives to meet humanity's deepest existential needs by setting them within a lived acknowledgement of the divinity through the process of sacralization. "Whatever it is," Chenu continues, "this religion springs from the nature of man—from his instincts, whether reasonable or not, and from his aspirations, whether consistent or not."[1]

In the continuation of this passage, Chenu describes the essential difference between this movement and that essential to Christian faith:

> *Faith,* as such, proceeds in exactly the opposite way. Considered phenomenologically, the act of the believer has a totally different inspiration from the religious act just described.... Faith is not the action of a man ascending toward the Divine. It is the act of response to and of communion with a personal God, who on his own initiative enters into conversation with men and establishes a communion in love. In accord with the logic of love, this God enters into the life of the "other" and makes himself man in order to bring this act to its full reality.... All this may seem to the unbeliever nothing but myth and illusion, but it is the very object of faith and governs its design and structure. In faith we are dealing with an event. We are no longer in nature but in history.[2]

As Chenu points out, we approach this question in the midst of a cultural experience in which cosmic reality is being desacralized: nature can no longer provide a symbolic access to the transcendent in the way in which it did in the past. This cultural development calls for the recognition that the new locus in which religions must find the sacred is the human person and the stories and history which give expression to human existence. From the vantage point we have in history—situated in the midst of the cultural shift of secularization—we are in a position to recognize more clearly the profound harmony which exists between our deepest human needs and the manner of God's dealings with us: it is in a sacred history that God's ways have been expressed for us.

A History as the Locus of the Sacred

In the next chapter, we shall consider more fully the questions raised by the claim that the truth of faith finds expression through a history. In the present chapter, we must make clear the nature of this claim—a claim which concerns, as Chenu has pointed out, "the very object of faith" and "governs its design and structure." This is the unprecedented novelty which the Judeo-Christian tradition introduces into humanity's religious quest.

The Jewish scholar Robert Alter notes the peculiar genius of the faith tradition of the Old Testament as it is reflected in the biblical record.[3] It contrasted with the approach of contemporary religious traditions in their sacralized interpretation of the human situation.[4] These interpretations turned away from the overwhelming enigma confronting anyone who seeks to understand the significance of human history, to the cyclical paradigms of mythology. The Hebrew imagination, on the other hand, was captured by the working out of God's purpose in history; it was therefore vitally interested in "the concrete and differential character of historical events."[5] If fiction and other imaginative literary forms are incorporated into the biblical literature,[6] these elements are completely subordinated to the purpose which gives it unity: "The ancient Hebrew writers...seek through the process of narrative realization to reveal the enactment of God's purposes in historical events."[7] Of its nature, a commitment to the history of free, human agents in its concrete, differentiated reality leads this literature to register two dialectical tensions: one "between the divine plan and the disorderly character of actual historical events," the other "between God's will, His providential guidance, and human freedom, the refractory nature of man."[8]

The Christian scholar G. von Rad underlines the originality of Old Testament faith in similar terms: "Cultures such as those of Egypt and Babylon knew no possibility of salvation but a return to primeval sacral orders which found expression in myth and the cycle of festivals."[9] Israel's faith, on the other hand, "emphasized the unique character of any events that had occurred" as contributing to the ongoing drama of their relationship with "the living God." As a consequence, von Rad notes:

> a survey of the great moments of her history gives us the impression of a lack of repose—the nation is always on pilgrimage—and the constant emergence of new religious ideas seems to leave her a stranger in time.

The great moments of her history were seen as points of departure, as "archetypes of mighty predictions"; the God who had entered into covenant with them was a God of promise, so that with the passing of time Israel "swelled Yahweh's promises to an infinity" and, "placing absolutely no limit on God's power yet to fulfill, she transmitted promises still unfulfilled to generations to come." The literature which is the record of their faith "can only be read as a book of ever increasing anticipation," a book "in which expectation keeps mounting up to vast proportions."

As von Rad goes on to comment, left to itself, the Old Testament becomes a baffling enigma because, if it has no sequel, its unbounded expectation "points straight into the void." For Christian faith, however, it does not stand alone. This faith acknowledges that, in what God has done for the world in Christ, the fulfillment of the former testament's infinite promise is realized. In him the two testaments have their unity as the self-disclosure of God in the events of human history.[10]

The novelty of God's revelation in the life, death and exaltation of Jesus of Nazareth is not the message of God's gracious love and his justifying mercy,[11] though these are certainly more clearly enunciated through the Christ-event. The real novelty of this message is to be found in the manner in which that generosity and love have been finally incarnated in human history: "We preach Christ crucified," Paul declares, "Christ the power of God and the wisdom of God. For the foolishness of God is wiser than men, and the weakness of God is stronger than men" (1 Cor. 1: 23-25).

The Christ-event reaches its supreme moment in the cross and its glorious aftermath. It is a disclosure of the depths of the divine mystery before which all human and religious wisdom is confounded and reduced to silence. In the words of the great Protestant theologian Jürgen Moltmann:

> Must one not abandon all that has been imagined, desired or feared in respect of "God" if one is to understand God...in the crucified Christ? Can one still understand the crucified Christ on the presupposition of a concept of God imported "from elsewhere"? On the contrary, must one not understand this "God and Father of Jesus Christ" completely in the light of what happened on the Cross?[12]

During his earthly ministry, the Saviour was not concerned to proclaim himself in the message he brought. His whole concern was the kingdom, the coming rule in love of the one whom he called "God and Father." As the New Testament proclamation developed, and it was recognized that Jesus was one with his Father in the glory of the divine name, the proclaimer became also the one proclaimed. Thus it was recognized that the essential purpose of the Christ-event was to lead creation into a meeting with the depths of the divine mystery: God's astounding "purpose which he set forth in Christ as a plan for the fulness of time" (Eph. 1: 9-10; cf. Rom. 16:25; Col. 1: 26-27). For those who would be genuine followers of Jesus, the ultimate reference of the gospel message must always be the divine mystery itself. The human existence of Christ is the revelation of this mystery, the living affirmation of God's purposes for humanity and for the whole of creation. Today we benefit greatly from a renewed awareness of the man Jesus and the trajectory of his life, long eclipsed by a dominant emphasis upon the Savior's divinity. This appreciation must find its proper balance by our recalling that Jesus' whole concern was to bring humankind to know the Father whose ways overturn our familiar world as he establishes his "kingdom."[13]

The truth of the gospel message, therefore, is the truth which is declared through the presence-in-history-for-us of the divine mystery. In the revelation to Moses of the divine name (Exod. 3: 1-5), the economy through which this truth is communicated is already established. It is this economy which shapes the whole covenant experience of Israel. John Courtney Murray describes the divine self-disclosure made through this economy as involving an "immanence in history," a "mode of absence," and a "mode of transparence."[14] It is as if God would reply to Moses' question thus:

Who am I? Human words can never express who I am; but *I will be with you.* And as you relate to my unspeakable mystery, through all the vicissitudes of our covenanted history, you will come to know me, as I give expression to my ways. In your uncertainty, you will know my unfailing fidelity; in your frailty and failure, you will know the holiness which makes it impossible for what is unworthy to share in the future I have in store for you; but you will also know my compassion, as my saving justice restores what is broken and lost, to bring forth what is worthy of my name; you will come to know the greatness of my plan—a plan which, in the end, will be the full expression of my wisdom and love, throughout the whole of creation.

This dispensation is not abrogated in God's self-disclosure in Christ; rather, in Christ the divine transparence finds it ultimate expression. Those who look upon Christ's life and death "from a human point of view" (2 Cor. 5:16) will never recognize the divine self-disclosure it contains; this recognition belongs to those who know him in that faith which is the gift of the Spirit. Faith finds God in a personal attachment to the Saviour, the master who calls to discipleship, the Lord who shares all things with the Father in the Spirit.

The Gift of Faith

In itself, knowledge is an overwhelming mystery. It involves the subject's capacity to transcend the limits of differentiated existence, to enter into the existence of the other *as other,* so that, according to the Aristotelian aphorism, "The mind becomes all things." The faith of which we have been speaking, however, is an infinitely greater mystery. Indeed, the great theologians of Christian tradition have seen faith as measured by the greatness of the divine mystery itself.[15] Through this gift, we become alive to the active presence of the living God in the events of our history: "No one has ever seen God; the only Son, who is in the bosom of the Father, he has made him known" (Jn. 1:18). Through the presence of God's spirit, we are touched by the depths of the divine life itself:

> God has revealed to us through the Spirit. For the Spirit searches everything, even the depths of God. For what person knows a man's thoughts except the spirit of the man which is in him? So also no one comprehends the thoughts of God except the Spirit of God (1 Cor. 2: 10-11).

The gospel recollections of Jesus recall him as laying great emphasis upon a faith which is open to recognizing and appropriating the first intimations of the kingdom. Walter Kasper sums up the meaning of this faith:

> Faith is open to something other, something new, something to come.... It is a description of the essence of faith to say: faith is participation in the omnipotence of God.... Faith is existence in receptivity and obedience.[16]

Lucien Cerfaux's description of the meaning of faith for Paul shows Paul completely attuned to the mind of the Saviour:

> An intervention of God and his Son is accessible to us.... The righteousness of God is the divine principle of the Christian order, and faith is the corresponding human attitude, which is in this sense the foundation of the new order.[17]

The economy established by Christian faith is far more in tune with the existential needs of ordinary men and women than the remote hierophanies created by the sacralization process. The sacralizing tendency so typical of the religious project set up firm boundaries between the sacred and the profane orders. In contrast, the Christian faith recognizes the ultimate hierophany as given in the secular reality of Jesus' life and shameful death "outside the gate" (Heb. 13: 12). The meaning which the process of sacralization has typically given to the distinction between the sacred and the profane is radically modified by the paradox whereby Christ "by his death demolished all mere worldliness."[18] The truth of Jesus Christ discloses and addresses the deepest dimensions of that existence which we share with all human beings as we know the same hopes and fears, and struggle with the same problems and challenges.[19]

Faith Overcomes the Ambiguities of Humanity's Religious Project

---

Our analysis of the process of sacralization has made clear the ambiguities and distortions to which it is prone. It is not surprising, therefore, that the truth of Christian faith calls for a resolution of these ambiguities and challenges these distortions. It follows that those to whom the revelation of this truth comes as a grace and a gift are called thereby to a prophetic mission: since the God who is revealed to them is the God of all peoples, they must proclaim the life-giving message of who-God-is to all the peoples of the world.

The No-Gods of the Pharaohs

Walter Brueggemann spells out in a very concrete fashion the way in which this challenge to the distortions of sacralization was brought to the consciousness of Israel.[20] According to the biblical record, the part played by Moses in the development of this prophetic awareness can scarcely be exaggerated: for Israel he was the "paradigmatic prophet."[21] In the thirteenth century, B.C., under the leadership of Moses, the faith of Israel was created, as it were, almost *ex nihilo*. A new social realism—an intersecting of the political and the theological—appeared which can be explained only as based upon what was essentially a revelation of God as acting in history. The *status quo* which this revolutionary realism confronted received its legitimation from mythological lore produced by the sacralization process. Its religion was one of a "static triumphalism," sanctioning the social world of the Pharaoh. Its political order was one of "oppression and exploitation." The "alternative religion of the freedom of God" exercised on behalf of his people in the Exodus, however, reduced the mythic pretensions of the Pharaoh's religion to nothing.[22] To follow the living God is to know that the gods of the Egyptians are no-gods, propping up the existing regime with their illusory authority; it is to enter into a new order of politics founded upon a justice and compassion which are learned from God.

Brueggemann's analysis leads to the valuable insight that the prophetic truth essential to Christian faith makes it clear that authentic religious and socio-historical issues cannot be separated. Those who neglect one or the other of these orders will move towards unacceptable positions: either towards a liberalism in which political activism neglects the authentic demands of a transcendent reference, or towards a conservatism which makes concern for the transcendent an alibi which absolves the religious person from accepting responsibility for political reality. In the end, each of these positions is unfaithful to the truth of the gospel.[23] Brueggemann concludes:

> The urging I make to those who would be prophets is that we not neglect to do our work about who God is and that we know our discernment of God is at the breaking points in human community.... Prophecy cannot be separated very long from doxology or it will either wither or become ideology.[24]

The Subtle Distortions Attendant upon Sacralization

Today we are in a position to recognize that the processes characteristic of religion as it establishes its institutional forms can compromise the gospel truth in many subtle ways. As Chenu observes, psychological, cultural, social and national contexts "provide it with a ground to grow in, but they also threaten to suffocate it."[25] Because these processes are "pre-reflexive," as Chenu says, "religion by itself is never clear about itself and its operations."[26] Not only can it lead to the neglect of responsibility for the world, which scandalized Marx and Nietzsche, but it can also produce an illusory validation of self-interest. Chenu writes:

> One can without injustice ascribe to it the deviations of superstition and magic, the ritualistic clear conscience, search for the marvellous, "absenteeism" from the world, and "alienation."[27]

Faced by this issue, Protestantism has undertaken a radical criticism of religion, so severe at times that it is in danger of leaving no place for authentic religious forms.[28] While some Catholic authors have recently taken up a position close to that adopted by Protestantism,[29] in general the Catholic tradition has given too little attention to the self-criticism the whole question calls for.[30] A balanced criticism must recognize that religious expression often degenerates into an inauthentic "religiosity."[31] According to Gregory Baum, Catholics have neglected to give sufficient attention to the "pathology" of religion to be found in the biblical literature.[32] This pathology, as Baum points out, identifies various kinds of inauthentic religiosity. Idolatry, in the broad New Testament sense of that word, is a self-interest which easily erodes the unconditional loyalty which belongs to God, and sets up in his place some other reality or institution. Superstition seeks an illusory protection in ritual forms. Religious practices, the scriptures warn, can become an occasion of hypocrisy and legalism when externals become an alibi from genuine responsibility and commitment; they can lead to blindness and hardness of heart when groups cling to flattering illusions and the privileges associated with the exercise of office.

The Christian faith does not call for the abolition of religion, but for the removal of its ambiguities.[33] The truth of Christian faith certainly gave rise to a movement in the direction of desacralization. It provided an unprecedented order of sacral concepts; as Schürmann observes, when it made use of traditional religious terms, these were transformed by the meaning they were now made to carry. They must give expression to aspects of the eschatological event achieved in Christ, now recognized as the source and measure of all that is authentic in religious ritual.[34] Moreover, in the contemporary world, Christian life should be governed by a principle of economy which is alive to the fact that "in our modern, technical, godless world considerable caution and restraint are required in the use of all symbols of the 'holy.' "[35]

Because theology is the interpretation of faith, we have begun our inquiry into the nature and forms of theology by seeking to clarify what faith is in itself. Reflection upon the secularization of contemporary Western culture has assisted towards this understanding. Not only does this development provide a challenging context for faith today, it also leads to a clearer understanding of the remarkable claims essential to Christian faith. Interpreting secularization as a reversal of the process of sacralization which has played such a large part in the development of the world's cultures, we have seen that this process is not inimical to Christian faith, for faith seeks access to the divine mystery, not through the symbolic sacralization of nature, but through the events of history. Indeed, faith revolutionizes the dialogical relationship between humanity and the divine mystery. Much will be further clarified concerning the full implications of this claim as we proceed in the chapters which follow to discuss the manner in which the characteristics of an authentic theology derive from the nature of faith itself.

PART TWO

From the Dimensions of Christian Faith
to the Principles of a Sound Theology

CHAPTER THREE

Coming to Terms with the Historical Character of the Christ-Event

Speaking of the revolution the Judeo-Christian faith has introduced into the religious quest, Chenu notes that faith deals, not with nature, but with "an event," an event which constitutes "the very object of faith and governs its design and structure."[1] In this and the following chapters, we propose to explore the implications of this principle, as we seek to clarify the principles which should animate a wholesome theology. If the various dimensions of the Christ-event "govern the design and structure" of faith itself, they also determine the nature and characteristics which should belong to theology if it is truly an interpretation of faith, "faith seeking understanding."[2] The present chapter takes up that aspect which has shown itself to be fundamental to faith: its essential reference to historical events.

An Order of Truth Which at First Seems Unfamiliar

God's self-disclosure—the essential concern of faith—is realized through the unfolding of the story of a people and, in particular, in the events with which that story comes to its climax: the life, death and resurrection of Jesus of Nazareth. In other words, the truth which we are called to accept in faith is a truth embodied in a history.

We shall not be able to appreciate the full implications of this statement if we do not go beyond the notion of truth inherited from the Greeks, a notion which has tended to dominate the awareness of Western culture for many centuries. According to this conception, truth is seen as an *idea*, an eternal concept or proposition, to be possessed by the mind. Although the Western tradition is strongly influenced by this way of conceiving truth, upon reflection we shall recognized that we are not unaware of another notion of truth: the truth of some remarkable gesture, the truth which is lived out in the witness of a heroic and dedicated life, the truth we want to live in the totality of our own lives.

In the address which Alexander Solzhenitsyn prepared at the time he received the Nobel Prize, he made reference to this order of truth. Recalling the classical metaphysical principle that beauty and truth are identified with being in its integrity, he pointed to the manner in which great literature expresses a truth which is to be found in the living reality of its own world: "The convincingness of a true work of art is completely irrefutable," he writes, "and it forces even an opposing heart to surrender." Portrayals which manipulate or force the truth, he notes, do not endure and end by convincing no one. But a true masterpiece

> bears within itself its own verification.... Those works of art which have scooped up the truth and presented it to us as a living force—they take hold of us, compel us, and nobody ever, not even in ages to come, will appear to refute them.[3]

The truth which concerns us in Christian faith is of this kind. The noted French biblical scholar Pierre Benoit sums up in simple terms the manner in which God has expressed his own truth in the history he has shared with his people, a history that is lived before it is told:

> Salvation according to the Bible is a goal of history, a history that God lives with men.... God establishes...Israel.... In order to build it up, his Spirit breathes everywhere, in minds, in hearts, in bodies. His inspiration guided the whole group, but singled out certain privileged individuals to lead the people. One of the fruits of this education of the People of God is the Holy Bible, which embodied the main points of divine teaching.... Before impelling to write, the Spirit impelled to speak; before impelling to speak, he impelled to act.[4]

The Greek notion of truth, isolating the abstract, objective dimension of the human encounter with reality— what Benoit calls its *dianoetic* dimension—pointed the way towards the project of scientific investigation so important and fruitful in the development of Western civilization. The more comprehensive Semitic notion found in the scriptures, however, is closer to ordinary life experience. This notion is concerned before all else with existential truth, and calls for a response from the whole person. It is a truth concerning human destiny, which is found, *known,* in and through involvement and commitment:

> For a Semite "knowing" is an activity involving his whole being. The way to God is through obedience and service rather than by contemplation. In the Bible, "hearing" is more important than "seeing," because perfection consists less in contemplating the mystery of the divine essence than in heeding the appeals of God's love.[5]

Walter Kasper brings to light important theological implications of this dynamic truth embodied in the history of God's people.[6] He points out, with Benoit, that it is a truth which vindicates itself by being lived. It is linked with the covenant promise and is grasped by whose who place their trust in that promise. Its possession involves at once a remembering of past events and an expectation of the promise they contain. The truth of God's "word," therefore, is not static; it involves a dynamic process in which each fulfillment embodies a further promise. Its ultimate dimension is eschatological; indeed, according to this truth, nothing less than the living God constitutes in reality the future of this people.

Of its nature, this truth calls for expression through a prophetic witness inspired by the Holy Spirit. It is the role of the prophet to articulate the appeals of God's love present in the great things he has done for his people. Through the prophet's leadership the people as a whole learn to heed God's call to a destiny for the sake of the whole world. In other words, because their history becomes the embodiment of the truth of God's saving ways, this people as a whole has a prophetic mission in the midst of all the peoples of the world among whom God's ways will finally be expressed.

Today, as the distinctive characteristics of the Greek and the Semitic notions of truth have come to be appreciated, it is customary to emphasize the contrast that exists between them. While this is appropriate and necessary, it is important to recognize that, when they are compared, they are not in opposition but have a complementary nature. Benoit sums up this complementarity as he describes the nature of biblical truth: this truth

> certainly comprises a "dianoetic" aspect insofar as it carries an "idea" that is directed to the intelligence. But it also includes, more than does the Greek *logos*, a dynamic aspect: it is power-laden. The Hebrew *dabar* signifies not

only "word" but also "thing," or, more exactly, the "background" *(hintergrund)* of a thing wherein resides its deepest meaning.[7]

Let us now consider some of the questions which the historical medium of the truth of faith has raised in contemporary theology.

A Challenging Question for Contemporary Theology

Having recognized the historical nature of the medium through which the truth of Christian faith is grasped, contemporary theology is confronted by a not inconsiderable problem. It is not a problem which is peculiar to theological inquiry. Indeed, in the words of the French scripture scholar Ignace de la Potterie, it is one which "dominates all modern thinking in our Western world."[8] The problem assumes a challenging form for the theologian, however. In the words of de la Potterie: "The cardinal question that the theologian must face is that of the connection between absolute truth and historical contingency in the economy of revelation and the history of salvation."[9] This same question, he notes, confronts scriptural scholarship as it seeks to express the relationship between the Jesus of history and the Christ of faith.[10]

Down through the ages, interpreters of Christian faith have not hesitated to attribute an absolute character to the Word of God and the truth it expresses. While this interpretation was made within the perspective of the Greek understanding of truth—as an eternal concept or proposition to be possessed by the mind—the problem did not come to light with full clarity. But when theology's interpretation of the truth of faith must acknowledge that it does not come to us in the form of "words from heaven" but as embodied in historical events, it faces a considerable difficulty.

Modern historiography has renounced any pretensions to being able to recover in any absolute fashion the facts of the past; all that it would claim to do is to make possible a dialogue between the contemporary observer's point of view and these facts as they are attested to by the evidence they have left in our world. This dialogue is as much shaped by the subjective values and preoccupations of the observer as it is by the reality of the persons and situations with which the observer is entering into dialogue.[11] This recognition may seem to demand the conclusion that theology's claim to be the interpreter of an absolute truth is unacceptable. A. Loisy adopted a position of this kind:

> Historical phenomena with their relativity and limitations are the *complete object* of a scientific and historical study. An analysis that would look only for the truth behind the phenomena, that is a sort of world to which the phenomenal representation is related, is definitely excluded and outdated.[12]

Walter Kasper's Approach to the Problem

Speaking as a theologian, Walter Kasper is of the view that "history is today our biggest problem."[13] As he wrestles with this problem, Kasper makes a number of points which may well serve to clarify its nature and point the way towards a satisfactory solution. Together with most contemporary Catholic theologians, he sees the truth possessed by faith to be found in the Christ-event itself: "God's relinquishing of himself into history in Jesus Christ."[14] If that truth is expressed in propositions, these are derived from the Christ-event and look to it as an ultimate norm to which they are absolutely subordinated.

Kasper emphasizes the radical nature of the change in outlook brought by historical consciousness.[15] On the one hand, ancient thought took for granted "the idea of a cosmos with eternal laws of being" in which the movement of history was seen as "accidental changes to a permanent substance.... History was a phenomenon within the framework of an encompassing order." On the other hand, Kasper points out, for modern thought,

> history is not a moment in an encompassing order; on the contrary, every moment is a moment within a history which the next moment makes relative. In this view reality does not have a history; it is itself history through and through.[16]

Clearly, in order to enter as completely as possible into the contemporary mindset, Kasper takes up a philosophical position with far-reaching implications. Has he sufficiently explored this position? One may well judge that he neglects some basic philosophical distinctions and, in doing so, makes more difficult the finding of a satisfactory solution.

Kasper identifies two false responses to the challenge.[17] There are some believers who respond by retreating into an "inner sphere of faith," dismissing historical issues as irrelevant to faith, and appealing to the Church's dogmas as an ultimate which does not have to be interpreted within the context of history. For others, the problem is met by interpreting the faith "existentially"—Kasper has in mind a position such as that adopted by Rudolf Bultmann—so that "the individual venture of faith" is an ultimate in itself, no longer dependent upon the content of specific historical events: the events of the life of Jesus do not possess, in this view, an enduring normative significance, but occasion a call to an existential decision. In both of these cases, as Kasper observes, history no longer has any meaning for faith, and because "the relation to history which constitutes the Christian faith is denied...the essence of Christian faith is called into question."[18]

The principles of modern historiography, Kasper judges, must contribute to the solution of the problem. While rejecting the "existential" solution just mentioned, he wishes to do justice to its "relative truth and legitimate concern."[19] He echoes the insights of modern historiography, as he points out that faith does not grasp the truth of revelation through a neutral

> assent to the truth of objective facts of salvation. God's action in history is never simply one fact among others; it cannot, like others, be neutrally observed and checked.[20]

If all historical judgment calls upon the subjective resources of the interpreter, faith's recognition of the significance of historical events comes through a subjective conversion which is a gift of God's Spirit:

> Only a person who is prepared in faith to break out of the world of the measurable and calculable, out of his comfortable and automatic habits, and entrust himself to the newness of the world of faith, can recognize God's salvation in history.[21]

Whatever the difficulties arising from the philosophical position he has adopted, Kasper is determined to affirm both objective and subjective dimensions in faith's grasp of the truth. He upholds "the objective character of salvation history." While maintaining that the "subjective historical aspect is of considerable importance...even crucial," he is concerned "to rebut the subjectivist tendencies" which would undermine revelation's objective content.[22]

We have already quoted an earlier work in which Kasper stressed the eschatological character of the truth possessed by faith, the truth of God in itself, the future of humankind. Kasper relates this theme to the problem we are discussing, stressing its implications concerning the provisional character of doctrinal statements during the Church's time of pilgrimage:

> As an eschatological phenomenon, the Church must again and again go beyond itself and enter afresh into its own future.... The Church does not possess the truth in any simple way, but must keep looking for it afresh...since just to say the same thing in different situations one has to say it differently each time.[23]

Kasper also introduces a dialogical dimension to the faith's grasp of the truth:

> In the single reality of Christianity we must...hold to two aspects: the word which is uttered in history and the answer that is uttered in history.[24]

This opens up a vast perspective which situates the Christian witness within the broader drama of humanity's religious strivings: the record of this historical dialogue provides "a standard by which to judge all other peoples"—for the same dialogue "takes place in principle wherever human beings trust themselves to the transcendence which opens to them in their freedom."

Models of the History-Truth Relationship

A valuable framework for critical reflection upon Kasper's position is provided by de la Potterie's survey of "the principal models of relationship between history and truth."[25] This scholar identifies three models which have emerged in the history of Western thought. The first conceives truth as "separated from history." He points to three varieties of this model. For the Platonic tradition, truth in the last analysis is "identical with the idea of the thing." Rationalism had much in common with the Platonic view: for it, purely rational knowledge grasps the truth when it is properly critical. Extrinsicism is the name given by de la Potterie to a view of the truth espoused by nineteenth-century theologians which derived from the prevailing climate of rationalism. To the rational truth championed by the latter, these theologians opposed "truth *divinely* revealed"; and, whereas previously truth has been spoken of by theologians in the singular, "nineteenth-century theology became increasingly accustomed to...speaking of *the truths* of faith; such a practice meant a risk of absolutizing in formulas the revelation of God in Jesus Christ."[26]

The second model described by de la Potterie conceives truth as "immersed in history." He points to two variants of this model. Historicism identifies truth with what is recoverable by strict historical method. Hegelianism, in its idealist form, conceives truth as reality's becoming through a growing awareness of the Idea, the absolute, which draws all of history into the process of its finding of itself.[27] In its pragmatic form, the Hegelianism of Karl Marx equiparates truth with *praxis*—that is, with social effectiveness produced in the course of history.[28]

The third model, which sees truth as "immanent in the human person," is that of existentialism. For this model, truth is found in the human person's existential response and commitment. It has two forms. An agnostic or atheistic form acknowledges no objective truth outside personal consciousness. Christian existentialism, on the other hand, while emphasizing existential consciousness as the locus, or place, where truth is to be found, understands this consciousness as involving a relation to God, and therefore admits the existence of an objective foundation of truth.

Against the background of the review he has made, de la Potterie's conclusions are very enlightening. He maintains that the Christian faith "uses the word 'truth' in a sense that is proper to itself"[29]—something which he judges needs to be more fully pondered by contemporary theology. This notion finds expression in the scriptures and has remained alive and operative in the Christian tradition. According to its central meaning, this truth focuses on God-as-revealed.[30] Comparing this understanding with the conceptions he has reviewed, de la Potterie finds that, while this Christian notion avoids their "partial approaches," it gathers the various aspects they emphasize into a synthesis: the truth of revelation is grounded in historical events, it registers the presence of the transcendent, it is in the process of self-disclosure, and it shows itself as addressing our deepest existential concerns. What has already been said concerning the truth of faith as a truth which is *lived* before it is *told,* and concerning the essential contribution of the resources of the inquirer to the outcome of a dialogue with the facts of the past, is of obvious importance in this holistic interpretation.

It is only the revelation-event itself which, as a normative point of reference, makes such an integration possible.[31] As revelation, Christian truth "takes place in history."[32] This acknowledgement avoids the narrowness of historicism because, while it conceives Christian revelation as having taken place in the events of history, it implies, on the other hand, a vertical dimension, "the presence and self-manifestation of [God's] mystery at the very heart of historical events."[33] In other words, the truth of revelation is achieved in an openness to the transcendent. This truth's reference to the events of history has a twofold aspect: it looks to the foundational event in Jesus of Nazareth, but its dominant reference is eschatological, looking forward to the final triumph of God's plan being realized in and through him.[34] Further, the notion of truth which Christian faith derives from the revelation-event complements its stress on the historicity of truth, its openness to the transcendent mystery of God and its eschatological orientation, with a recognition that this truth touches the believer at the existential level, being appropriated by being lived.[35]

The analysis he has made, de la Potterie concludes, has important lessons for contemporary theology:

> As compared with the Christian model, the other models make us think of an organic whole that has been reduced to fragments, of a shattered unity. On the other hand, it can hardly be denied that in modern theology the notion of truth has not preserved the synthetic character it had in scripture and early tradition. It has become overly conceptual and thus cut itself off from the history of salvation and from the lived faith of Christians.[36]

This review of the different ways in which truth and its relationship to history have been understood in our Western tradition helps us to appreciate more fully the approach taken by Kasper. He grounds the truth of faith in the historical events of salvation history, at the same time showing himself sensitive to the insights of modern historiography and its recognition that our interpretation of the events of the past necessarily involves the subjective qualities and concerns which the inquirer brings to the task. He develops this aspect in a way which draws on Christian existentialism's understanding of the function of the faith dimension in the believer's recollection of the events of the sacred history God has shared with a chosen people.

Concerned, however, to preserve the notion of truth which he is defining from being excessively conceptual, Kasper distrusts the notion of "a cosmos with eternal laws of being" and an understanding of history as involving "accidental changes to a permanent substance."[37] In taking this philosophical position, he perhaps runs the danger of not leaving sufficient basis for an openness to the presence of the transcendent. Does his stress upon the eschatological character of the truth of revelation succeed in upholding the absolute character of the truth of God accessible to us through Christian faith and proclaimed by the Church to successive ages? This is a question which we must consider further in a later chapter.

Conclusions

This chapter has raised a very challenging issue. As we conclude it, let us list the principal lessons it has for us concerning the theologian's task.

1. Today's theology must be grounded in the unambiguous acknowledgement that *the faith which it interprets finds in historical events—especially the Christ-event—the essential medium of God's self-disclosure.*

2. This acknowledgement calls for a clear taking of position with regard to the relationship between the absolute truth possessed by faith and human history. This taking of position will find *in revelation-as-truth a controlling principle* which makes possible an appreciation of the different perspectives which have been adopted in the history of Western thought, and a critical understanding of their complementary positions.

3. The truth with which faith is concerned has from the first had *an eschatological character:* it will be definitively possessed only in the fulfillment of the promise it constantly affirms. This eschatological reference, which was greatly obscured for many centuries in Christian thought, must be recognized as absolutely fundamental to the interpretation of faith, whatever may be theology's immediate area of concern.

4. Because the truth possessed by faith finds in revelation-as-truth its controlling norm, theology must recognize that *the truth which is its ultimate concern is the TRUTH ITSELF which God is:* God, who is the future towards which the saving history of humanity moves.

This important insight, which will be explored further in a later chapter, is inescapable once it is recognized that revelation cannot be an ultimate in itself. Of its nature, it exercises a mediating function.

CHAPTER FOUR

Probing the Full Incarnational Implications of the Christ-Event

The present chapter is concerned with the incarnational nature of the Christ-event[1] through which God's truth is finally disclosed to Christian faith, and its implications for a sound theology. "The Word was made flesh" (Jn. 1: 14). The astounding nature of this affirmation becomes clear when it is set against its Old Testament background. Isaiah 40:6-8 declares: "All flesh is grass.... The grass withers, the flower fades; but the word of our God will stand for ever." The first verse of John's Prologue has already underlined the divine greatness of the Word ("the Word *was* God"); now that Word is said to have made our human nature his own in a way that stresses its transitoriness, mortality and imperfection—all, in fact, that at first glance seems incompatible with God.[2]

And it is through this incarnation that God's definitive self-disclosure is to take place.It does so in a fashion that is beyond human devising:

> The passing of the irony of the crucified messiah into the faith of the Church is manifestly a liberation of consciousness from its worldly limits.... Such trueness to *life* (the fact that the mission of Jesus failed and the evangelists are at pains to emphasize this) is, well, it's simply uninventable.... The early Church did not bypass the cross. It did not pass from this bitter disappointment into another dream, the ecstasy of the Hellenistic mysteries. It

gloried in the cross and found there the very coining of *its* mysteries.[3]

The relevance of these observations to the contrast which has been drawn in our first chapter between the sacralized symbols of the religious quest of humanity and the locus of divine disclosure provided by God's sacred history is dramatic and clear.

A Flesh-and-Blood Reality

The Christ-event belongs to the flesh-and-blood reality in which our human existence is immersed. Coming to terms with this condition has always presented a challenge to religious consciousness. The efforts of religious traditions to establish our existence in the order of the transcendent easily made coming to terms with the material dimension of human existence seem something of a compromise. The Hellenistic world to which the Christian faith was first announced stressed the spiritual dimension of human existence at the expense of its materiality. Plato, whose influence was immense for many centuries, looked upon the human spirit as imprisoned in matter, away from its true homeland. The Neo-Platonic view of the universe, which greatly influenced the early Christian centuries, saw the human spirit as a divine spark which had emanated from the supreme divine source into the realms of matter and darkness; they saw human destiny as a struggle to find the way back to the divine order of the spirit. The religious traditions of the East[4] and of the West have constantly sought the way along paths similar to this. An *angelism* which drew back from the full implications of the incarnation has appeared in many forms. Notable among them were Puritanism in the Protestant tradition, and Jansenism in the Catholic tradition.

This inclination to draw back from the implications of our material condition is very seductive. One of the earliest distortions of Christian faith was a refusal to acknowledge that the Saviour had come "in the flesh," seeing his bodily aspect as no more than a phantom appearance—hence the name for this heresy: *Docetism*. The Johannine tradition reacted vigorously against this tendency, which was to trouble the Church for many decades through the teaching of the Gnostics (cf. 1 Jn. 1: 1; 4: 2-3). In the early years of the second century, the letters of the martyr bishop Ignatius of Antioch warned insistently against it. A century later, the theologian Tertullian coined the phrase "The flesh of Christ is the hinge of salvation"—*Caro Christi cardo salutis*—a pun that emphasized the Church's opposition to this stubborn heresy.

The critical assessment we can make today of the influence of the sacralizing tendency, with its compromising of the proper integrity and autonomy of mundane reality, makes us aware of the subtle forms this tendency can assume. The incarnation of the Saviour was not only the revelation of God's ways; it was also an affirmation of the human condition, as destined to find fulfillment in a full identification with the material universe which is God's creation, not in some flight from it. The Christian mystery is not a mystical enlightenment which liberates us from the limitations of our material existence. Christian faith acknowledges the presence of the living God in the midst of those limitations. God's final achievement will take place in human flesh and blood—those of Jesus of Nazareth and our own—and it is on these terms that the Christ-event is the absolute reference point for all that faith has to tell us. It is not a coincidence that the abiding sacramental celebration of the mystery of Christ is made possible through the "body" and "blood" which have been "given" for us.

Rudolf Bultmann, as we have seen, has endeavored to interpret the existential decision to which faith calls us independently of the flesh-and-blood reality of Christ's existence among us. Theology will be seriously impoverished if it succumbs to this tendency. We shall return to this question in considering the *realism* proper to the Christ-event. However, in the present context we must speak of another aspect of the human existence of the Saviour coming to be appreciated more fully by contemporary theology, an aspect which theology must explore if it is to acknowledge the fulness of the incarnational truth embodied in the Christ-event.

The Story Which Expresses the Human Existence of Jesus of Nazareth

---

To be human means more than having a human nature; it means having a personal story, having an existence and an identity—a cause—which is progressively clarified and affirmed by the choices and commitments made in the course of one's life. This second pole of awareness demanded by the incarnation of the Word emerges from, and must be seen as integral with, what we have just considered.

Clearly, this aspect of the incarnation is one with the historical economy we considered in the last chapter: God's truth is expressed through historical events; its final expression is given in a human story. The humanity through which "Jesus interprets God," writes Hans Urs von Balthasar, "is not an inert, mechanical alphabet simply used to put the absolute into words"; as the interpreter of God, Jesus "speaks with his whole existence of flesh and blood." Through the Holy Spirit, the whole drama of Jesus' life "was the eternal Father's self-offering and self-interpretation."[5]

Today the renewal of biblical studies is enabling theology to reflect in a new way upon the implications of the gospel story of Jesus. As the Dutch theologian Edward Schillebeeckx has observed, these studies are leading us towards the point at which "the problem of the historical Jesus" will disappear from theology. Scholarship is establishing beyond all doubt that "the interpretation of Jesus in faith" made by the New Testament is inseparable from a "specific historical person, the broad outlines of whose career can be established by historians."[6] Schillebeeckx stresses the importance of distinguishing between "a historical-critical picture of Jesus," the product of strict academic investigation, and "the spontaneous, living story of Jesus down the ages."[7] This distinction has great importance. Some events, some lives, have an impact which subsequent generations cannot disregard or forget. We may have only a sketchy knowledge of the details of the careers of Socrates or Mahatma Gandhi, but the causes to which they dedicated their lives had a revolutionary significance which the world can never forget. The analogy helps us to understand the impact the story of Jesus of Nazareth has had as it was passed on in the New Testament and in subsequent ages.[8]

Like Us and With Us

The living story of Jesus—in those various details to which modern scholarship gives us a far more sensitive access—is the final embodiment of the truth of God. In the words of the great Swiss Protestant theologian Karl Barth, this life is a "self-attesting reality": Jesus is

> the man who, even in our human situation and within our human history, has lived and lives and will live this eternal life, this Stranger whom we cannot overlook or remove...because as such He is at home among us and like us and with us, belonging as we do to our human situation and history. It is because it is the life...of this near Neighbor even in all His otherness, that this life is called light, revelation and Word.... This life of a man like us...is a declaration.... It is an address, promise and demand, a question and answer.... Confronted and compared with His life, the life which we live or describe as such is only a vacuum and darkness.[9]

We are reminded that it is in the cross that the story of Jesus reaches its overwhelming climax. In the cross we are confronted with a gesture which embodies the unconditional finality of God's love for us. Recall the words of Moltmann already cited:

> Must one not abandon all that has been imagined, desired or feared in respect of "God" if one is to understand God...in the crucified Christ?

In Paul's words:

> We preach Christ crucified, a stumbling block to Jews and folly to Gentiles, but to those who are called, both Jews and Greeks, Christ the power of God and the wisdom of God. For the foolishness of God is wiser than men, and the weakness of God is stronger than men (1 Cor. 1: 23-25).

A life like ours, a story like ours, is God's medium of communication. Contemporary reflection, in recognizing the limitations of the Greek conception of truth, is led to seek a more holistic point of view. It recognizes that truth is embodied in our stories: the story which expresses the existence of each of us, the story (or history) we *live* together, and the stories that we *tell* as we recall the significance of it all. There is much here that is of great value to theology as it seeks to understand the medium that God has chosen. It would be true to say that, previously, under the influence of the truth conception stemming from the Greeks, theology tended to presume that the coin of revelation was concepts from God; a more holistic awareness recognizes that the concepts of doctrinal statements are a secondary currency, translating the truth of history and story into another idiom, as it were—an idiom with severe limitations which we disregard at our peril.

The Theology of Story

"God made man because he loves stories" (Elie Wiesel). In the last decade important work has been undertaken by theologians such as John Shea and Terrence Tilley, exploring our new appreciation of the significance and importance of "story."[10] Theology must give increased attention to these important questions.

The analysis we have made in this and the previous chapters points to an important distinction which could be brought out more clearly by the authors we have mentioned. Like "history," "story" is an ambiguous term: it may refer to the story we live or to the story we tell. When there is question of the sacred "history" of God with his people, and its climactic moment in the "story" of Jesus of Nazareth, the two are essentially linked: the *told* story—which, as we have seen, may at times employ symbolic and imaginative elements—has no meaning for Christian faith except as a conveying of the truth of the *lived* story. It is events of history which are "the very object of faith" governing "its design and structure": even though "this may seem to the unbeliever nothing but myth or illusion."[11] To allow this to become unclear is to disregard the incarnational implications of the Christ-event.

In his important work, *Faith in History and Society: Toward a Practical Fundamental Theology,* J.B. Metz underlines the importance of narrative in the life of the believing community, as it becomes the "subject" of the truth which lives on in the Church, as tradition, through the presence of the Spirit.[12]

Conclusions

The considerations we have made in this chapter point to conclusions which are important for the development of a wholesome theology.

1. The incarnational character of the Christ-event challenges theology to *concentrate its attention upon the human condition in its totality* as the locus of God's self-revelation in history. In particular, theology must recognize as contrary to the genius of the Christian faith, the tendency so common within religious traditions to turn away from a complete acceptance of our fleshly and material condition.

2. Because the truth of God is finally expressed through the "story" through which Jesus is the embodiment of God's eschatological intervention on behalf of humankind, it is *in this story that the theologian finds the basic currency of revealed truth.* Doctrinal statements are the translation of this truth into a secondary currency, the limitations of which one disregards at one's peril. By the same token, the story that is *told* of Jesus in the Church's confession of faith is utterly dependent upon the story that he *lived*, and which constituted the eschatological event of God's self-disclosure.

CHAPTER FIVE

An Openness to the Gift of Spirit

It emerges as axiomatic from what we have seen in the preceding chapters that it is only through the gift of God's Spirit that one may assent to revealed truth as it is embodied in the Christ-event. The New Testament community were aware that, just as Jesus had fulfilled his destiny in the power of the Spirit, so too it was through the same Spirit that they were able to recognize that the cause to which the life of Jesus had been given, and the tragedy of his shameful death, were not scandal and foolishness but the demonstration to the world of God's power and wisdom (1 Cor. 1: 23-24).

It was a revelation of the depths of the mystery of God: "God has revealed to us through the Spirit," Paul wrote, in verses following those we have just cited, "for the Spirit searches everything, even the depths of God.... No one comprehends the thoughts of God except the Spirit of God." He then points to the conversion which is necessary if the believer is to know the truth brought by the Spirit:

> We impart this in words not taught by human wisdom but taught by the Spirit, interpreting spiritual truths to those who possess the Spirit. The unspiritual man does not receive the gifts of the Spirit of God, for they are folly to him, and he is not able to understand them because they are spiritually discerned. The spiritual man judges all things (1 Cor. 2: 10-15).

The Son and the Spirit

Our stress upon the historical character of Christian faith's access to the mystery of God has directed attention to the Christ-event, the mission carried out by the Son who came forth from the Father. The text we have just cited reminds us that in the divine self-expression which takes place in our world the mission of the Son is inseparable from that of the Spirit. The Son's total concern was the kingdom: the rule of love to be established by the one whom he called his God and Father. From the first, the Son's union with the Father was realized through the Spirit of love which united them, the Spirit who searches everything, even the depths of God.[1]

The neglect in the Western tradition of the role of the Spirit in the Christian life in general, and in the work of theology in particular, may be related to the different characteristics of the two missions. That of the Son's incarnation belongs to the arena of human history; that of the Spirit, being interior and invisible, is not as readily recognized and described. Walter Kasper helps us, in words we have already cited, to situate the believer's meeting with the Spirit, and the conversion it involves, within the framework of personal experience:

> Only the person who is prepared in faith to break out of the world of the measurable and calculable, out of his comfortable and automatic habits, and entrust himself to the newness of the world of faith, can recognize God's salvation in history.[2]

Conversion in the Life of the Theologian

Bernard Lonergan's study *Method in Theology* has made an important contribution to an understanding of the theologian's task.[3] In the judgment of Lonergan, conversion has a fundamental importance in any disciplined intellectual inquiry. Against this background, he discusses the conversion called for in the theologian.

Lonergan describes the theological project in terms that bring out what it has in common with other disciplines. He distinguishes various specialties which contribute to the total project and describes their interrelationship. Lonergan relates conversion to the functional specialty he calls foundations. Whereas the previous specialties he has identified concern the identification of positions which have emerged independently of the inquirer, and the interaction these positions have provoked,[4] foundations establish the bases upon which the inquirer will adopt a personal position.[5] This calls for a clarification of where one situates oneself, in the intellectual, moral and religious orders. This clarification takes place at the level of human consciousness, "on the level of deliberation, evaluation, decision"; it involves a decision "about whom and what you are for and, again, whom and what you are against,"[6] a decision whereby one becomes "fully conscious...about one's horizons, one's outlook, one's world view."[7] Lonergan concludes:

> Such a decision is anything but arbitrary. Arbitrariness is just unauthenticity, while conversion is from unauthenticity to authenticity. It is total surrender to the demands of the human spirit: Be attentive, be intelligent, be reasonable, be responsible, be in love.[8]

As Lonergan points out, however, horizons are not necessarily adopted in a fully deliberate fashion: "For the most part, people merely drift into some contemporary horizon."[9]

It is clear, however, that the horizons which have been adopted determine, finally, the quality of the judgements which are arrived at:

> The fact of the matter is that proof becomes rigorous only within a systematically promulgated horizon, that the formulation of horizons varies with the presence or absence of intellectual, moral, religious conversion, and that conversion is never the logical consequence of one's previous position, but, on the contrary, a radical revision of that position.[10]

In the judgement of Lonergan, the religious, moral and intellectual dimensions of conversion are profoundly interrelated:

> Normally it is intellectual conversion as the fruit of both religious and moral conversion; it is moral conversion as the fruit of religious conversion; and it is religious conversion as the fruit of God's gift of his grace.[11]

For Lonergan, therefore, religious conversion through the gift of the Holy Spirit is fundamental to the theologian's project:

> Religious conversion is being grasped by ultimate concern. It is other-worldly falling in love. It is total and permanent self-surrender without conditions, qualifications, reservations. But it is such a surrender, not as an act, but as a dynamic state, that is prior to and principle of subsequent acts. It is revealed in retrospect as an undertow of existential consciousness, as a fated acceptance of vocation to holiness, as perhaps an increasing simplicity and passivity in prayer.[12]

It is helpful to relate this conversion, which brings an openness to the wisdom which comes from above (Jas. 1: 17), to the consideration of our previous chapters. It is clear that we are touching once more upon that existential level of decision which we have recognized as crucial at different points in our discussion. As Lonergan points out, the horizons which are adopted in the conversion process—in all its dimensions: intellectual, moral and religious—are not arrived at by a process of demonstration. They derive from a more complete surrender to the demands of a meeting with meaning in all the subtlety of its various dimensions.

A Connaturality with the Divine Mystery

Lonergan's contemporary analysis helps us to appreciate the nature and importance of the conversion process. Coming from a very different historical context, Thomas Aquinas' analysis of the nature of infused contemplation brings out other aspects of the growth in faith and prayer which should be part of the life of a theologian. Among the gifts given in and through the presence of the Holy Spirit, Aquinas distinguishes gifts which are given for the enriching of the Christian life of the recipient, and those, such as prophecy or healing, which are given for the manifestation of the Christian mystery and the edification of the Christian community.[13] Among the gifts which of their nature enrich the believer's life in Christ, Aquinas distinguishes the gifts traditionally called virtues and the gifts known as "the seven gifts of the Spirit."[14] Aquinas' virtue does not have the overtones the word has assumed in contemporary parlance; in his vocabulary it meant literally a strength, a dynamic confirmation towards the good, superadded to the human person's basic inclinations. Among the infused virtues, Aquinas points to the distinction which should be made between the theological virtues of faith, hope and charity (which, as their name implies, give the capacity to relate immediately to the divine mystery itself, as it is revealed in what God has done for us in Christ) and moral virtues (which give the capacity to relate to created things in a manner which is according to the believer's new destiny in Christ).[15]

The theological virtues and the seven gifts of the Holy Spirit are intimately linked. Of themselves, the virtues would operate in a manner connatural to the nature of their human subject (by way of deliberation and calculation). It is the function of the seven gifts to enable the human subject to act with a divine connaturality, by a kind of Spirit-given instinct, to use St. Thomas' term.[16] Thus the function of the seven gifts is inseparable from the union with the Holy Spirit achieved through faith, hope and charity, so that these virtues are, for Aquinas, "like roots, as it were, of the gifts."[17]

The instinct, or connaturality, of which Aquinas speaks comes through a progressive conversion, and develops with the habit of prayer and contemplation. It is necessary, if the theologian is to recognize the demands of the divine truth and relate them to changing cultural and intellectual contexts. It is only in this way that the theologian can undertake a ministry of the gospel among believers which is truly prophetic and which forms and inspires a prophetic people, able to recognize the signs of the times.

The issue we are speaking of underlies the discussion that has taken place in recent times of whether one can properly speak of a spiritual sense of the scriptures. In the name of a disciplined and fully accountable interpretation of the scriptures, some scholars distrust this concept. Raymond Brown, a Catholic scholar who has made an important contribution to the advancing of contemporary scriptural studies, indicates important limits that the spiritual sense must not transgress if it is to meet the demands of the text's literal sense.[18] But Brown's discussion of the *sensus plenior*[19] is very rational, and does not seem to have taken into account sufficiently the "ways of the heart," which have been so important for the finding of the spiritual sense which opened up the horizons within which the great interpreters of the Bible undertook their task.

It is interesting to compare Brown's view with that of Henri Crouzel.[20] This author cites Origen's view that the charism of the exegete is the same as that of the sacred author. As a result,

> the voice which God makes the soul hear, even in connection with the text, is tied to no words and no objective sense of words.... If the soul, once in contact with God, feels him leading it, it must surrender to his leading.[21]

The essence of the problem is evident in the phrase "tied to no words and no objective sense of words." Raymond Brown would object, and justly, that it is difficult to see how a sense could be given to the words of scripture which was in no way contained in the literal sense of the words themselves and their relationship to the literal meaning of cognate passages.

But the point which Crouzel is making—in a somewhat confused way, certainly—is an important one: what is conveyed by the words of the scriptures cannot be limited to what the calculations of an exclusively historico-critical exegesis can yield. Such a meaning will be constrained by the limitations of what can be established within the forum of a strictly rational inquiry. A "spiritual" reading of scripture adds to what rational analysis has to affirm (though never contradicting this affirmation) what a loving knowledge tells of the mystery of God. As Pascal says in his often quoted dictum: "The heart has its reasons which reason does not understand."

This loving knowledge does not bring to light new objects, but it grasps familiar objects in a new and deeper way. A mother's appreciation of her child is not a subjective fiction; nor is it necessarily a knowledge of realities others may not observe; but her love leads her to apprehend the wonder that is in her child in a way that is not possible for one who does not love the child as she does. Those who, like Origen, St. Bernard and John Henry Newman, have been admired for their elaboration of the spiritual sense of the scriptures have—through the gifts of the Holy Spirit—attained a loving knowledge of the Word of God which makes them alive to the greatness of the simple message from the depths of the heart of God which is the real burden of the scriptures. Alive to God's ways, through the connaturality or instinct of which Aquinas speaks, they have been able to recognize the implications of the divine truth in a way that would not be possible to one making a purely rational inquiry.

In this context, we may note that today it is being recognized that a historico-critical inquiry into the original intention of the sacred author is not sufficient to bring to light what the scriptures have to say to later times. Such an inquiry certainly provides controlling norms which are essential to an authentic interpretation, but it must be complemented by bringing the text into dialogue with the sensibilities and insights of the readers' world.[22] The connaturality which comes through the Spirit's gifts will play an important part in the discerning of the divine truth to be found through this dialogue.

Conclusion

What we have seen contains an important lesson for those who are entering into the theological project.

Since the truth of God embodied in the historical reality of the Christ-event is recognized only through the presence and gifts of the Spirit, *a life of conversion, openness to the Spirit, and that connaturality with the ways of God which is the fruit of prayer are necessary for the theologian* if the challenging simplicity of the message of the Christian faith is to be interpreted in a life-giving way for God's people.

Important as they are, human industry and skills can never replace these things.

CHAPTER SIX

The Context of the Ecclesial Community

What we have seen in the previous chapters makes it clear that the believing community provides the context within which the believer has access to the truth of God essential to Christian faith. We are concerned, as we have said, with a truth which is lived before it is told. The history in which this truth is expressed belongs to a community, a people living out the drama of their relationship with God. To possess it in its fulness, the believer must enter completely into the life of the people of God as—through the abiding gift of the Spirit—it *remembers, celebrates and witnesses to* the great events which had their climax in Christ. The Saviour's assurance "I am with you always, to the close of the age" (Mt. 28:20) is fulfilled within the context of the life of the Church, "built upon the foundation of the apostles and prophets, Christ Jesus himself being the cornerstone...a dwelling place of God in the Spirit" (Eph. 2:20-23). The implications for the theological inquirer are unmistakable. It is these implications that we shall discuss in the present chapter.

A Truth Which Lives On
In Word and Sacrament

It was Augustine who stressed the importance of these two categories as establishing the substance of the Church's communion in the Christian mystery.[1] The Word of the Scriptures and the sacramental rituals, which plunge the believer into the achievement of God in the Christ-event, are the extension of the incarnational order which has already been discussed in Chapter Four.[2]

Through Word and Sacrament God overcomes the barriers of space and time to make the reality of what was done for the world once-for-all in Christ accessible to all peoples and cultures. In Word and Sacrament we recognize the generous way in which God has accommodated his design to the deepest needs of our nature. It is connatural to us as humans to express our truth through both words and gestures. From the first, as we have seen, humanity's project of relating to the transcendent has been through the mythology and lore which attempted to shape a world in which access to the divine was possible, and through the festal celebrations and rituals in which this access was lived out. This pattern is taken up in the Word and Sacrament which are the life of God's people.

In the plan of God, the Christ-event was not to be confined to one moment of time; it belongs to all peoples and cultures. Through the Christ-event, God's ultimate achievement is realized; all that remains is for the whole of creation to be taken up into this achievement. In a real sense, all subsequent time is lived in the presence of this final moment of God's plan, through the presence to the world of the risen Lord, "the last Adam" (1 Cor. 15:45). From the beginnings of the Christian community's life in the Spirit, its sharing in this final moment was realized, not only through the Word which told of what God has done, but also through the sacramental rites—first and foremost among them, baptism and the Eucharist—in which they were caught up in the destiny of "the last Adam," as "members of his body."[3]

It is not difficult to recognize that the understanding of Word and Sacrament we have outlined implies their organic unity in Christian life. In both secular and religious life, lore and ritual have always had a mutuality. In the life of the believing community, the Word proclaims and invites participation in the sacramental mysteries; for their part, the sacraments are never enacted without recalling through the proclamation of the Word the great things God has done. The fulness of God's truth, therefore, will be possessed only through this vital unity of Word and Sacrament in the Church's life. The implications, for those who seek the truth of God given through faith, are clear.

Both sides to the Protestant-Catholic divide of recent centuries must carefully ponder this truth. The evangelical inspiration of Protestantism has led to an emphasis upon the Word. The Catholic tradition, on the other hand, has insisted upon the place of the sacraments in the Christian life, recognizing that they are essential to the incarnational economy established by the Christ-event. Today we can acknowledge that each of these emphases has something important to teach the believing community. A one-sided approach, however, seriously impoverishes Christian faith. The Protestant tradition has run the danger of being left with a disembodied Word which was incapable of nourishing fully the incarnational genius of Christian faith. In our time, the Catholic communion—especially through the teaching of the Second

Vatican Council's Constitution on Divine Revelation, *Dei verbum*—has acknowledged that it needed a profound renewal in its appreciation of the place which must be given to the Word of God in the Church's life.

A Truth that Rules the Church

The Catholic-Protestant divide to which we have re-ferred was occasioned, in part, by a confused under-standing of the Church's role as bearer, or subject, of the truth given to the world in the Christ-event. The Protes-tant movement, taking its stand upon the sovereignty of the truth given in the gospel, failed to give full acknowl-edgement to the mutuality which exists between the Word of God and the Church.[4] Their Catholic oppo-nents, on the other hand, were so concerned to champion this mutuality that their insistence that the scriptures should be read as "the Church's book" seemed to com-promise the sovereignty of the divine truth. Obviously, this is a question that theological inquiry within both of our traditions must clarify. Once more, each side to the Catholic-Protestant divide is giving expression to a valid concern which must be upheld in a satisfactory solution to their differences. The sovereign authority of the once-for-all truth given to the world in the Christ-event must be maintained. This authority finds expression in the di-vinely authored Word of the scriptures and in the divine action present in the sacramental rites. This expression is absolutely normative. The recognition that it has been realized through the use of human agency within the be-lieving community—and in such a fashion that its full import can be appreciated only within the context of the life of that community—must not obscure the sovereign authority with which it must rule the life of the community as a *norma normans non normata.*[5]

Walter Kasper points to important consequences of this reaffirmation of the absolute sovereignty of the divine truth in the renewal of Catholic theology. In his judgment, Catholic theology of the past couple of centuries is to be criticized for making use of the scriptures within a framework established, not by the message of the scriptures, but by the Church's dogmatic teaching. This reversal of right order betrayed a failure to give practical recognition to the authority of the Word as it is found in the scriptures. If this sovereign authority is acknowledged, the Church's teaching will be presented "within the framework of scripture's testimony"[6] and as a service given to that testimony. Not only must dogma serve as an interpretation of the message of the scriptures, but the interpretation of dogma must always be made in the light of the scriptures.[7]

On the other hand, the fact that the believing community of the Church is the bearer, or subject, of the divine truth which expresses its sovereignty in her midst challenges the Protestant tradition to a fuller recognition of the fact that

> dogmatic theology is a function of the Church; she constantly renews her dogmatic awareness of the faith at its sources and makes it a living awareness by carrying out her mission today.[8]

The Mind of the Church Provides
the Analogy of Faith as a Criterion

Basic to the Catholic tradition's understanding of it-self is the assumption that the truth of God will always be accessible within a living communion which is faith-ful to the revelation given to the world in the Christ-event[9]—because, through the gift of the Spirit, it has kept faith with the Church of the apostles. Acknowledging that important qualifications must be made,[10] Catholics understand this communion to be present in all its essentials in the tradition in which they are united. This means that—provided it is properly interpreted—the living faith in which the Catholic communion is united may serve as an index for those who seek to remain in "the faith which is once for all delivered to the saints" (Jude 3).

Theology has made use of a phrase of St. Paul to re-fer to this index. The exercise of prophecy within the Christian community, he says, should be regulated by the "proportion [Greek, *analogia*] of faith" (Rom. 12:6). In other words, the danger of self-deception which is obviously present in those who seek to give expression to God's ways in the midst of his people must be offset by a critical assessment of what they have to say: whatever purports to be an expression of faith should be accepted as such only if it is in accord with the "one faith" (Eph. 4:5) in which believers are united.

Three Criteria

But how is the analogy of faith to be applied? The Second Vatican Council gave consideration to this question.[11] In the Constitution on the Church, *Lumen gentium* (no. 12), three criteria are given for the recognition of the faith in which the Church's communion is united. The first and most fundamental of these is the *sensus fidei* (sense, or instinct, of faith) produced by the Spirit.[12] We are concerned here with the existential response to which all who live in the Spirit by faith are called. Its origin is not to be found in the directives of authority, nor in democratic consensus, but in the connaturality with the divine truth which life in the Spirit brings.

Though this norm is clearly of great importance for the believer, because of its simplicity it is often neglected. Moreover, if it is to be used, a discriminating interpretation is called for. Unanimity is not necessarily a pointer to the analogy of faith, but may come from a prevailing theological fashion. The faith in which the Church is united will have as its central point of reference the mystery of Christ; in other words, it is the fruit of genuine discipleship.[13]

The Church's common faith provides a particularly reliable guide when it involves the united witness of Eastern and Western Churches and therefore indicates a common faith which has existed since the first millennium—for instance, in the acknowledgement of the divine identity of Christ, of the nature of the Eucharist, of the Church as a mystery authored by God.

The second criterion indicated by the Council serves as a complement to the first. It is obvious that the connatural awareness of the truth of God to which we have referred is open to subjective distortion. Religious enthusiasm is notorious in this regard. This danger is offset by measuring what purports to be the living faith of the Church against expressions of Christian truth which have shaped the history of the believing community. As the Council says, citing the letter of Jude, the Church must uphold "the faith once delivered to the saints." The faith of the believing community shows itself to be more than a subjective projection by expressing itself and defining itself in a meeting with the norms provided by the record of the faith of the originating Christian community to be found in the scriptures, and with the testimony provided by the witness of other ages. This dialogue with the norms provided by the witness of the past is important if the Church's understanding of God's truth is not to be distorted by the pressures of current views and passing intellectual fashions. A sensitive use of this second criterion pays special attention to the witness of those who have been venerated by the Church for their expounding of the Christian faith—the "Fathers" and "Doctors" of the Church.[14]

The third criterion mentioned by the Council is "the lead of the sacred teaching authority." It should be noted that this criterion is mentioned after those we have already explained. The exercise of pastoral authority presupposes and serves the other criteria by helping them to find expression. This authority is not the mediating source of divine truth, but a service which recognizes and articulates the faith living in the Church through the presence of the Spirit.[15]

It is evident that authoritative teaching on the part of those who, as pastors of the Church, have received a special gift of the Spirit, has a special place in the life of the believing community. The dogmatic formularies which they have upheld within the Church by their authority have always been seen as providing a "rule of faith" for the believing community. The discussions of the two Vatican Councils made it clear, however, that this teaching does not arise from some independent access to revealed truth on the part of the authoritative teachers: it is an expression of the faith living in the whole Church. While they are assisted by the gift of the Spirit proper to their calling and office for the maintaining of Church order and the public rule of faith, the pastors must maintain a constant dialogue with the Church's tradition, with the living faith of the community over which they preside, and with the theologies which interpret the truth living in the Church through the categories of contemporary awareness. This dialogue brings a mutual benefit, as the International Theological Commission noted in a document published in 1973: through it

> the magisterium can acquire greater understanding of the truth of faith and morality to be preached and defended; the theological comprehension of faith and morals, strengthened by the magisterium, acquires certainty. The dialogue between magisterium and theologians is limited only by the duty of preserving and explaining the truth of faith.[16]

The Interpretation of Authoritative Teaching

The authoritative expression of the Church's faith calls for a careful interpretation. Its import, or content, must be clarified by identification of the questions it has set out to answer, and by an analysis of the context which was essential to the meaning of those questions. The nature of the authority with which the pronouncement was made must be determined. Definitive teaching, which commits the Church irrevocably to a position and excludes all who do not hold it from the Church's full communion—in order to put it beyond all doubt for the believing community—is the ultimate use of teaching authority. It has been rare in the Church's life, serving as a kind of emergency procedure to be used in time of crisis in order to preserve the Church from doctrinal anarchy.[17] Authoritative teaching,[18] which is not by way of definition as just described, has an authority within the community of believers which goes beyond the force of the arguments proposed in its support, since it is related to the gift of the Spirit promised to the Church's pastors.[19] This latter authority varies greatly in quality. This must be judged through the manner in which it is exercised (the authority of the teaching of the Second Vatican Council, for example, none of which is definitive, is greater, all other things being equal, than that of a papal encyclical; the Constitutions of the recent Council are more weighty than its Decrees; matters dealt with in passing in an authoritative document are of less significance than the essential teaching which the document is concerned to propose, and so forth).[20]

The interpretation of authoritative expressions of the rule of faith is intimately associated with the question of whether a human formulary can give expression to the truth of God given to the world in the Christ-event. We must take up this question at length in the next chapter.

Conclusions

The considerations of this chapter make it possible for us to enunciate further principles which should guide the theological inquirer.

1. Because the bearer, or subject, of the truth given to the world in Christian faith is the believing community of the Church, it is *the Church's life in Word and sacrament which provides the context* within which theologians must seek an understanding of that truth; the living faith of the believing community provides the analogy of faith which is an important index of theological truth.

2. If the analogy of faith is to provide a genuine index, it must be carefully interpreted. It will be recognized: (a) in the *sensus fidei* (i.e., the instinctive recognition of the truth of God by the believing community), (b) in *the dialogue the Church must continue in every age with the Word of God in the scriptures and with the witness of past ages* in their life in Word and Sacrament, and (c) in *the authoritative rule of faith* upheld by the Church's pastors.

CHAPTER SEVEN

The Realism of the Christ-Event

The theologian's task is the interpretation to each age of the truth of God given to the world in the Christ-event. We have already seen something of the contemporary debate concerning the relationship between truth and history. Without entering further into that debate, we can recognize that truth and realism are in a sense synonymous: to possess the truth is to be present to reality itself. What we have seen in preceding chapters already makes clear some aspects of the realism of Christian faith: God's truth is embodied in the events of history; the Christ-event, which brings this history to its final climax, is by way of incarnation. If we are to clarify the foundations of a wholesome theology, we must explore more fully the implications of the realism which inevitably asserted itself in the development of Christian thought.[1]

Human Language and the Expression of Divine Truth

The incarnational realism of Christian faith presents the theological enquirer with a paradox. It is this paradox (which has given rise to many of the tensions and debates at the heart of the Christian tradition) that the present chapter must discuss. On the one hand, this incarnational realism sees the divine self-disclosure as having taken place through the events of a saving history which has its climax in the Christ-event itself and is perpetuated in the mysteries of Word and sacrament constituting the Church's life "in Christ." It recognizes, therefore, that this truth can never be adequately grasped in the form of human propositions. But, on the other hand, the Christian faith understands its own mystery as a sharing in, a coming alive to, the things of God in themselves; and it has confidently responded in every age to whatever distorted the truth to which it must give witness. After an initial hesitation, the living voice of the Christian community has confidently passed beyond the terminology and thought patterns of the scriptures to make use of the resources of human categorization provided by other cultures[2] in giving expression to the message and implications of Christian faith.[3] This paradox presents the theological interpreter with two poles which must both be maintained. If the dialectic to which they give rise is neglected, the Church's living faith will suffer.

Medieval Scholasticism's Approach

It is interesting, in the light of what has just been said, to look back at the development of Christian thought during the Middle Ages—a development which provided the background to the Reformation movement of the sixteenth century. As medieval Scholasticism gave more and more attention to the task of categorization, it ran the obvious danger of neglecting the other pole of Christian awareness: the overwhelming mystery of God as it is revealed in the Christ-event, a mystery which human language can never adequately express.

The rationale of medieval Scholasticism did point, however, to the principles which put beyond all doubt the severe limitations of the project it had taken up. The "negative theology" of Aquinas, for instance, was alive to the fact that, whatever may be truly said of the divine mystery is said only by way of analogy—an insight which carries the inescapable implication that what is proper to the divine analogue infinitely transcends the meaningfulness which may be derived from created analogies in the making of theological assertions.[4]

Moreover, the analysis the medievals had undertaken pointed to the distinction which must be made between proper and improper assertion by way of analogy. Thus, for instance, one may say that a thoroughbred is "good"; one may say that the martyr's courage is "good"; and one may say that God is "good." Clearly, the predication in these assertions has a communality of significance, but this communality is only by way of analogy; what is affirmed in each case is, in the end, of essentially different orders. This is proper analogy: on the basis of the communality which exists, the predication is made without qualification in each case. When, on the other hand, we say that God is the "rock" upon which we can rely forever, the predication is by way of metaphor: what is predicated is said by way of a figure of speech which calls upon the symbolic capacities of the imagination. This is improper analogy: what is predicated cannot be said without qualification in each case.

The terminology "proper"/"improper" can easily give rise to a serious misunderstanding. What is referred to is the manner of predication. The distinction in no way implies that the truth conveyed by an improper analogy is in any way inferior to that conveyed by proper analogy. The reverse may well be the case. One may well judge that the development of medieval Scholasticism—and, even more, that of twentieth-century Neo-Scholasticism—reflects something of the misunderstanding we have just indicated. The categorization of proper analogy absorbed the whole attention of the theological interpreter in a way which clearly gave to understand that the figurative expression of Christian truth, so fundamental to the scriptural message, belongs to an inferior order.[5]

The Christian faith's incarnational message—the truth of the divine self-disclosure which was made in the saving history of Israel and in the tragic story of Jesus of Nazareth—will never be given fitting expression if our only currency is the proper analogy to which the Scholastics gave their principal attention. In fact, the scriptural record which embodies this message gives pride of place to metaphor, symbol and rhetoric, and the capacity they have to go beyond the austere assertions of proper analogy and the "negative theology" to which it gives rise. The forms of expression used by the scriptures—making use of all the resources available to human language for the expression of existential truth—constitute, as it were, a dynamic of converging lines, leading the hearer ever closer to the mystery of the living God, which it evokes and which it affirms as standing just outside the listener's purview as an overwhelming reality.

Sixteenth-Century Misunderstandings

The essential tragedy of the Reformation crisis of the sixteenth century, it may be judged, was the failure of protagonists on both sides of the debate to recognize the significance of Luther's rediscovery of the rhetoric of the scriptures and the power which that rhetoric possesses to lead the Christian community to the heart of the message of Christian faith. Despising the "rancid logic" of the dogmatics of the Scholastics, Luther turned what should have been a distinction into a rejection. For their part, not recognizing the potential and importance of the "new theology" Luther was proposing, his Catholic opponents evaluated his teaching through a theological idiom which was incapable of appreciating its essential genius. In many ways, this false opposition has lived on in the interaction of the Catholic and the Protestant traditions until our own day.

Today we are in a position to recognize that the truth which is embodied in history and story (both lived and told), on the one hand, and the derivative truth expressed in doctrinal propositions, on the other, are not necessarily opposed but may be complementary.

The Evaluation of Doctrinal Statements: The Problem for Contemporary Theology

Ignace de la Potterie's analysis, to which reference has been made in an earlier chapter, helps us to situate the question which constitutes, in the judgement of one of its leading Catholic exponents, theology's "biggest problem."[6]

While Western awareness was dominated by the Greek notion of truth, all aspects of the problem concerning the relationship between the events of God's saving history and the truth given to the world in that history could not emerge with clarity. We have already seen that Kasper's treatment of the problem which has emerged leaves some issues unresolved. On the one hand, he hesitates to acknowledge a "metaphysical structure of order" which may be "disengaged from all the detail of history and salvation history": the "things that happen are theologically...the real 'nature' of things.... Theologically there is only one permanent fact, that man has been called by God in history and asked for an answer."[7] But, on the other hand, he recognizes that, unless some "permanent element in history" is identified, the historical approach to truth will become "an all-embracing relativism."[8] The real problem of understanding the abiding validity of doctrinal statements still remains. As Kasper remarks: "Without the courage, one could almost say the rashness, to make definitive decisions and statements, the Christian faith would be denying its own nature."[9]

If Kasper looks towards Hegel for the solution to the problem, Edward Schillebeeckx discusses it within a framework provided by contemporary existential thought. He notes that if the truth which was embodied in history is to be appropriated by later ages, the existential "experience" of the believers of later ages must involve an accurate evocation of, and identification with, the existential experience of the originating faith-community.[10] The Christian tradition makes this possible by providing a searchlight which recovers the story of Jesus: "Our faith does not go back to 'heavenly words,' but to an earthly event." This event is made known to later believers through the experience of redemption and liberation it brought to those who first experienced them.[11]

If the truth given to the world in the Christ-event is not given in "heavenly words," then the framework Schillebeeckx outlines is fundamental to our question. But we must still face the question of whether this sharing in the revealed truth by successive ages has given rise, in the doctrinal pronouncements of the Church, to expressions of that truth which have an abiding validity. In the last lines of the work we have quoted, Schillebeeckx speaks of the "liturgical mysticism" which "found an appropriate expression in Nicaea and Chalcedon."[12] Reading the pages which precede this passage, one may well conclude that for Schillebeeckx the magnificently simple affirmations which are the very substance of the Church's liturgy do not really mean what they say. Such a position would be at variance with what is demanded by the analogy of faith discussed in the previous chapter: the community of believers, learned and simple, have not heard the words which nourish the Church's faith in this fashion.

Terrence Tilley faces the problem that concerns us, as he attempts to relate the truth of "story" to the doctrinal statements of credal formularies. The solution he suggests represent another approach. According to Tilley, "doctrines are live or dead metaphors"; but metaphors are not true, nor are they false;[13] therefore the question of whether doctrines are true or false becomes meaningless. Tilley is led to conclude: "The truth of a religious tradition...is borne, not in its doctrines, but in its stories."[14] But is this an acceptable solution? Those who have taken part in the dramatic debates which produced the credal formularies of the Christian tradition would be astonished to find that they were engaged, not in the defense of the truth and the exclusion of error, but in the devising of good or bad metaphors. Tilley has failed to take into account the distinction between proper and improper analogy to which attention has already been drawn.[15]

The Enduring Worth of Doctrinal Statements: The Contribution of Bernard Lonergan

Bernard Lonergan takes up our question—one which is essentially metaphysical and epistemological—more directly than the authors we have mentioned. While fully acknowledging and concerning himself with the problem raised by contemporary historical awareness, Lonergan points the way to a "critical realism" which provides a solution which is less esoteric than those we have just considered, and fulfills far more clearly the expectations coming from an understanding of the analogy of faith such as it has been explained.[16]

In Lonergan's judgment, the project of intellectual inquiry can be properly understood only if one distinguishes two manners of knowing, or being present to reality. On the one hand, we are confronted by the world insofar as it is grasped by way of immediacy. But the reality which we experience is also "a world mediated by meaning."[17] This latter world is vast and subtle in its dimensions. As reflective intelligence grasps the present, it sets it in a context of the past that led to it, and the future that flows from it. Perceiving the actual reality of our world, we are also aware of what is possible and probable in it. The world mediated by meaning not only confronts us with facts, it also presents us with subtle realities such as the interrelatedness which we know as right and duty, of which only reflective intelligence can acknowledge the existence. This world is illuminated by travelers' tales, by stories, by legends, by literature—all of which contribute to our perception of its meaningfulness. The measured understanding of philosophy, science and history mediates further dimensions of meaning; religion, faith and theology do the same at another level.[18]

Once this distinction—between reality as grasped by way of "immediacy" and reality as "mediated by meaning"—is recognized, we are confronted by the uncertainties and ambiguities it implies: this is

> an insecure world, for besides fact there is fiction, besides truth there is error, besides science there is myth, besides honesty there is deceit.[19]

These uncertainties and ambiguities can be resolved only by identifying and applying the subtle "criteria of reality" called for if we are to come to terms satisfactorily with the world mediated by meaning. One of these criteria, Lonergan acknowledges, is certainly immediate experience; but to make this the sole criterion would have disastrous consequences for the project of intellectual inquiry. The world mediated by meaning is "not just given." Over and above what is given by way of immediacy, there are aspects of reality—such as those which have already been indicated: past and future, possible and probable, rights and duties, etc.—which are accessible only through understanding's accurate exploration of the meaning which mediates reality to the inquirer. In Lonergan's words, the world mediated by meaning is a vast "universe that is intended by questions, that is organized by intelligence, that is described by language, that is enriched by tradition." Exploration of this universe must be measured by the criteria of "relevant understanding, of accurate formulation, of correct judgment, of prudent belief."[20]

Lonergan speaks of the philosophical position we have just described as a "critical realism."[21] In his judgment, many of the frustrations of modern philosophies have their origin in the unsatisfactory manner in which they have negotiated the relationship between the world of immediacy and the world mediated by meaning.[22] According to Lonergan's "critical realism," in the world mediated by meaning "the objects to which we are related immediately are the objects intended by our questions and known by correct answering."[23] In other words, meaning (that of questions and of propositions answering questions) mediates reality itself. Lonergan's realism, in fact, involves a critical reassertion of something we take for granted as we live in the world mediated by meaning—namely, that the true meaning we give to our questions and answers about the world in which we live tells us about the reality, or being, of that world.[24]

It was necessary to clarify the philosophical position presupposed by Lonergan in his approach to the question of the enduring validity of doctrinal statements. This philosophical position takes a clearly defined stance with regard to the function of meaning. Indeed, it is difficult to see how the question can be discussed in any other terms. We can now pass from these philosophical presuppositions to the application they must find in doctrinal assertions: for as Lonergan writes, "Insofar as Christianity is a reality, it is involved in the problems of realism."[25]

In making this application, Lonergan is concerned, therefore, with the mediation of reality by meaning. He invokes the distinction which is basic to his position. The truth given to the world in the Christ-event belongs, in the first place, Lonergan points out, to the world of immediacy: in the Christ-event

> there is a new man in Christ Jesus, and that new man is primarily, not the fruit of one's own free choice, but the effect of God's grace.... It is not confined to some metaphysical realm so that experiencing it would be impossible. It can come as a thunderclap.... But more commonly it comes so quietly and gently that it is conscious indeed but not adverted to, not inquired into, not understood, not identified and named, not verified and affirmed. For, as you know, consciousness is one thing and knowledge another.[26]

But the truth which is grasped in immediacy is also mediated by meaning:

> It is mediated by meaning in its communicative function inasmuch as it is preached. It is mediated by meaning in its cognitive function inasmuch as it is believed. It is me-

diated by meaning in its constitutive function inasmuch as it is a way of life that is lived.[27]

The Christian community therefore faces all the ambiguities of a reality mediated by meaning. It is only the resolution of these ambiguities which can establish the validity of doctrinal statements.

Lonergan provides a model of this process in his analysis of struggles with the ambiguity of doctrinal assertions which took place in the third, fourth and fifth centuries: struggles which produced dogmatic statements concerning the relationship between the Father and Son.[28] In his judgment, the theological essays of Tertullian and Origen were flawed because they failed to establish satisfactory criteria of doctrinal realism: Tertullian's identification of the incorporeal with the non-existent—derived from Stoicism—implied an apprehension of reality in terms of immediacy, and led him to attempt to express the relationship between the Father and the Son through simile and metaphor derived from the material order—comparing them to root and shoot, spring and stream, the sun and its beam.[29] Origen, on the other hand, was led by his Platonic stance to equate the real with idea. Both of these essays issued in a doctrinal position which later theology has judged to be flawed with an implicit subordination of the Son to the Father.

Doctrinal inquiry was to find a genuine solution, according to Lonergan, in a procedure which passed beyond these early essays:

> There was the object in the world of immediacy and the object in the world mediated by meaning. The first is immediately experienced in the data of sense or of consciousness. The second is immediately intended in the questions we raise but mediately known in the correct answers we reach.

Thus, beyond the approaches to the question of doctrinal assertions adopted by Tertullian and Origen,

> there is a third possibility in which one's apprehension of reality is in the world mediated by meaning, where meanings in question are affirmations and negations, that is answers to questions for reflection.... It is this third view that we find in Christian preaching and teaching and, more generally, in Christianity as a reality mediated by meaning.... It is this third view that is implicit in conciliar pronouncements.[30]

For Lonergan, Athanasius provides an authentic model for this realism.[31]

Let us express in simple and concrete terms what Lonergan is claiming for doctrinal assertions. According to his critical realism, the reality of the Christ-event is known by the believing community, on the one hand by way of immediacy, and on the other through the mediation of meaning (in the language of the scriptures and in the Church's living profession of faith). The ongoing life and witness of the Church calls for a reaffirmation, in new terms, of the truth given to the world in the Christ-event. This is especially the case in those moments in which the community's life in that truth is threatened with doctrinal anarchy; but it is also necessary if that truth is to find expression in new and changing cultural contexts. Insofar as—through the meaning they contain—they do mediate the reality of the Christ-event, doctrinal statements have a lasting validity. One thinks particularly of those to which the Church has committed itself absolutely. They obviously call for a complex process of interpretation if the meaning they incorporate is to be grasped accurately. Statements such as those contained in the Church's doctrinal definitions do not, however, pretend to be an adequate or comprehensive expression of the meaning to be found in revealed truth.

Properly defined questions, "intending" reality, and the answers given to them constitute the procedure which must be used by all inquirers after truth; it is a procedure which is limited by its very nature, pretending to answer only the questions which have been asked. This is the procedure which critical realism must employ to reaffirm the revealed truth. When this realism claims that doctrinal assertions can have a lasting validity, therefore, this claim is very modest indeed. These assertions do no more than answer particular questions which have been faced by the believing community. If they concerned only a limited aspect of the divine truth, the questions taken up by the dogmatic teaching of the early councils of the Church were questions having a meaning all can grasp. They are questions which—once they are raised—have to be answered if the Church is to be certain that its faith remains one with that "which was once for all delivered to the saints" (Jude 3).

It is for the historian, of course, to identify these questions; it must not be presupposed that they will always be obvious to the reader, particularly if the reader is not well informed as to the historical and cultural context in which they arose. Though the language in which they were discussed is very remote from our contemporary situation, it is possible for contemporary scholarship to identify the questions faced by the believing community in the period Lonergan has considered: Is Christ bodily, or merely a phantom appearance? Is the one who saves us a creature or not? Is the Son only another aspect of the one who is Father? Is Mary the mother of the one who is God? Is the one who is one in being with the Father one in being with us? Just as these questions are intelligible to all believers, so too are the answers given to them in the Church's dogmatic pronouncements.

Lonergan is careful to point out important implications of his analysis as far as the meaning conveyed by the language of doctrinal statements is concerned. The

language used by the councils of the early centuries
(language hammered out by keen debate, it is true) must
not be misunderstood in a way which would inflate its
import: "In interpreting the councils, it is desirable not to
assume that the participants possessed, or the conciliar
decree intended, some precise technical meaning."[32] He
exemplifies this general observation by making reference
to the terms "nature" and "person," which play such a
prominent part in these early doctrinal statements.
Something may be clearly identified, "intended," in the
world mediated by meaning—so that questions can be
asked about it and answers given concerning it—before
it can be precisely defined:

> Socrates asked for definitions...of fortitude, temperance,
> justice and truth. While no Athenian could afford to admit
> that he did not know what the words meant, it was true
> that none, not even Socrates, could produce the desired def-
> inition.

When, later, Aristotle essayed philosophical definitions
for such things, they "involved the enormous shift from
the common sense Socratic viewpoint to the elaborate
systematic viewpoint of the Aristotelian corpus."[33]

In doctrinal statements the same process has gone
on. It would be quite inaccurate to read back into the
early dogmas speaking of "nature" and "person" the
interpretation given to these terms by later theological
discussion. These interpretations must stand or fall by
the arguments their proponents can bring forward.
Lonergan notes that Augustine is sensitive to the
principle he is enunciating:

> If one follows the lead of Augustine and profits by the ex-
> perience of Socrates, then one will explain the meaning of
> "nature," "person" and "hypostasis" in the decree of Chal-
> cedon by saying that "nature" means what there are two of
> in Christ while "person" or "hypostasis" means what there

is one of in Christ. Nor is there doubt about what is the one and what are the two. For in the prior paragraph the subject is the one and the same Son, our Lord Jesus Christ. Of this one and the same there is the four-fold predication of opposed attributes.[34]

Modest as these assertions are, for the critical realism of Lonergan they are of immense value:

> For a nominalist the subject of the statement, the Son, our Lord Jesus Christ, is just a proper name and two or perhaps three titles, while "truly God" and "truly man" involve the addition of further titles. But if one acknowledges the reality of the world mediated by meaning, then the subject of the statement is not just a proper name with certain titles but primarily a reality and, indeed, a reality begotten of the Father before all ages.[35]

Lonergan's critical realism, therefore, in contrast to a naive realism, recognizes the severe limitations which are inherent to doctrinal statements. As answers to questions concerning the truth embodied in the Christ-event, these statements are capable of a realism which has an enduring validity. But their capacity to mediate the reality of the Christ-event is severely limited on several scores.

In the first place, the meaning they register can be identified only by a careful historical inquiry. Secondly, they are limited by reason of the limited nature of the questions which they use to intend reality. Thirdly, they are further limited by reason of the lack of definition attendant upon the elements of meaning made use of in the questions asked and the answers given—as we have seen, meaning may identify objects of questioning even though they are beyond precise definition, especially when these questions and answers concern the revelation of the divine mystery. In other words, doctrinal statements are limited by reason of the fact that the language and notions which must be made use of in expressing the meaning which mediates the divine reality can have only an analogical function as they refer to this reality.

Something should be said about this last issue, which is not discussed by Lonergan in the article to which extensive reference has been made. The world of meaning which belongs to faith has an intrinsic limitation, since faith does not grasp the reality it knows comprehensively, but "in a mirror dimly" (1 Cor. 13:12). Faith is always pursuing a fuller understanding of the divine mysteries it is given to know. That fulness will come in the final vision: "Now I know in part; then I shall understand fully, even as I have been fully understood" (1 Cor. 13:12). Theology must never lose sight of this limitation and the humility it calls for: the reality of God's mystery can be spoken of and known by faith only through a language and finite concepts which are no more than an analogical expression of the eminent reality which is, in itself, beyond the grasp of created concepts.[36]

Conclusions

The matter dealt with in this chapter has important lessons for the theologian:

1. A faithful witness to the truth embodied in the Christ-event calls for *new expressions of its once-for-all meaning* in all the cultural contexts of human history. The realism essential to Christian faith and its unity in every age (Eph. 4:5) make it clear that such a translation must take place.

2. On the other hand, contemporary historical and philosophical awareness makes clear the challenges involved in this process—challenges which can be adequately met only if the theologian reflects critically upon the *epistemological implications* of the transposition of truth and meaning from one historical context to another. The theologian who does not undertake this reflection will certainly base his or her work upon philosophical assumptions; such assumptions, made but not reflected upon, will threaten the quality of what is achieved.

3. It would be naive, moreover, to judge that the meaning of doctrinal statements of another era will be immediately accessible to the reader who does not appreciate the cultural and historical situation which produced them. *Critical scholarship is called for* if the documents which record the witness of Christian faith—whether they be essays of theologians or the official pronouncements of Church authorities—are to be properly interpreted.

4. Bernard Lonergan provides a model of critical reflection which, on the one hand, justifies the possibility

of translating the meaning of these documents into new contexts, and, on the other, makes clear the *severe limitations* which the theologian must recognize as intrinsic to the process.[37]

CHAPTER EIGHT

The Essential Message of the Gospel Embodied in the Christ-Event

Too often the Christian faith has been presented as a complex code requiring assent. Not infrequently, theological analysis has led the scholar to become engrossed in particular questions which emerge in this analysis. As a consequence, the unity and simplicity of the message embodied in the Christ-event, which should be the central concern of faith, has been lost sight of. It is clear that this essential message should provide one of the formative principles of wholesome theology.

The renewal which is associated with the Second Vatican Council has recognized that the message of the gospel should have a central place in the Church's life and mission. This recognition has been slow in coming. One of the tragic aspects of the crisis of the sixteenth century, as we have already noted, was the failure on the part of the Catholic party to recognize the importance of Luther's central concern for the gospel. Conscious that he was breaking away from the prevailing "Scholastic theology" and contributing to a "new theology,"[1] Luther sought to use the message of the Bible to shape this theology; he allowed the scriptures to speak through their own idiom and rhetoric. Thus "he found his way back to the beginnings of a biblical theology in which the story of Abraham or of Christ happens anew for every reader"[2]; this theology leads to the climatic moment of the believer's meeting with the story of the cross and the message it contains. For Luther, the power unleashed in a direct dialogue with the message of the scriptures inevitably gives rise to a "destructive tension."[3] But this tension was not inimical to the true genius of the Catholic tradition:

> What is exciting about Luther is that he burst the framework of the old Church without thereby leaving it, and that he does not establish a "new Church" whose "reformist configuration" would be a function of its rejection of Catholicism.[4]

The rupture which came was due in part to his Catholic opponents' failure to appreciate the value of Luther's new mode of theological discourse. One searches in vain in the documents of Trent for an echo of the "gospel" theme which was giving such an impetus to the Protestant movement: in fact, the term *gospel* appears only once or twice in the indices of the published documents of the Council of Trent. Trent did produce a remarkable text on the organic unity of scripture and tradition in the gospel.[5] But this text—which derives from the work of John Driedo, who had been engaged in controversy with Protestants—was soon forgotten, and the theme did not reemerge in the later work of the Council.

Catholicism's lack of interest in this theme in later centuries is echoed in the meager articles on "gospel" in Catholic encyclopedias published prior to the Second Vatican Council. Without a doubt, the impulse towards renewal which found expression in the Council involved a new awareness of the gospel as "the fundamental law of the Christian economy."[6] Reflecting the insights of a renewed biblical scholarship, the Council redirected attention to the long-neglected text of Trent to which we have referred, which speaks of the gospel as the "source of all saving truth and moral teaching."[7] The Council spoke of the gospel message as the "leaven" of liberty and progress, of fraternity, unity and peace for a renewed humanity.[8] But it is significant that this fine text looked to missionary efforts in lands still to be evangelized, rather than to the dialogue with the gospel which is the very nature of Christian faith. In fact, reflecting this long neglect, both English versions of the Council's documents omit "gospel" (in the sense of message) in their indices. They each have a substantial list of references under "Bible"; but there is no focus in these entries on the *message* of the Word of God.

This lack within the Catholic communion has been redressed since the Council. Pope Paul VI's Apostolic Exhortation *Evangelii nuntiandi* (1975) endorsed the declaration of the 1974 Synod of Bishops that evangelization is "the essential mission of the Church"; he added,

> It is a task and mission which the vast and profound changes of present-day society make all the more urgent. Evangelizing is, in fact, the grace and vocation proper to the Church, her deepest identity. (no. 14)

These words have been echoed by John Paul II: "Evangelization is the essential mission, the distinctive vocation and the deepest identity of the Church."[9]

Without a doubt, the great strength of the Protestant tradition, and the source of its vitality, has been its recognition of the absolute authority of the Word of God in the scriptures, and its emphasis upon the gospel message which is the heart of the scriptures. In the long centuries during which the Catholic communion's only exchange with the Protestant tradition was a polemic which concentrated upon perceived differences, Catholics failed to recognize how much the genius of the Protestant movement has to contribute to the life of the Christian Church as a whole: in the judgement of one leading Catholic ecumenist, it is possible and necessary for this essential genius to be reconciled with the Catholic Church "as a prophetic movement of permanent significance and import."[10]

A Message About God

The message which faith must recognize in the truth embodied in the Christ-event concerns God and the mystery of God's self-giving. As Karl Barth writes, echoing the sensitivity of the Protestant tradition:

> The event of the existence of Jesus Christ [is a] self-attesting reality....[It is] a declaration....It is an address, promise and demand, a question and answer.

This message comes through Jesus Christ, who, in this sense, is himself the gospel, the embodiment of the message: "We preach Christ crucified" (1 Cor. 1:23). In Christ is given "the revelation of the mystery which was kept secret for long ages but is now disclosed" (Rom. 16:25-26). This message is the declaration of who-God-is-for-us. It is the ultimate source of joy for the world.

The dialogic moment of the believer's encounter with the gospel truth brings a meeting with the Word of love from the heart of the living God.[11] Various New Testament texts which set out to give an ultimate expression to the message of the gospel do so in terms of love. Paul writes:

> I live by faith in the Son of God, who loved me and gave himself for me (Gal. 2:20).

God's love has been poured into our hearts through the
Holy Spirit which has been given to us (Rom. 5:5).

If God is for us, who is against us?... For I am sure that
neither death, nor life...nor anything else in creation will
be able to separate us from the love of God in Christ Jesus our Lord (Rom. 8:31, 38-39).

John speaks in similar terms:

God so loved the world that he gave his only Son, that
whoever believes in him should not perish but have eternal life (Jn. 3:16).

In this the love of God was made manifest among us, that
God sent his only Son into the world, so that we might
live through him (1 Jn. 4:9).

The novelty of the New Testament's gospel message, as has already been pointed out, is not the message
of God's love, but the manifestation of that love in the
life and death of the Saviour. The Saviour's new commandment is more than the call to love one another: it is
the call to love one another as he has loved us (Jn.
13:34).[12]

Hans Urs von Balthasar sums up the astounding and
overwhelming content of this message:

In Jesus Christ, to whom the revelation in creation and
history leads...God freely manifests himself (be he never
so deeply veiled)...as gift, as love and therewith as self-
surrender.... God wills to be with me, for me and in me.
This now, in theological terms, is the "dazzling darkness"
of the divine beauty: it is not that which remains inacces-
sible when God has manifested himself in Christ, rather it
is on the contrary the splendour which breaks forth from
this love of God which gives itself without remainder and

is poured forth in the form of worldly powerlessness: the superabundant power of the light and meaning of Love.[13]

The-Truth-Itself Which God Is

In the end, the truth which is conveyed in the Good News is not *a* truth about God, but the-truth-itself which God is. To know by faith *the* truth which is embodied in the Christ-event is to enter into a meeting with the living God and his gracious designs for us. From this truth shine forth all those challenging paradoxes which we recognize as the hallmarks of the gospel, and which we instinctively acknowledge we must embrace if we are to be the Lord's true disciples. This meeting with the living God, revealed in Jesus Christ, challenges the very foundations of human existence. It invites us to enter a new order, where human wisdom looks like foolishness, where poverty is divinely precious and renouncing all is possessing all, where weakness is divinely efficacious, where the lowly are raised up and the powerful of this world are reduced to nothing, where the ordinary, the everyday reality of each man and woman is the locus of God's coming. It calls the one addressed to set out on a journey which will end in the kingdom. It promises that this way will lead to nothing less than the possession of all with God in love. It calls to a relationship which can only be one of submission and discipleship, to an identification with the ways of Jesus, even to the folly of the cross as the pathway to glory; it calls to a complete identification with the compassionate ways of the Father.

It is important to recognize that this transcendent reference in no way compromises the taking up of responsibility for the world. The message of the gospel calls those who receive it to enter into a dialogue with the reality and aspirations of humanity's common project, in order that the "signs of the times" may help them to enter more deeply into the all-embracing plan of God.[14]

Key to the Hierarchy of Truths

The presentation of revealed truth, as we have already noted, has frequently lacked cohesion. The believer has been confronted with a code made up of disparate assertions: the Trinity, the incarnation, original sin, grace, the Church, sacraments, and so on. Today those who are alive to the task of evangelization recognize that this is a degeneration. In other words, it is important to find the unity and coherence of the truth which is given to the world in the Christ-event.

Protestant scholars have seen this problem as one of identifying a canon or rule within the canon of the New Testament—that is, of finding a central affirmation which would provide an axis of reference within the confusing variety of perspectives and immediate concerns to be found in the theologies of the New Testament. The teaching of the Second Vatican Council has invited the Catholic communion to reflect upon the same issue. In the context of ecumenism, the Council pointed out that "in Catholic teaching there exists an order or hierarchy of truths, since they vary in their relationship to the foundation of the Christian faith."[15] Elsewhere the Council points to the ruling principle of this hierarchy: the essential affirmation of the scriptural message, which is free from all error: "that truth which God willed to put into the sacred writings for the sake of our salvation."[16]

This truth is surely the truth of the gospel which we have discussed.[17]

What we are discussing provides, it is clear, the proper context and measure of the search for Christian unity to which we are called today. Ecumenism must be a dialogue within the dialogue which is the essence of Christian faith: the dialogue which is realized when the gospel message is met by the response of faith. This is a dialogue which is authentic only when it is submitted to on the terms essential to the gospel itself. In that submission, the Lord's disciples must find their unity together.

Conclusions

The lessons for the theologian in the considerations of this chapter are simple and clear:

1. Faith will not have found its proper focus, and theology will not fulfill its task of interpretation within the believing community, if both faith and theology are not animated by *a concern to make clear the centrality of the gospel message* embodied in the Christ-event: the message of who-God-is-for-his-people. Particular doctrines and elements of the Christian economy find their *full significance only in the light of their relationship to this message.*

2. Because this message concerns the ultimate mystery of God and his loving self-giving, faith and its theological interpretation should always be undertaken as *a journey into the greatness of the divine mystery,* as an anticipation of what is prepared for us when faith gives way to vision (1 Cor. 13:12).

3. Properly understood, the call of the gospel is an invitation to identify with *the best interests of humanity,* because identifying with the ways of God demands this.

PART THREE

One Faith, Many Theologies

CHAPTER NINE

The Origins of Theological Pluralism

Today students of theology will encounter a bewildering variety of theological approaches. They may well ask themselves whether such a situation is healthy: how can the one divine truth embodied in the Christ-event give rise to such a variety of points of view? Our analysis of what the theologian's task involves will lead us to conclude that this pluralism is both acceptable and desirable. Moreover, an understanding of the formative principles which give rise to differentiated theologies will make possible a critical assessment which situates particular theological achievements within the theological project as a whole and makes clear their contribution to the interpretation of Christian faith.[1]

Failure to achieve such a critical point of view will give rise either to parochialism or to eclecticism. Theological parochialism fails to appreciate the valid contribution made by theological approaches which make use of perspectives and resources different from one's own. If such a point of view was almost inevitable in other epochs, contemporary historical and cultural awareness provides a comparative view which makes such parochialism unpardonable. On the other hand, however, the recognition that a variety of theological approaches is legitimate and desirable should not lead the theologian to adopt an eclectic position in which he or she can identify with a confusing variety of points of view, but not find a measure against which they can be evaluated and integrated. In this chapter and those which follow we propose to take up these questions.

The Greatness of the Truth of Faith

What we have considered in the preceding chapters has already made us aware of the overwhelming nature of the truth which is grasped by faith and which must be explored by theology: it is the divine truth itself, God revealed in all the greatness of the divinity as "for us" (Rom. 8:31). More than once Paul is moved to wonder as he considers what he calls "the mystery" revealed to the world in Christ: "O the depth of the riches and wisdom and knowledge of God! How unsearchable his judgments and how inscrutable his ways" (Rom. 11:33). He gives glory to God for

> the revelation of the mystery which was kept secret for long ages, but is now disclosed...according to the command of the eternal God, to bring about the obedience of faith (Rom. 16:25-26; cf. Col. 1:25-28).

This truth is so varied in its aspects and so rich in its implications for human existence, that already in the normative record of the New Testament a variety of theological approaches made their appearance, reflecting the situations and personal resources of their authors.[2] Ever since New Testament times, the theological project—an essential part of the life of the believing community—has been enriched by the efforts of great thinkers and traditions of thought. Addressing the International Theological Commission in 1979, Pope John Paul II referred to the variety of theologies existing in the Church from earliest times: "One can speak of a healthy pluralism" in the life of the contemporary Church, he said.

Called for by the Incarnation

Over and above the immensity of the divine truth which theology must interpret, the fact that the truth given in the Christ-event is given by way of incarnation, and yet addressed to all peoples and cultures, makes the multiplication of theological perspectives inevitable. In the Christ-event, God's truth is given to the world, not in words from heaven, but through "the language of a human life"[3] as, acting out "the logic of love...God enters into the life of the 'other' and makes himself man" in order to enter in to a "communion of love" with us.[4] Thus, the "scandal of particularity," as it has been called, was the inevitable consequence of the incarnation. God's truth was given in a human existence which was lived out and had its immediate meaningfulness within the framework of a particular culture and historical situation—that of first-century Palestine. But this truth is given for all peoples and cultures. Its interpretation must make it accessible to all by transcending particular cultures: that in which it first became incarnate, and those in which it becomes reincarnated in successive ages.

Each interpretation making it available to a new cultural tradition establishes a new theological perspective. Moreover, as time passes, particular cultural traditions undergo profound transformations, calling for new essays of interpretation which make the divine truth available to those living within that cultural tradition. In the words of the International Theological Commission:

> Because of the universal and missionary character of the Christian faith, the events and words of God's revelation must be, time and again, rethought, reformulated and lived

again within each human culture, if they are to give a real answer to the problems rooted in the heart of every human being, and if they are to inspire the prayer, the worship and daily life of the people of God. In this way, the gospel of Christ leads every culture towards its fulness, while subjecting it to a life-giving criticism.[5]

The Complexity of the Human Response to the Gospel Truth

In the previous section, we have considered the way in which the greatness of the divine truth itself gives rise to a plurality of theological constructs. We must now turn our attention to the ways in which theological diversity has its origin in the response of those who receive the divine truth. The truth embodied in the Christ-event comes to each individual believer and to each believing community where they find themselves—in the midst of their human experience. Their appreciation of the truth embodied in the Christ-event will be influenced by the culture they have received from previous generations; individuals and shared traditions will be disposed by their own experience to recognize and explore particular aspects and implications of that truth.

John Henry Newman, the nineteenth-century English cardinal, reflected upon the way in which, in the course of history, an idea expresses itself according to the dispositions of those receiving it.[6] The problem Newman faced was that of the immense transformations that are evident in Christian truths as they have been transmitted down through the ages: the "increase and expansion of the Christian Creed and ritual and the variations which have attended the process."[7] Could the faith of the

Church in the nineteenth century truly be said to be one with that of the first Christian centuries? His studies convinced him that an affirmative answer could be given to this question once it was recognized that

> from the nature of the human mind, time is necessary for the full comprehension and perfection of great ideas, and that the highest and most wonderful truths, though communicated to the world once for all by inspired teachers, could not be comprehended all at once by the recipients.[8]

In a process which involves reciprocity, Newman points out, "an idea not only modifies but is modified"; it not only shapes history but it is influenced by historical and cultural circumstances.[9] He concludes:

> And the more claim an idea has to be considered living, the more various will be its aspects; and the more social and political is its nature, the more complicated and subtle will be its issues, and the longer and more eventful will be its course. And in the number of these special ideas, which from their very depth and richness cannot be fully understood at once, but are more and more clearly expressed and taught the longer they last—having aspects many and bearings many, mutually connected and growing out of one another, and all parts of a whole, with a sympathy and correspondence keeping pace with the ever-changing necessities of the world, multiform, prolific, and ever resourceful—among these great doctrines surely we Christians shall not refuse a foremost place to Christianity.[10]

In applying the general principle Newman has identified, we may distinguish various orders of influence which helped to shape the interpretation of revealed truth offered by different theologies. The examples given in this chapter are proposed by way of illustration of the factors which are at work in the shaping of particular theologies; a more comprehensive overview of the development of theology will be given in a later chapter.

Cultural Influences

The Christian faith must be interpreted within a wide variety of cultural contexts. The increased historical sensitivity which has emerged in the last century helps us to understand how profoundly we are influenced in our outlook by our culture. History gives rise to constantly evolving human situations, shaped and reshaped by a multiplicity of cultural factors. As Lonergan's analysis makes clear, this process is constantly remaking our world: the very meaning of life and human experience is placed in an endless variety of new perspectives and frames of reference. And as we become aware of this, we are becoming freed from the assumption that our way of interpreting the meaning of the human situation is absolutely normative.

As the Christian faith expresses itself in and through different cultures, it will reflect their peculiar insights and sensibilities. In fact, the divine truth embodied in the Christ-event was first expressed in and through a concrete culture. In principle, as we have seen, it could have been expressed in and through any of the world's cultural traditions, at any stage in their development: the human life which provided the "language" of revelation could have been lived in India or China, it could have been lived in another epoch. In a very real sense, as we have seen, theology is called to effect the translation of the divine truth into the lived reality of all the world's cultures. Today, as we review the history of the spread of the Christian faith, we are confronted by the challenging fact that, having effected the transition from the Semitic culture which Jesus shared with his contemporaries to that of Hellas, the believing community has failed to carry this process forward, tending to make the Western expression of the Christian mystery normative for the whole world, and failing to recognize that it is the Christ-event itself which must provide this norm.[11]

Historical Influences

But it is not only cultural factors which shape theological interpretations. They are also affected by the historical situations in which they are made, and by the challenge of contemporary events.

The development of Christian awareness and the emphases which have emerged in theological traditions have been profoundly influenced by the controversies which have marked the course of the Church's history. The Christological and Trinitarian disputes of the early Christian centuries left their mark upon later theology, as we are only today coming to appreciate with the help of increased historical awareness. So easily theology *re-acted* to particular situations and difficulties rather than charter its own course through reference to its own cardinal principles. The crisis of the sixteenth-century Reformation, we can now recognize, brought a profound polarization and reaction on both sides of the Catholic-Protestant divide. Today, Catholic thinkers can recognize the unfortunate consequences of this reaction within Catholic theology of the Counter-Reformation era, from the sixteen to the twentieth century. The emergence of Protestantism as an alternate Christian movement led to an overwhelming preoccupation with the formulating of a theological rationale which responded to what were perceived as the positions adopted by Protestantism. No doubt, on the Protestant side of the divide a similar pattern can be recognized.

Historical influences derive not only from events within the life of the believing community but also from the ongoing developments of history at large. In the judgment of M.-D. Chenu, the essential features of the theology of Aquinas, for example, are related to the challenge inherent in the emergence of a new social reality in the twelfth century. The disintegration of feudalism, through the emergence of a new order of free cities and commerce, contained the seeds of a historical development which has continued until our own day. It also brought an end to the monastic system's dominance of the sacralized order which was the Church's life during the era of feudalism. Chenu sees these developments as having inspired a rediscovery of the essential dialogue which must take place between the message of Christian faith and the mundane order—a dialogue which was inhibited by the sacralizing ideals which had captured the monastic movement.

He sees this dialogue as having found expression, at the popular level, in the evangelical brotherhoods which were so widespread at the time, of which the movement presided over by Francis of Assisi was the outstanding example. At another level, Albert and Aquinas entered into the dialogue by taking the revolutionary step of basing their theological project upon the scientific realism of Aristotle, rather than upon the philosophical tradition of Plato which the sacralized medieval culture had found so congenial.[12]

In the modern period—at a later stage of this same development—the cultural shift of secularization which we have considered, and the related development of a new humanism, have had a profound effect upon the development of contemporary theology since the work of Friedrich Schleiermacher (†1834). This is something which we must consider in more detail in a later chapter.

The movement of "liberation theology" which is capturing the imagination of Christians throughout the world is another example of theology's response to historical developments. The renewal of Christian faith taking place in our own day finds itself confronted with the ugly forms of exploitation and injustice which have emerged in societies such as those of Latin America, as the new marketing possibilities of an integrated world economy arouse the greed of the economic establishments of these countries and of interests in countries which profit from this exploitation. Those who interpret the message of Christian faith within this historical situation are compelled to take up the challenge it brings.

Personal Factors

Some of the greatest minds in the history of Christian thought have given to their theology a spirit and outlook which reflects not only the cultural climate and the history of their time but also the personal drama of their own lives. We shall find this to be the case with many of those theologians whose work we shall discuss in later sections.

The luminous center of Paul's theological achievement is the recognition, forced upon him at the time of his conversion, that God's intervention in Christ had overturned the basic convictions of Pharisaism to which he was so committed. Taking his stand upon the Law's declaration that one who dies on the gallows is "accursed by God" (Deut. 21:23), he had been determined to eradicate by all means at his disposal the movement which proclaimed one who had been crucified as the Christ of God. His meeting with the crucified Jesus on the road to Damascus forced him to interpret his faith within a completely new framework, as he penetrated the mystery whereby God brings reconciliation and hope to the world through the Saviour's cross and resurrection: "We preach Christ crucified, a stumbling block to Jews and folly to Gentiles, but to those who are called…Christ the power of God and the wisdom of God" (1 Cor. 1:23-24). It is this central focus which dominates Paul's interpretation of the Christian message.

There is little doubt that the somber tones which characterize Augustine's theological vision reflect the historical experience he shared with his contemporaries as the ancient world slowly disintegrated around them.[13] But it is Augustine's conversion experience after a long personal struggle which left a decisive mark upon the theological synthesis which he developed within a perspective of the mystery of sin and the grace of God.[14]

Like Augustine's, Luther's interpretation of Christian faith was influenced by both historical and personal factors. The positions he adopted were certainly a "protest" against the inadequacies of the Church's life in the late Middle Ages, but it was a profound conversion experience which provided the real inspiration of Luther's theological project.[15]

John Henry Newman once complained that his work had been, for the most part, not something undertaken by reason of personal choice, but what circumstance had thrust upon him in the course of his long and sometimes tumultuous career. His theological vision was certainly profoundly influenced by his perception of the vast changes which were taking place in the modern world;[16] but it was the struggle carried out within the arena of his own personal conscience, to identify the authentic bearer of the Christian tradition, and then to communicate his understanding of that tradition to others—first Anglicans, then Catholics—which shaped his theological achievement.[17]

Existential Concern:
A Radical Subjective Factor
Shaping the Essays of Theology

When we come to interpret the major shifts which mark the history of theological development, we shall suggest that it is the location and form assumed by existential concern within particular historical contexts which provides the key to this development.

What do we mean by "existential concern"? Human existence is shaped by and has its ultimate worth from the responsible decisions and commitments which are the stuff of personhood. The daily concerns which are taken up by personal decision and commitment are, in the end, the expression of an all-embracing and ultimate concern which gives meaning to personal existence. It is this concern which polarizes human life. In it the explosive energies which shape human history have their source.

Karl Rahner begins to analyze for us the implications of existential concern when he points out that an "unobjectified knowledge about oneself" is "a basic condition of the spiritual subject which is present to itself"; through this unobjectified knowledge, the human subject has a "transcendental ordination to the totality of possible objects of knowledge and of free choice." And, as a consequence, "spirituality, transcendence, freedom, the ordination to absolute being" are "the most primitive data of consciousness, possessing transcendental necessity, and of all-embracing significance." This transcendental significance, however, is grasped only through the themes and objects of more immediate and commonplace concern, and this is achieved

> with the greatest effort and then only in a long history of the spirit, hidden beneath the extremely changeable history

of terminology, and only with very mixed success, and the greatest difference of opinion as to their interpretation.[18]

It is clear that the manner in which men and women living in different historical situations represent this ultimate concern to themselves is going to have a profound influence upon theological development, because it is this concern which shapes their efforts to relate their existence to the transcendent ground of all existence. If Christian faith claims that the Christ-event gives a name and a face to the divine mystery, the normal starting point of the theologies which set out to interpret it will be one with this existential concern, and their development will be linked with the function of this concern in particular cultures.

In different cultural, historical and personal situations, existential concern will be differently experienced. Recognition of this helps us to understand important developments which have taken place in the history of theology, as we shall see.

Methodological Principles Which Shape Particular Theologies

What we have seen in the section of the present chapter which has just concluded has to do with what we may call extraneous factors: the various dispositive influences which have contributed to the formation of particular theologies. We turn now to the intrinsic principles which are at work in their development. When a great theology emerges from the particular soil in which it is nurtured, it has its own distinctive characteristics and an individualized spirit and life which is independent of that soil. The history of Christian thought makes it clear that theologies with very different characteristics may emerge from the same milieu. Such differences come, as B. Mondin has pointed out, from internal principles at work in their formation; these principles are of two very different kinds.[19]

Structuring Principles

Mondin calls the first order of principle determining the shape of a theology "the architectonic principle." He describes it as "that fundamental mystery of revelation which is chosen by the author as the basis on and around which he organizes all the other mysteries and events of the history of salvation."[20] The insight being expressed is an important one. The genius of particular theological achievements is profoundly linked with the perspective within which their author has come to appreciate the truth of faith which he or she sets out to interpret. It may be suggested, however, that one should speak, not of the "fundamental mystery" which provides this perspective, but of that particular aspect of the one Christian mystery—given to us in the Christ-event—which provides the orientation and perspective that characterizes the theologian's approach to the divine truth. In this way we avoid the tendency we have already mentioned, which would dissolve the one vision of faith in a catalogue of more or less dissociated "mysteries."

As Mondin notes, the manifold content of the truth conveyed by the Christ-event establishes

> central and fundamental points around which to arrange all the others: grace, the covenant, the Trinity, the Incarnation, Christ's passion, the Resurrection, the Church, the Eucharist, etc.[21]

Investigative Principles

The second order of principle Mondin points to he calls "hermeneutical principles." These are the resources which are made use of in the interpretation of the Christian mystery. In principle, any human resource which helps towards an understanding and interpretation of the human situation can contribute to the theologian's task, because the Christ-event touches human existence in its ultimate dimensions and depths. As John Paul II declared in 1979,

> The truth that we owe to humanity is the truth about human existence.... Thanks to the gospel, the Church has the truth about human existence. This truth is found in an anthropology that the Church never ceases to fathom more thoroughly and to communicate to others.[22]

It is not surprising that many theologies have made use of philosophy as their chief investigative principle. Mondin gives examples from the history of theology: the Fathers used the philosophy of Plato; Rahner has used transcendental Thomism; Bultmann has made use of Heidegger's existentialism; Paul Tillich has used ontological existentialism; Moltmann has used E. Bloch's philosophy of hope; G. Gutierrez has used the Marxist analysis of society.

But the task of interpretation to be undertaken by theology can be fully carried out only if other resources are not neglected. Today, as Mondin points out, investigative instruments other than philosophy are being employed: "psychology, psychoanalysis, history, anthropology, politics, sociology, etc."[23] The resources used may be not only academic disciplines but also "ordinary knowledge which is neither systematic nor rigorous...spontaneous, non-technical philosophy, practical more than speculative."[24] The history of theology indicates, in fact, that it would be wrong to expect that theologies which made use of such resources would be inferior to those making use of strictly academic disciplines.

Whatever their form, Mondin notes, these investigative resources will be able to serve theology satisfactorily only "when it is a question of a view or a culture already positively open to Transcendency, or not necessarily closed" to such an orientation.[25] He points out that some resources which, at first sight, seem closed to the transcendent may well contribute to the work of theology. Philosophical systems which are "apparently closed or even actually closed" in the form they have been given by their proponents, may not be so closed

> in virtue of their own first principles. For this reason, if they are considered according to their appearances or even according to their original utilization, they do not offer any link with the word of God. The philosophy of Aristotle seemed such to the Fathers of the Church and to many Scholastics; and the philosophies of Heidegger and Bloch seem such to most people today. But St. Thomas succeeded in showing that the principles of Aristotelian philosophy, as such, do not involve any closing, any reduction of reality; and, therefore, he was able to assume them to a great extent for his interpretation of the Christian message. Today many scholars think that the same can be done with the philosophies of Bloch and Heidegger, freeing them from the meshes imposed on them by their authors.[26]

Mondin makes the observation that Protestant theologies have not always fully appreciated this second order of principle, thus raising an issue which is important if we are to make a critical evaluation of twentieth-century theologies. Deriving the main light of their theological enterprise from the mystery itself, and rightly recognizing that this light must be sovereign in their enterprise, they have distrusted the introduction of "human wisdom." It should be noted with Mondin, however, that not all Protestant theologians have adopted this stand.

Speaking rhetorically, Paul certainly stresses the contrast, and declares the inadequacy of human wisdom in the understanding of the Christ-event (cf. 1 Cor. 1:20; 2:4-5). But it in no way follows that theology's employment of human resources is disqualified, provided that it is utterly subordinated to the light of God's truth. Indeed, as we have seen, the incarnation calls for the use of such human knowledge if the truth embodied in the Christ-event is to be brought to all peoples and cultures. The incarnation implies that what is essentially and authentically human is saved and owned by God: as the Son saved us through his human experiences and response, so too we live out our life in his mystery through all that is authentically human in us.[27]

Basing his stand upon the gospel message expressed in the rhetoric of the scriptures, Luther rejected the Scholastic method of late medieval theology. Karl Barth has taken a similar stand in the twentieth century.[28] If some Catholic theology has left itself open to the criticism that it seemed to submit the revealed truth to the canons of reason, it must be made clear that such theology is a degeneration, and not representative of the true genius of the Catholic tradition.

Mondin's distinguishing of the two orders of formative principle which contribute to the form assumed by particular theological essays opens the way to a critical reflection upon the widely differing forms these essays have assumed in the history of Christian thought. We shall pursue this reflection in the chapters which follow. But before that, we must consider in more detail the manner in which existential concern provides a key to the understanding of the history of theological development.

CHAPTER TEN

The Changing Focus of Existential Concern

Existential concern—the concern to find an ultimate significance and value in human existence—is a theme which has become familiar in the course of these pages. It is this concern, as we have seen, which is the source of humanity's restlessness and of the developments which occur within our history: sometimes amazing in the creative achievements to which they give rise, sometimes explosive and destructive in their impact. The concern of which we speak has its source in human nature itself. It has a fundamental place in the theology of Karl Rahner, as we have already seen. As Rahner has observed, human existence is a paradox: in itself, it must ultimately be recognized as constituted by a void. One may respond to this paradox with the cynical laughter of the damned, and despair of finding anything beyond the void of human existence; or one may recognize that it constitutes a call to set aside the illusions of self-sufficiency and respond to the invitation to a meeting with the Other who is Being itself. Human existence is, in the end, an invitation to set out on a journey which leads ultimately into the unfathomable fulness of the divine mystery. It follows, therefore, that the struggles which make up human history are inseparably linked with the question of God. And, as a consequence, the changing focus of existential concern in different historical periods is an essential key to our understanding of the developments which have taken place in Christian theology down through the ages.

From Sacralized to Secularized Cultural Setting

In discussing the secularization which has taken place in Western culture, we have had occasion to reflect upon the outcome of humanity's religious quest for a lived relationship with the transcendent, and upon the ambiguities of the sacralized order which this quest has established in a long succession of cultures. The gospel was first announced to a world in which it was taken for granted that human existence has meaning only through its relationship to the divine transcendent. The challenge brought to Christian thought by contemporary secularization makes us aware that, in this sacralized context, the revolutionary nature of the truth given to the world in the Christ-event was easily lost sight of. Christian awareness was happy to rely upon a "religious *a priori*"[1] which was really alien to the genius of Christian faith.

If—in creating an order of symbols which gave access to the divine—the process of sacralization had tended to "divinize" the world of nature, the Judeo-Christian tradition brought a revolutionary shift in this order of things when it proclaimed and witnessed to the fact that the transcendent One had not remained in unspeakable mystery but had made a self-disclosure, through a history shared with a chosen people, that the unconditional expression of divine love and fidelity given to the world in the Christ-event removes the ambiguities which our religious strivings could never overcome. The full impact of this revolution is only now making itself felt in Christian theology.

It may be suggested that the disappearance of the religious *a priori* in the culture of modernity constitutes a watershed which divides the history of Christian thought into two periods. In each of these periods, the task of theology has been undertaken in a very different spirit. Moreover, the manner in which the Catholic and the Protestant traditions have negotiated the transition across this watershed has proved to be very different.

It is only recently that the Catholic theological tradition has made the transition. Distrusting the spirit of modernity, as we have seen, Catholicism maintained a cultural tradition—whether in the Catholic regions of Europe and the New World, or in the subcultures which united Catholics in other parts of the world—in which the religious *a priori* which had been inherited from the Middle Ages gave a fundamental orientation to the theological task. During the present century, especially through the work of the Second Vatican Council, this situation has changed, giving rise to far-reaching developments in Catholic theology.

The Protestant tradition, on the other hand, made the transition considerably earlier, though it was only in the present century that the problems of coming to terms with modernity have begun to find an entirely satisfactory solution within Protestant theology. Having journeyed by very different paths across this divide, the Catholic and the Protestant traditions, as we shall see, now find themselves on common ground as they take up the theological task and share their achievements within the context of today's secularized culture. The Orthodox tradition, one may suggest, is in a position similar to that of Catholicism before its recent negotiation of the divide. That theological tradition, whether in its home countries or in the New World, still functions within a culture or subculture which is established upon a religious *a priori*.

The Distinctive Theological Traditions of the Byzantine and the Latin Churches

---

During the first decades of its history, the Christian Church wrestled with the immense task of translating the Christian message from its original Palestinian setting to that of the Hellenistic world. In the judgment of Karl Rahner, we are, at long last, on the threshold of the next step in the process which was thus initiated:

> There are three great epochs in Church history, of which the third has only just begun and made itself observable officially at Vatican II. First, the short period of Jewish Christianity. Secondly, the period of the Church in a distinct cultural region, namely, that of Hellenism and of European culture and civilization. Third, the period in which the sphere of the Church's life is in fact the entire world.[2]

Rahner described the Christian Church's activity with regard to the world outside Europe during the period just ending, as

> the activity of an export firm which exported a European religion as a commodity it did not really want to change but sent throughout the world together with the rest of the culture and civilization it considered superior.[3]

It is important to keep this perspective in mind in surveying the development of Christian theology to the present day. In fact, for all practical purposes, until the immediate past, theological development has taken place only within the context of Western culture. An immense work remains to be done in giving expression to the Christian faith in the other great cultural traditions of the world. It is for that reason that we have spoken in the title of the present section, not of the theologies of the East and the West, but of two theological traditions within the community of Western culture.

The traditions of the Byzantine and the Latin spheres of influence had much in common. Most fundamentally, existential concern derived from the same Hellenistic culture, and its concern for immortality provided its starting point. During the early Christian centuries, most theologians made use of the Platonic scheme of things in their interpretation of the divine self-disclosure through the Christ-event. Doctrinal development in both spheres was shaped, in large part, by the Christological and Trinitarian controversies of the period; and the ecumenical councils these controversies occasioned were the milestones which marked this development.[4]

Beyond these common features, however, the history of separate theological developments in the two halves of Christendom was marked by the characteristics of the differentiated cultures in which they had their beginnings. The Latin tradition was heir to the pragmatic genius of the Romans, a genius which expressed itself in its codes of law and administration, and in its feats of engineering. Thus the approach of the Latin Church was marked by a matter-of-fact spirit, and was to become engrossed in questions of ecclesiastical order and moral discipline, problems which gave rise to the Novatian and Donatist heresies. It was not until the beginning of the fifth century that Augustine's controversy with Pelagius and his followers concerning grace and freedom raised a theological issue of first importance in the Latin Church, and even then the center of interest was predominantly moral rather than speculative and metaphysical. Meanwhile, the Eastern part of Christendom—heir to the culture which produced the philosophical achievements of the Greeks—became passionately involved in the dogmatic controversies which threatened to tear the Byzantine Church and Empire asunder. Christopher Dawson sums up the contrasting characteristics of these two traditions, characteristics which are of great importance to one setting out to achieve a critical appreciation of their achievements:

> Theology in the West found its centre and principle of organization in the doctrine of Grace; the Sacraments are conceived primarily as Means of Grace, the Christian life as the Life of Grace. In the East theology is the doctrine of the Consubstantial Word. The sacraments are conceived as mysteries of illumination, and the Christian life is seen as a process of deification by which humanity is assimilated to the immortal nature of the Divine Word. Thus the tendency of Western theology finds its representative and embodiment in St. Augustine, the Doctor of Grace, whose influence dominates the whole medieval development, while the typical representative of Eastern theology is to be found in Origen, who continued to influence the development of Greek Christian thought through the medium of Athanasius and the great Cappadocian Fathers, Basil and the two Gregories.[5]

Catholic Theology from the Medieval Period to the Second Vatican Council

---

In the Latin Church, the Middle Ages saw the development of a new Christian civilization. This medieval culture produced the sacralized context within which the medieval scholar took up the theological task. The medieval cathedrals and the immense influence of the monastic movement stand as monuments to the religious *a priori* of this medieval culture. Chenu describes its sacralized world view as being realized "in a Church which has absorbed the world, in a humanity where the triumphant serenity of the monastery holds sway."[6]

Because our age does not share in the context provided by this medieval culture, the theological discussion of a thinker like Thomas Aquinas can strike contemporary readers as very remote from their concerns. His purpose was, not to awaken a recognition of the importance of the questions he took up, but to achieve their precise articulation. Their importance was already established by the religious *a priori* of medieval culture. The disputations of the Scholastic "schools" are far removed from the existential concerns which challenge modern awareness.[7]

There can be little doubt that the transition from the medieval era to that of modernity is associated with the recognition that mundane reality must find its proper autonomy by being freed from the tutelage in which it was held by the sacralized culture of the Middle Ages. It is to the great credit of Aquinas that his Aristotelian project began to establish the principles which made possible a recognition of the proper autonomy of mundane reality of which we are speaking.[8] Unfortunately this development was not appreciated in a Scholastic tradition which would soon degenerate into the nominalism[9] which was to dominate the immediate context of the Reformation disputes of the sixteenth century.

Thus, instead of responding positively to the emergence of modernity—the world of commerce, the free cities which were the beginnings of autonomous political regimes, an intellectual culture no longer under ecclesiastical tutelage—Catholic theology reacted negatively, isolating itself in a tradition of thought which endeavored to maintain continuity with the traditions of the Middle Ages. The Reformation crisis only increased this unfortunate alienation from the creative movements developing within Western civilization, as the Catholic tradition found itself confronting not only the spirit of modernity but also the Protestant Reformation movement. As Walter Kasper has remarked:

> These two movements, Humanism and the Reformation, were to have a profound effect on the shape of modern theology. Despite their differences and antipathies, they both shared the same outlook on one point.... Both opposed Scholasticism's use of rational argumentation in theology and the Scholastic method in general.[10]

Kasper describes how, through this isolation, Catholic theology fell on hard times. Out of step with the movement of the prevailing culture, this theology

> when it is challenged...must uphold its claim to absolute, universal truth in a "dogmatic" way. This explains why we encounter a *theologia dogmatica* only from the seventeenth century on. And this new emphasis upon the ecclesiastical character of dogma could easily degenerate into doctrinaire clericalism and excessive concern for the magisterium. It could easily foster a ghetto outlook and make dialogue impossible both within the Church and outside.[11]

The efforts of Catholic theologians who attempted to enter into dialogue with the ongoing developments of Western culture—such as Moehler in Germany and Newman in England—were distrusted. In the first years of the twentieth century, the "Modernist crisis" was met with a repressive severity which greatly hampered the development of Catholic scholarship.

Pope Leo XIII's directive[12] that Catholic seminaries were to adopt the theological method of Scholasticism, particularly that of Aquinas—a policy which was enjoined once more by the Code of Canon Law when it was promulgated in 1915—was an attempt to bring a new vitality to Catholic theology. This measure encouraged the development, in subsequent decades, of scholarship which has made it clear that contemporary insights are not incompatible with the analytical method of a sound Scholastic tradition, as the work of scholars such as Matthias Scheeben, M. -D. Chenu, Karl Rahner and Bernard Lonergan has made clear. But it also had the unfortunate effect of fostering the development of a superficial Neo-Scholasticism, inspired more by the prevailing Counter-Reformation ideology[13] than by a healthy spirit of creative scholarship.

If the enjoining of a Thomistic approach ran the danger of seeming to give a new encouragement to the Church's resistance to the spirit of modernity, by the second quarter of the twentieth century it was becoming evident to many Catholic scholars that theology and the Church's life in general needed a profound renewal if they were to face up to the challenges of the age. The way towards this renewal was sought in a return to the sources of Christian faith. Biblical theology's exploration of the categories in which the Christian message was first presented made it clear that the categories of Scholastic thought had been excessively absolutized in the theological movement we have just described. The work of scholars such as Yves Congar and Henri de Lubac brought home the same lesson through their exploration of the doctrinal development of other ages, particularly the patristic period. It was this movement of return to the sources which prepared the way for the theological renewal initiated by the Second Vatican Council.

The Protestant Tradition
Comes to Terms with Modernity

In a very real way, Luther's efforts to formulate a "new theology" were related to a recognition that the medieval order was passing away, and it was clear that Protestantism was not destined to cling to the sacralized culture of the Middle Ages. The Reformation movement's protest was directed against the popular piety of the sacralized culture of the Middle Ages, which was the distorted shadow-side of the incarnational and sacramental genius of the Catholic tradition. From the beginning, as a consequence, the Protestant movement ran the danger of rejecting not only these abuses but also the fulness of the incarnational implications of the truth given to the world in Christ. It was a danger that it did not always avoid: as John Macquarrie writes,

> Protestant theology, from Calvin to Barth, has despised natural theology and depreciated natural law; it has minimized human achievements, and sometimes taught a doctrine of "total depravity"; it has sharply distinguished between "church" and "world," and has sometimes taught that God cares only for the "elect."[14]

As a result of this situation, though the Protestant tradition was earlier in responding to the existential concerns of modernity, it has been hampered by the inadequate resources at its disposal as it sought to come to terms with the mundane reality which is so fundamental to the existential concerns of modernity.

The interaction between the Protestant tradition and the spirit of modernity has been long and difficult. The response of Friedrich Schleiermacher (†1834) to the challenge of finding a way of negotiating the transition from a culture established upon a religious *a priori* to a culture in which this assumption was no longer present had an immense influence upon the development of Protestant theology during the nineteenth century. Richard R. Niebuhr compares Schleiermacher's place in modern theology to that of Kant in modern philosophy, in that "it is his critical reflection on theological issues that sets the basic problem for the succeeding nineteenth century and the greater part of the twentieth."[15]

Until the end of the eighteenth century, "religion" was seen as the foundational dimension of a whole culture. The attempt to describe religion as a distinct sphere of individual activity—registering the ongoing desacralization of Western culture—made its appearance at the beginning of the nineteenth century with the rise of the social sciences. Schleiermacher's treatise *On Religion: Speeches to Its Cultured Despisers* was one of the first writings that treated religion as an isolable subject; it is also remarkable in that it addressed directly the incipient secularization of the times. In this book and in his later treatise *The Christian Faith,* Schleiermacher set out to interpret the Christian faith in terms of religion as a universal human experience. He interpreted religion as a response to reality, irreducible, on the one hand, to the rational analysis with which thinkers such as Kant had concerned themselves, and, on the other, to morality. He saw each of these as having a real dependence on religion, which he judged to be *sui generis*, a primordial response to reality, a feeling of absolute dependence before the infinity and transcendence which characterizes the divine.

If his understanding of religion is influenced by Romanticism's reaction to the Enlightenment in the nineteenth century, he is speaking of something very close to what we have described in contemporary terms as existential concern. Schleiermacher invited his contemporaries to discover this neglected dimension of their experience. The theological synthesis he proposed at once vindicated and interpreted the Christian faith against the criterion provided by this dimension, as the most authentic form of religion. *The Christian Faith* was the first systematic theology of modern times and has left its mark upon subsequent theological development:

> So firmly entrenched are Schleiermacher's ideas in the spirit of the times we call modern...that very little published today of a theological nature does not borrow consciously or otherwise from some facet of his thinking.[16]

Nevertheless, Protestant theology, as it developed in the twentieth century—in the thought of Karl Barth, Emil Brunner, and Rudolf Bultmann—saw Schleiermacher's project, and the "liberal theology" which had embarked upon the path he had proposed, as compromising what is unique and essential to the truth of the Christian mystery. This was so because Christian faith was being interpreted as able to be measured by the general principles of "religion," a human universal: in Barth's words, they made the Christian faith no more than "the revelation of religion."[17] This was, Barth declared, to turn things upside down. He attacked in the prevailing liberal theology what he called the "dreaded results of the reversal of revelation and religion."[18] Revelation's "superiority, which does not allow us even to consider religion except in the light of revelation," had been lost sight of, and revelation and religion had been put on the same level.[19]

The Neo-Orthodox movement within Protestant theology set out to reaffirm the great dogmatic truths of the Christian tradition. Barth (†1968) and Bultmann (†1976) set about this task, each in his own way. Barth called for the recognition that the infinite qualitative difference between the Word of God and human thought must provide the basis of a dialectical meeting with God's Word. In the dialectic of this discussion, God's Word must stand as the absolute measure, not human thought. Bultmann's efforts to restore the transcendent biblical message to a central place in Christian awareness set out to disengage the *kerygma* and the existential challenge it brings to every age from the "mythological" forms which made the message of the *kerygma* meaningful for the New Testament community.[20]

Barth and Bultmann thus stand at an important threshold of Christian theology. Their thought represents the recognition within the Protestant tradition, that the "liberal" approach built upon the foundations provided by Schleiermacher did not provide a satisfactory response on the part of Christian faith to the challenge of modernity and the secularization it brought. A new beginning must be made. Dietrich Bonhoeffer (†1945), the German theologian who had already made his mark when his life was ended at the hands of the Nazis at a relatively early age,[21] criticized the way in which these two thinkers set about that task. This criticism serves as a good introduction to the period in which we now find ourselves, and to the challenges it faces.

Bonhoeffer applauded Barth's contrasting of God's "revelation" and the human project of "religion," and his call for the recognition of the sovereign nature of revelation. But he considered that Barth had not come to grips with the challenge of secularization. Bonhoeffer believed that the emergence of a "radically religionless" culture—one with the religious *a priori* removed—demanded the expression of the truth of revelation in categories other than those indebted to the religious cultures of the past. It was not sufficient, as Barth did, merely to confront humanity with the message of revelation in its infinite qualitative difference from human wisdom—which Bonhoeffer characterized as "a positivism of revelation."[22]

Bonhoeffer was also critical of Bultmann's attempt to remove a religious dimension no longer meaningful to contemporary culture. It, too, he found not thoroughgoing enough, with the consequence that it did not fully disentangle itself from the "liberal" approach:

> You can't, as Bultmann supposes, separate God and miracle, but you must be able to interpret and proclaim *both* in a "non-religious" sense. Bultmann's approach is fundamentally still a liberal one (i.e., abridging the gospel), whereas I am trying to think theologically.[23]

During the final months of his life, Bonhoeffer was planning a work which would present a "non-religious interpretation of biblical concepts."[24] If the religious *a priori* found God in the extremities of human existence, his theology would present God as "the beyond in the midst of life":

> I should like to speak of God, not at the boundaries but at the center, not in weakness but in strength; and therefore not in death and guilt but in man's life and goodness.[25]

Concerned to proclaim the gospel in its integrity, his interpretation of the faith would find its center in the Christ-event:

> Our relation to God is not a "religious" relationship...but our relationship to God is a new life in "existence for others," through participation in the being of Jesus.[26]

If Bonhoeffer's tragic death made it impossible for him to complete his project, he had made it clear that in the coming age theology's task must be an interpretation of the Christian faith made independently of the ambiguous support it had received in the religious cultures of the past.

Protestant and Catholic Traditions Take Up a Common Task

As we have seen, Catholic and Protestant traditions of theology have traveled by different paths as they have come to terms with the spirit of modernity and the de-sacralized culture which it has produced. Though the genius proper to each of these traditions gives rise to a dialectical relationship between them which has much to contribute to the project of Christian theology,[27] they now find themselves engaged in the common task of interpreting the truth given to the world in Christ within a secularized culture. Facing this common challenge, these two traditions are coming to recognize how much they hold in common, and denominational differences are far less apparent than previously in the theological contributions made by thinkers on both sides of the divide.

The theological achievement of Hans Urs von Balthasar was one of the first evidences of this common enterprise. Though he received his basic theological formation in Catholic faculties in the first half of the twentieth century—he was a friend and colleague of Karl Rahner—von Balthasar was an admirer of Karl Barth,[28] and his theology reflects Barth's influence. It has come to be held in high regard in both Catholic and Protestant circles. In considering his approach in a later chapter, we shall see how this approach—if it is more open to the incarnational dimension than Barth's—takes its stand, like Barth's, upon the sovereign nature of revealed truth. For von Balthasar, the act of divine love revealed in Christ is a self-attesting reality which overwhelms the creature with its incomparable beauty and establishes itself as the transcendent norm of all truth and goodness.

We may well judge that von Balthasar's theology stands with Barth's as far as Bonhoeffer's criticism is concerned. While they insist that theology must make its starting point the recognition of the sovereign nature of revelation, neither Barth nor von Balthasar takes us beyond what Bonhoeffer calls "a positivism of revelation." Their work must be supplemented, as Bonhoeffer saw, by a theology which shows more directly how the message of revelation speaks to the concerns of a culture which is no longer impelled by a religious *a priori* to assume that revelation is of fundamental importance in the interpretation of the human situation. It is to this project that the energies of contemporary theology are directed.

At first sight, contemporary theology could seem to be in a state of chaos, with almost as many approaches as there are practitioners. A recognition of the function of existential concern in the theological project, however, provides a key which helps us to understand what is taking place. The situation of theology on either side of the divide established by the emergence of secularization is very different. Theologies which interpret revelation to a culture established upon a religious *a priori* address an existential concern which is established and defined. Theologies which interpret the truth given to the world in Christ to a secularized culture—one in which the religious *a priori* is no longer present—are challenged to explore the existential concerns of that culture, in order that they may bring about a meeting with the divine truth in and through these concerns. What at first sight seems a chaotic development of widely differing theological approaches may be recognized as the prelude to a new meeting between the divine truth and the deepest concerns of humanity, as gifted theologians explore the possibilities that exist for such a meeting in today's world. We are on the threshold of a development which promises to enrich Christian theology greatly.

The thinkers who have caught the attention of the theological world working within the context of today's secularized culture in the West may be differentiated, therefore, according to the nature of the existential concern which their theology has addressed. We shall conclude this chapter by listing some of the theologians who have contributed to this task. The work of some of them will be discussed in greater detail in a later chapter.

Locations of Existential Concern

Although Teilhard de Chardin did not consider himself a professional theologian—a fact which made it easier for him to disregard the theological establishment of the Catholic Church of the first half of the twentieth century—his theological reflections fit into the framework we have just described. Because these reflections addressed concerns which were foreign to the climate of Catholic thought at the time, his work was looked upon with suspicion by Church authorities. However, the wide appeal his thought had at the time of the Second Vatican Council shows that it was taking up the concerns of believers who found themselves more and more challenged to enter into dialogue with the secularized culture they shared with their contemporaries. Working within the scientific milieu, Teilhard found himself forced to make his own the existential concerns of those involved in this project. He related these concerns to the revelation of the cosmic Christ in the Christ-event, and sought to understand how the implications of this revelation can speak to a scientific age.

Paul Tillich, as we shall see, grasped very clearly the challenge which the present age presents to theology, and he saw that this challenge must be met by bringing the message of Christian faith to the existential uncertainties of our age. The great influence which he has had in twentieth-century theology indicates that his approach has been one with which many have been able to identify.

The work of Karl Rahner parallels, in the Catholic tradition, what Tillich contributed to Protestant thought. The great attention his work commands today reflects a recognition—within a Catholic community finally taking up the positive challenge of modernity and secularization—that the message of Christian faith must be addressed to and interpreted within the framework of those concerns which arise from the primordial experience of human existence in itself. As we shall see, Rahner explores our experience of existence as a confrontation with the horizon established by the mystery of absolute being. In a later chapter we shall fill out further details of the work of Tillich and Rahner.

The challenge brought by secularization is so radical that it is not surprising that, once the Protestant and the Catholic traditions had crossed the divide and met the challenge head on, it provoked a crisis which shook the project of theology to its foundations. This crisis found expression in the "death of God" debates in the 1960s. We have seen how Bishop J.A.T. Robinson's work *Honest to God,* published in 1963, became one of the most widely read religious books ever published. In writing this small volume, the author had no intention of making any contribution to scholarship; he merely intended to make available to the general reader some of the recent developments in theology as it faced the challenge of secularization. It became, however, a catalyst which occasioned a wide-ranging discussion of the impact of secularization upon contemporary theology.

Within Protestant circles, Thomas Altizer[29] is representative of those who became deeply involved in the crisis. It also had a profound effect upon the work of the Catholic theologian Edward Schillebeeckx. The challenge of communicating the Christian truth to a secularized culture has led him to abandon a theological method which belonged to the tradition of Aquinas, and to set about implementing a method established upon categories more accessible to the contemporary Western mind.[30]

One important element in the theological project of the later Schillebeeckx is an appeal to the hope which is such a remarkable dimension of our deepest existential experience, in order to find a manner of speaking of the divine mystery which is intelligible to a secularized awareness. In this, he is one of a group of contemporary theologians who have made use of the thought of the Marxist Ernst Bloch, whose philosophy of hope is one of the important achievements of twentieth-century thought. Other theologians making use of Bloch's insights are J. Moltmann and J.B. Metz. In an approach which is not dissimilar, the work of Wolfhart Pannenberg seeks to interpret Christian faith by relating it to the existential concern which compels us to seek an understanding of the significance of human history and its finality. We shall have occasion to look at these theologies more closely later.

The theologies of hope have been complemented in recent decades by theological movements which have undertaken a further exploration of the meeting between the truth of God given to the world in the Christ-event and the mundane reality within which the existential concerns of our contemporaries are experienced. Thus, two important theological movements have emerged in our day which may be described under the general heading of "theologies of *praxis*." *Praxis* is a truth which is tested in the living, rather than by academic criteria. These latter, which have, for the most part, ruled the theological project down through the ages, are not incompatible with *praxis*. They are indispensable to the theological project, but they should be given a place which is relativized by its relationship to *praxis*.

It will be recalled that we initiated our discussion of theology and its task by pointing out that the truth which is given to the world in Christ is a truth which, before being told, is lived in the covenanted history that comes to its climax in the Christ-event and in the Church's discipleship, through which the Christ-event is made present to every age. We noted that, for most of the Christian era, this notion of truth has been lost sight of and replaced by one derived from the scientific project which had its beginnings in Greek philosophy. Giving *praxis* an essential place in the elaboration of theology's interpretation of Christian truth is, therefore, a development of great importance—provided that those doing so avoid the obvious danger of setting *praxis* in opposition to the theoretical criteria which must also contribute to the theological task. Both are, in the end, indispensable to that task.

It is not difficult to recognize that *praxis,* which is a testing of truth in the living, is inseparable from existential concern. The truth which, before all else, concerns humanity is an existential truth known through being lived. Theological *praxis* brings the truth given to the world in Christ into the arena of people's existential experience, so that this truth may disclose itself in being lived.

The best known theology of *praxis* is the "liberation theology" which has developed in Latin America. There, *praxis* brings the full message of the gospel into contact with the social reality of that troubled region, in a way which contrasts with the intellectualized theology inherited from the Old World, and with its inability to come to terms with the immense problems faced by the believing community. This theology speaks to an existential concern which, before the injustice of social structures that prevent human development, becomes alive in a new way to the life-giving implications of the gospel truth. The work of G. Guttierrez, J. Sobrino and L. Boff, carried out on this basis, has captured the imagination of theologians throughout the world. [31]

The "political theology" of European and North American thinkers sets out to make use of *praxis* in the elaboration of an interpretation of Christian truth which faces much more subtle issues than those raised by the blatant injustices to be found in third-world countries. Harvey Cox's *The Secular City,* published in 1965, was an early attempt to elaborate a theology which spoke to the existential concerns associated with the political developments of first-world countries. There can be little doubt that political developments in the Western world during the twentieth century confront us with radical issues. These developments may be related to the spirit of modernity which has shaped today's secularized culture. If, as we have suggested, modernity is established upon the recognition of the proper autonomy of mundane reality and secular institutions, this recognition has immense implications which, although anticipated by thinkers such as Nietzsche, have fully dawned upon the West only in the present century: responsibility for the shaping of the historical project of humanity rests with humanity itself.

The violent upheavals which have marked the history of the present century are the practical outcome of this recognition, as the vast energies latent in human history have been released, and attempts have been made by each end of the political spectrum to assume the initiative and shape the future development of the Western world. The terrible nature of the struggles which have ensued confronts us all with the immensity of the existential issues raised by this dramatic development. They are issues which confront the Western world at every level of political involvement. Thinkers such as J.B. Metz[32] and Jürgen Moltmann have recognized the challenge this situation brings to those who interpret the gospel truth. These issues can provide an opportunity for the message of the gospel to express itself in the midst of humanity's existential concerns in a manner which is unprecedented and just as dramatic as the work of the theologies of liberation.

CHAPTER ELEVEN

The Structuring Principles of Particular Theologies

Interpretations of the Christian faith which exert a lasting influence within the Christian tradition have a recognizable spirit and coherence. The distinctive character of these different theologies arises, first and foremost, from the way in which reflection upon the Christ-event has been structured, and this will usually come from some aspect of the Christian mystery which captures the attention of the theologian.

The central concern of the theologies of the early Christian Fathers, for instance, was the *salvation* brought to humankind by the Christ-event. Today's theologies often adopt a perspective which sees the Christian mystery as a source of hope for struggling humanity, hope in the final achievement of God for his people, which Jesus called the "kingdom"—an achievement which, while constituting the transcendent end-point of human history, already has its mysterious beginnings in what is authentic in today's world. From the time of Paul, other theologies have seen the *passover* pattern of the Christ-event (established by the dying and rising of the Saviour) as providing a formative focus. If we are to make a critical assessment of the work of the many different theologies which have appeared in Christian thought, it is essential that we identify the structuring principle or principles of this kind which they have made use of.

In fact, this influence may not be confined to *one* such principle. In Paul's theology, for example, we can recognize various structuring principles at work: he saw the Christ-event as embodying the *message* of the gospel; this message proclaimed *salvation* for humankind; it is through the *passover* pattern of the Saviour's death and resurrection, overturning all the expectations of human wisdom, that God is active on our behalf in Christ. These three principles help to shape his interpretation of the divine truth. As a general rule, however, one structuring principle will provide the main orientation of a distinctive theological achievement. In Paul's case, we will probably judge in the end that it is the third of the principles we have mentioned—the one provided by the passover pattern of the Christ-event— which shaped the most important contribution Paul has made to the Christian tradition. In the New Testament theology of John, the *incarnation* provides the dominant perspective, and within this perspective, as a subordinate principle, the *sacramental* dimension of Christian existence has had an important formative influence.

In the sections which follow we shall consider in turn a number of structuring principles which have been most influential in the essays of theologians, illustrating this from the work of well-known theologians.

The Christ-Event as a Communication from God to His People

Surveying the development of Christian thought, we may recognize this structuring principle at work in a wide range of theologies. It is already at work in the

New Testament. As we have pointed out, it helped to structure Paul's interpretation of the Christ-event.[1] And if Mark's Gospel gives expression to theological assumptions on the part of its author, the most fundamental of these is the recognition that the *story* handed on in the Jesus-tradition of the first generation of the Lord's disciples was the embodiment of God's "good news."[2] This assumption was taken up subsequently by Matthew, Luke and John. It has given rise to the paradox whereby the Christian tradition has given the title "gospel" or "good news," not to those texts of the New Testament (such as Paul's major letters) which have the form of an interpretative *proclamation,* but to those which simply *describe* the unfolding of the Christ-event.

The medieval theology of ST. THOMAS AQUINAS (†1274) belongs to a very different cultural setting.[3] The biblical theologies just mentioned are grounded in an approach to truth which is personal and existential. The analytical reflection of Aquinas adopts an approach to truth which derives from the Greek philosophical tradition—an approach which sees the truth as something objective, embodied in an eternal "idea."[4] He saw the Christian faith given in Christ as a *communication of the divine, eternal truth,* the upholding of which constituted the mission of St. Dominic's Order of Preachers, in which he had enlisted. Three passages representative of his remarkable theological synthesis are given in the *Supplementary Texts.*

The first of these is the body of the first article of the *Summa theologiae,*[5] a systematic handbook of theological questions. This article discusses the necessity of revealed truth. It is interesting to consider Aquinas' approach to this question against the background established by what we have seen in previous chapters. In the first place, his analytical approach relates the question to human existence as purposeful and responsible; if we are to attain, in an authentically human way, what is beyond the grasp of unaided reason, we must have access to a divine truth which is above reason. Secondly, he notes that even the truth concerning our ultimate destiny, which of its nature *is* accessible to reason, is easily obscured and distorted, and needs to be made clear and affirmed beyond all ambiguity by the truth of the faith. Our study of humanity's religious strivings has made us very aware of the ambiguities Aquinas is referring to.

In the second text, St. Thomas considers the "mission," or "sending," of the second and third persons of the Trinity, the Son and the Spirit, spoken of in the scriptures.[6] At first sight, this notion presents obvious difficulties: How is it compatible with the divine transcendence? Is not the one who is sent the subordinate of the sender? Does not the notion demand a departing from one place and a coming to be in another? Once more, Aquinas' approach is analytical. He analyzes what "mission" implies, concluding that it may have an analogical realization in the Trinitarian life of God.

The third passage[7] is included to indicate the manner in which Aquinas—whose normal manner of teaching theology was by way of a commentary upon the scriptures[8]—looked beyond the constraints which the Greek approach to truth tended to impose, showing himself sensitive to the mystery of divine truth given to the world in the Word made flesh. In this text, Aquinas asks whether Christ should have committed his doctrine to writing. He offers three reasons why this would not have been fitting. He argues, first, that Christ's manner of teaching should correspond to his excellence: as the most excellent of teachers, he adopted a way of teaching whereby his doctrine was imprinted on the hearts of his hearers. The excellence of the teaching itself also precluded transmitting it in writing, St. Thomas argues: his followers would have been prevented from being able to enter into the depth of this teaching, being locked into the limitations essential to verbal statements. His third reason looks to the transmission of Christ's teaching: Christ communicated his truth in a way which was beyond words, and his followers of every generation and culture must translate this one truth into preaching and writing.[9]

SERGIUS BULGAKOV (†1944), one of the leading Orthodox theologians of this century, adopted a theological perspective not unlike that of Aquinas. He called his theological synthesis "sophiology" because it is centered upon the divine wisdom *(sophia)* which is communicated in the revelation given in Christ. He was critical of Western theology for failing to incorporate this biblical dimension of the divine truth into the consideration of key theological issues. The Eastern tradition, he judged, can find its full expression only through the concept of wisdom, so profoundly meditated upon in the Old Testament, and finding its ultimate form in the Eastern Church's veneration of the Saviour himself as *Hagia Sophia* (Holy Wisdom). In this he was identifying himself with a tradition going back to Clement of Alexandria and Origen. Bulgakov saw this perspective upon God's revelation as providing an antidote to secularism's separation of the profane world from the living founts of spiritual and religious life. Through it he proposed a synthesis which united the material and the spiritual, God and man: for wisdom is present everywhere—in God in an infinite way, in man and creation in a finite way. The "seal" of the divine wisdom unites all things.[10]

In the twentieth century, the theology of KARL BARTH (†1968) is dominated by a reverential wonder before the breaking in of God's transcendent message through the Christ-event and through the Word of God living in the scriptures. The passage included in the *Supplementary Texts* shows Barth wrestling with an issue central to the perspective which shapes his theology, as he seeks to interpret the statement "We believe that the Bible is the Word of God."[11]

This passage is of interest, not only because it may serve as an introduction to the work of the great theologian and the dialectical method he adopted, but also because it deals with a problem which emerges from what has been discussed in the previous chapters. In order to provide a corrective to the "words from heaven" model which has prevailed in the understanding of revelation, we have stressed the manner in which God's truth is embodied in the Christ-event. For the "words from heaven" model, the scriptures have an obvious place at the center of the economy of revelation. What is their place in the perspective we have reinstated, and how are they related to the Christ-event? Barth sheds important light upon this question, not only for those who are tempted to fall into a "fundamentalism"[12] in their understanding of the scriptures as expressing the Word of God, but also for those of all Christian traditions who have too glibly given their assent to the proposition Barth is discussing.

This statement confronts us, Barth observes, with the "miracle" of faith's believing: an event in which the believer encounters and is overmastered by the lordship of the living God, so that barriers are transcended and the object which is encountered is the Word of God. Independently of this event, the fact that the Word of God is to be found in the scriptures cannot be proven: there is no "capacity or instrument" which could provide a measure making this proof possible.

Indeed, Barth points out, the "humanity of the Bible" constitutes a kind of scandal which impels us towards an opposite conclusion. The giving of God's Word in the earthly Jesus contrasts with the giving made in "the exalted and glorified humanity of Jesus Christ." The human form of the Bible's witness has more in common with the former than it does with the latter. This human form does not convey the Word by "direct impartation." It bears the Word of God by way of witness.

This analogy is scrutinized by Barth. Those whose witness we hear, speak to us as humans. As such, they may alienate us, given offense to us, show their capacity to err. If we analyze what they say before the forum of human wisdom, we shall never recognize what is brought to us in their witness. In a similar way, the scriptures, coming to us as human words, can give offense and be found wanting before the forum of human standards. But the inspiration of God's Spirit, whereby these words are a witness to the Word, also makes possible the "miracle" whereby faith recognizes the coming of the Word of God. What Word is it that we find in the scriptures? Is it a "lesser, less potent, less ineffable and majestic Word of God" than the second person of the Trinity? No, Barth replies, the Word which comes to us in the scriptures is the eternal Word himself. In the record of the scriptures, we are concerned with a great mystery which is an extension, as it were, of the incarnation itself. We cannot understand this mystery in a fashion which would be the equivalent of tying the Word of God to the Bible; instead, "what we must say is that the Bible is tied to the Word of God."

By way of conclusion, it is interesting to note the manner in which Barth touches indirectly upon the question of the validity of isolated doctrinal statements in the course of this passage. He contrasts, on the one hand, the divine truth itself—"the actual purpose, act and decision of God in His only-begotten Son, as seen and heard by the prophets and apostles in that Son"—and, on the other hand, particular doctrinal statements, in which the divine truth is "dissolved...into a sum total of truths abstracted from that decision, propounded as truths of faith, salvation and revelation." Something of an ambiguity exists in the contrast his dialectical approach makes.

He is drawing attention, it is true, to something which the Protestant movement has rightly underlined as of fundamental importance to all doctrinal interpretation: namely, the transcendent greatness of the message of the gospel, against which all human knowledge and wisdom must be measured, and not *vice versa*. But on the other hand, as we have already had occasion to point out, this insight must not be interpreted in a fashion which excludes the use of the resources of human understanding provided by the world's cultures, as the divine truth of the gospel is given expression in ever-changing historical and cultural contexts. In the course of this process, interpretation of the divine truth must give answers to the questions which emerge. The fact that these answers are not an *adequate,* or comprehensive, expression of the divine truth must not be seen as implying that they are of no validity—or, as Lonergan would express it, that their meaning does not mediate the reality of the divine mystery.

The point which has just been made serves as a suitable introduction to the work of HANS URS VON BALTHASAR (†1988). In this author's work we may also recognize the influence of the structuring principle we are considering: revelation is interpreted as a divine self-communication. A great admirer of Karl Barth,[13] von Balthasar is also critical of Barth's dialectical approach to the divine truth. As we have just seen, Barth extols the transcendent greatness of the divine truth by stressing its antithetical relationship to human wisdom and thought forms. Von Balthasar makes his own the insight Barth is concerned to emphasize; however, as he does so, he situates himself within the incarnational tradition of Catholicism. He sees the affirmation of the divine truth in our midst, not as a reducing of all other truths to nothing, but as the affirmation and upholding of the created order, as "everything of beauty found in this world is drawn up into a relationship to this inexhaustible standard."[14] Von Balthasar calls his theological synthesis "a theological aesthetics," because it is centered upon the beauty of the divine self-communication realized in the Christ-event. Clearly, the revelation of God must be presented as a teaching, a bestowing of the "truth" which completes and unifies our fragmentary knowledge; as salvation, it comes to us as the "good" which answers our deepest individual and social needs. But in the end, von Balthasar judges that the self-disclosure of God given in the Christ-event will be fully appreciated by Christian theology only if it is presented as the manifestation of the glory, the incomparably beautiful mystery of God's love. Within this perspective, the divine communication is a self-attesting reality—again we hear echoes of Barth—made credible without invoking humanly established criteria.[15]

This approach is explained by von Balthasar in the pages which introduce the second volume of his seven-volume work *The Glory of God: A Theological Aesthetics*.[16] Before the revelation of God in Christ, "everything in the world that is fine and beautiful is *epiphania* (manifestation), the radiance and splendour which breaks forth in expressive form from a veiled yet mighty depth of being," because "the event of the self-revelation of the hidden, the utterly free and sovereign God in the forms of this world, in word and history, and finally in the human form itself, will itself form an analogy to that worldly beauty"—calling it to authenticity and fulfillment—"however far it outstrips it."[17]

This analogy does not mean, however, that what is realized in God's self-disclosure is to be judged by principles or measures derived from the world of human experience. Its greatness must be, "no matter how strange the manner of its appearing, read off from the form of revelation and from nowhere else." It is this form which confronts us in its beauty as a self-attesting reality, "as a gift, as love and therewith as self-surrender" so that "the negating ineffability of the gift speaks only of the still greater overwhelming of man...through this 'ineffable' fact that God wills to be with me, for me, and in me"; it is this form which confronts us with "the splendour which breaks forth from this love of God which gives itself without remainder and is poured forth in" a "worldly powerlessness."

The terrible beauty of this divine love and self-giving von Balthasar sees as manifested in an incomparable way in the cross, whereby "going to the utmost point of what is not God, he can finally establish his lordship and his glory in what is other than himself, in man, and by the glorified *Kyrios* (Lord) fashion glory out of humanity and the cosmos." This expression of God's sovereign freedom on our behalf through a self-communication brings about the "drama" whereby God

> commits to the fray the last divine and human depths and ventures of love: the "ethical" is realized precisely in the figure of the "aesthetic": behind the perfection of each word, each gesture, each encounter of the Son of Man there stands, making it possible and bearing it, the harmony of divine and human "existence," life together with death, heaven together with hell.

The Christ-Event as Passover

The story of Jesus comes to its climax in the death of Jesus and its glorious but mysterious sequel in his risen triumph. As PAUL developed the theological synthesis through which he interpreted God's intervention in Christ on behalf of his people, this synthesis reflected, as we have seen, the way in which Paul had been forced to come to terms with the fact that God's final self-disclosure had taken place through the cross. In all probability, Paul the Pharisee undertook his campaign to stamp out the Christian movement, encouraged by the fact that he could appeal to the Law itself in his rejection of a crucified messiah: "A hanged man is accursed by God" (Deut. 21:23). His encounter with the crucified Jesus presented the most radical challenge imaginable to the position he had taken up. The reflection upon his previous position provoked by his conversion is echoed in the letter to the Galatians: "Christ redeemed us from the curse of the law, having become a curse for us—for it is written, 'Cursed by everyone who hangs on a tree' " (3:13).

It may well be that Paul's experience of personal failure led him into a deeper appreciation of God's strange decision to make the human failure and dereliction of his servant, Jesus, the source of life and hope for the world. The first two chapters of the first letter to the Corinthians give us a precious glimpse into Paul's coming to Corinth: "in weakness and in much fear and trembling" (2:3), after the humiliation which followed his brave speech in the Areopagus, at Athens. But the sense of powerlessness occasioned by this failure gave him a new closeness to the Saviour's cross and the hope it brought to a broken world: "I did not come proclaiming the testimony of God to you in lofty words or wisdom. For I decided to know nothing among you except Jesus Christ and him crucified" (2:1-20). And thus it is that Paul lays the foundations of the theology of the cross, the interpretation of the final self-disclosure of God which confounds all human wisdom and standards: "We preach Christ crucified, a stumbling block to Jews and folly to Gentiles, but to those who are called, both

Jews and Greeks, Christ the power of God and the wisdom of God" (1 Cor. 1:23-24).

Paul saw this theology of the cross as basic to the life of the whole Church; he reminds the Corinthians that—just as he has found a deeper sharing in the power of Christ's cross through his own experience of powerlessness—so, too, their own humble human resources can lead them to be open to a meeting with the message of the cross he brings: "God chose what is low and despised in the world, even things that are not, to bring to nothing things that are, so that no human being may boast in the presence of God" (1 Cor. 1:28-29). Because, in Paul's experience, it was a meeting with the risen Lord which forced him to come to terms with the cross, the significance he recognizes in the cross is intimately associated with the Lord's resurrection. Paul links these two as together constituting the saving intervention of God: "Jesus our Lord...was handed over to die for our transgressions and was raised for our justification" (Rom. 4:25). God's intervention thus has a twofold effect, at once overcoming evil and establishing humanity in the new existence brought by Christ. The faith which brings a new relationship with God in Christ is the owning of God's intervention on behalf of the world in the Saviour's death and resurrection, and the acknowledgement that, in raising Jesus from the dead, the Father has vindicated all that he lived and died for, and has shared with him his own "glory." The Father has made him a "life-giving Spirit," empowering him to bring forth the "new creation" (2 Cor. 5:17; Gal. 6:15) as the "last Adam" (1 Cor. 15:45), established "as the Son of God in power with the Spirit of holiness [or sanctification]" (Rom. 1:4).[18]

MARTIN LUTHER (†1546) consciously developed a "theology of the cross" as the centerpiece of his reformation program, making a contribution to Christian thought which has had a fundamental importance for the Protestant movement.

Luther found in the message of the scriptures a dialectical relationship between, on the one hand, the Law (which brings a deep awareness of moral impotence and depravity, yet, of itself, offers no remedy for this condition) and, on the other hand, the Gospel (which tells of the salvation given in Christ, prior to any effort or achievement on our part).[19] Echoing Paul, Luther sees this message as coming to us, first and foremost, in the cross.[20] In the crucified Christ—where Christian faith must recognize God as finally active on our behalf—all human initiative was reduced to nothing but sinfulness and darkness, and the ways of God were expressed in a manner which could never have been anticipated by a wisdom which is merely human:

> The visible...parts of God are set over against those which are...invisible...the humanity of God, his weakness, his foolishness...so that in this way those who did not worship God as made known in his works might worship him hidden behind his sufferings.... From now on, it could never be enough...nor could it benefit...to know God in his glory and majesty unless [God is known] at the same time in the humility and shame of the cross.[21]

Thus Luther contrasts the "theology of the cross," which is grounded in his recognition of God's self-disclosure in the cross, with what he calls the "theology of glory," a theology which interprets the faith in a way that neglects the wisdom revealed in the cross. Taking its stand upon human wisdom, this theology

> prefers works (i.e., its own achievements before God) to sufferings, and glory to the cross...power to weakness, wisdom to foolishness [because] through the cross, works are destroyed and the old Adam, who is rather inclined to be made stronger by good works, is crucified [and he is

taught] that he is nothing, and his works are not his own but God's.[22]

There is no doubt that Luther is pointing to something which should have great significance for Christian faith. Looking back from the vantage point of today's historical awareness at the confrontation in which he was becoming involved, we may regret, first, that his Catholic opponents were blind to the nature of this contribution, and, second, that the political climate of the times made it impossible for Luther to adopt a conciliatory approach which was alive to, and had some compassion for, the difficulty which the late medieval outlook had in appreciating what he was proposing. Moreover, as we have seen, the rhetorical form in which Luther proposed his "new theology" led him to expound his insight in a way which nullified all that would make dialogue and reconciliation possible between his contribution and what was valid in the position adopted by his opponents—this latter being summarily dismissed as "theology of glory."[23]

What we saw earlier about the development of doctrine and theological interpretation—in particular, Newman's analysis of the process—leads us to recognize that this development involved not only advances but also regressions: important aspects of the Christ-event which were appreciated in the New Testament or in earlier periods may come to be neglected. Today, we are able to recognize that this was certainly the case as far as the *passover* implications of the Christ-event are concerned.

There is something ironical in Luther's branding the position he is criticizing as a "theology of glory," indicating as it does his inadequate appreciation of the place of the resurrection in Christ's saving mystery. Luther shared with his Catholic opponents a theological perspective which neglected the essential place the resurrection must have in an adequate interpretation of the significance of the cross for Christian faith. Catholic theology has, for its part, been slow to recover an appreciation of the passover mystery which gives clear expression to the full message of the New Testament. This impoverishment has often meant that students of theology found their high expectations were disappointed when they came to study the redemptive meaning of the cross. An authentic faith instinct told them that the real grandeur of what God has done for us in Christ was not captured by a theological interpretation which explained the redemptive value of the Saviour's sufferings through the categories of sacrifice, merit and satisfaction. This impoverished appreciation—which came from Anselm of Canterbury (†1109)—left its mark upon the theological traditions of both Catholics and Protestants.

Today, the revival of biblical scholarship has pointed the way beyond this narrow perspective. In the mystery of the cross, an act of divine love has transformed the human existence of Jesus of Nazareth—an existence in which he shared the condition of our broken world and its evil and death—into the source of life and hope for all. Through the last Adam's life in the Spirit, he becomes the visible expression in this world of the final act of God's love: "The whole history of Christ from beginning to end forms a dramatic, effective sign in which God's saving purpose is set forth and through which his saving act comes to men.... But the essential core of this redemptive history was Christ's death and resurrection. That was when the essential transition took place and Christ passed from this world to a new order of creation" in which we are called to share.[24] The message of the scriptures makes it clear that our interpretation of what God has done for us in the cross of Christ must ground itself in an integration of the Saviour's cross and resurrection.[25]

The teaching of the Second Vatican Council registered an awakening to the central importance of the

Saviour's passover mystery within Catholic thought. If any single concept provided a structuring principle which gave unity to the teaching of the Council, it was this understanding of the paschal mystery, which brought the cross and the resurrection together in what was a return to the message of the New Testament and the early Church, and provided a framework which opened up a vision of faith that embraced the total destiny of humanity in the plan of God.[26] One would have to say, however, that appreciation of this integration has often been superficial. There is little evidence, for example, that the important insight Luther has given to the Protestant tradition has been fully acknowledged by Catholic theology.

The Protestant tradition itself has been challenged by contemporary developments to recognize that the "theology of the cross" which it inherited from Luther needs to be integrated more fully with an understanding of the significance of the Saviour's resurrection. This challenge has been taken up in a remarkable way by JURGEN MOLTMANN. This author's *Theology of Hope,* published in 1964, shared in the optimism and new hope reflected in the Second Vatican Council's emphasis upon the resurrection in its taking up the theme of the paschal mystery. His important study *The Crucified God,*[27] published several years later, on the other hand, situated itself squarely within the Protestant tradition's "theology of the cross."[28] His recognition of the significance of this tradition went back to the war and its aftermath: "A theology which did not speak of God in the sight of the one who was abandoned and crucified would have had nothing to say to us then." The theology which had provided a firm ground for faith in those difficult times came back to his mind when the movements of hope which dominated the early 1960s "met stiffer resistance and stronger opponents than they could stand" in the latter years of that decade.[29]

The Crucified God was his response to this situation, calling Christian awareness back to "the word of the cross" which is the "inner criticism of all theology, and of every Church which claims to be Christian," a criterion which "goes far beyond all political, ideological and psychological criticism from outside."[30] He outlines the main features of the theology of the cross proposed in *The Crucified God* in a passage reproduced in the *Supplementary Texts*.[31] Observing that the tradition of theology he is taking up goes back to Paul and Luther, he notes that today we can rise above "one-sided presentations" which neglect the relationship between the cross and the hope brought by the resurrection: "The theology of the cross is none other than the reverse side of the Christian theology of hope." He sees the theology of the cross as concerned primarily with the revolution Christian faith brings in humanity's "concept of God." Faith in the God revealed in the cross of Christ brings a liberation whereby humanity can confront the reality of the "demonic crisis" in contemporary society:

> Either Jesus who was abandoned by God is the end of all theology, or he is the beginning of a specifically Christian, and therefore critical and liberating, theology and life.

If Catholic thought has neglected the important insights contained in Luther's theology of the cross, it has an important contribution to make in the further dialogue which is called for in order that a common preaching of the "crucified Christ" may provide the basis of that reconciliation of Catholic and Protestant traditions for which we must all strive. This contribution calls for a further deepening of the recognition, in which we must all surely share, that the cross is before all else an ultimate expression of God's love. The Protestant tradition's theology of the cross has dwelt too exclusively, it would seem, on the abandonment of the cross, whereby the Saviour, having identified with us in the darkness and foolishness of the world we have made, shared with us the terror of a meeting with God's unspeakable goodness and holiness. But this identification—whereby, in Chenu's words, "in accord with the logic of love, God enters into the life of the 'other'"—was an ultimate expression of the mystery of God's love for the world, the love which the Saviour shared with his Father and to which he must give expression in our midst.[32]

The Christ-Event as Our Salvation

The existential plight of humanity is such that only God's intervention on our behalf in the Christ-event provides a way out. Those who first entered deeply into the living of the Christian faith recognized this truth very clearly, so that it became one of the dominant motifs of the New Testament. The secularization of contemporary Western culture, however, has led to a situation very different from that of the first century in which the message of the gospel was first announced; and, as a result, this structuring principle does not speak to us as it did to the first generations of Christian believers.

The many theologies which find expression in the New Testament are all influenced by this structuring principle. The name of God's chosen one, *Yeshua*,[33] means "Yahweh is salvation." A common name in New Testament Judaism, it took up a theme which had found expression countless times in the Old Testament and which was central to the New Testament's announcing of the Christ-event: "God our Saviour...desires all...to be saved and to come to the knowledge of the truth" (1 Tim. 2:3-4).

This aspect of the divine truth has had an immense influence upon Christian thought as the Christ-event was interpreted within the sacralized cultures which prevailed until the recent past. Many examples of theologies shaped by this structuring principle could be listed.

It was fundamental to the interpretation of the faith undertaken by the Church Fathers of the early Christian centuries. In fact, the "soteriological principle,"[34] which affirmed the achieving of the world's salvation in Christ as beyond all doubt for Christian faith, dominated the theological discussions of the patristic period so profoundly that it was made the basis of their interpretation of the incarnation itself.

ST. ATHANASIUS of ALEXANDRIA (†373), for instance, gave expression to this outlook in upholding, against Arius, the divine identity of the Word:

> Because death and corruption were gaining ever firmer hold on them, the human race was in the process of destruction. Man, who was created in God's image, and who in his possession of reason reflected the very Word himself, was disappearing, and the work of God was being undone. The law of death, which followed from the transgression [of Adam], prevailed upon us, and from it there was no escape.... What, then, was God to do?...*Who* was it that was needed for such grace and such recall as we required? Who, save the Word of God himself, who also in the beginning had made all things out of nothing? His part it was, and his alone, both to bring again the corruptible to incorruption and to maintain for the Father his consistency of character with all.... He saw how unseemly it was that the very things of which he himself was the artificer should be disappearing.... He saw and, pitying our race...he took to himself a body, a human body even as our own.[35]

In a very different context, the same soteriological conviction provided a basic impetus to Luther's search for a "gracious" God many centuries later. In our own century, the theological synthesis of PAUL TILLICH (†1965) may be seen as an interpretation of the gospel message as offering salvation: a way out of the anguish which besets the world of the twentieth century.[36] Tillich stood firmly within the Protestant tradition stemming from Luther; he judged, however, that the language with which that tradition had been accustomed to present the gospel's promise of salvation no longer speaks to to-day's secularized world. The gospel message of salvation, Tillich pointed out, has spoken in different ways to successive ages. In the early Church, it addressed an age preoccupied with death and yearning for immortality; in the Middle Ages and the Reformation periods, it spoke to those burdened with a sense of guilt and seeking the grace and favor of God. Today, he considered, it must speak to the experience of contemporary humanity, to the contradictions and precariousness of an experience of existence poised over an abyss of nothingness and tempted to lose all hope that the destructive powers of non-being can be overcome.

Contemporary existence, he observed, gives rise to a threefold anguish: the anxiety of uncertainty as to fate and death, the anxiety of individual and social responsibility and guilt, the anxiety that all existence will be swallowed up in meaninglessness. The faith which the gospel message brings is a courageous acceptance of existence in the face of these anxieties. This courage is born in the very depths to which the anguish attendant upon contemporary existence has led us. It comes from the acceptance of God as the "ground of all being," the "ultimate concern," "the God beyond God," inviting us beyond the comforting images of the divine which are the constructions of humanity's religious project—constructions which show themselves powerless to help us in our present need. This acceptance saves our being from meaninglessness and nothingness.

If Tillich's theology is developed within the framework of existential philosophy, the theological perspective to be found in the writings of HENRI NOUWEN makes use of a similar structuring principle within a framework provided by the insights into our existential needs provided by modern psychology. For the approach he has adopted Nouwen acknowledges his indebtedness to psychologist Carl Rogers. When one has the courage to enter where life is experienced as most unique and private, Nouwen declares, one "touches the soul of the community."[37] He cites Rogers:

> I have found that the very feeling which has seemed to me most private, most personal and hence most incomprehensible by others, has turned out to be an expression for which there is a resonance in many other people. It has led me to believe that what is most personal and unique in each one of us is probably the very element which would, if it were shared or expressed, speak most deeply to others.[38]

In one of his first publications, *The Wounded Healer,* Nouwen speaks of the wounds of contemporary humanity:

> They have been spoken about in many ways by many voices. Words such as "alienation," "separation," "isolation" and "loneliness" have been used as the names of our wounded condition. Maybe the word "loneliness" best expresses our immediate experience and therefore most fittingly enables us to understand our brokenness.[39]

In a series of publications which have made him one of the most widely read religious writers of the late twentieth century, Nouwen has explored the way in which the truth given to the world in Christ brings a healing for the wounds of which contemporary psychology makes us painfully aware. His writings have made an important contribution to the theology of our age which is shaped by a highly original use of the structuring principle we are considering.

The theologies of Tillich and Nouwen are the work of academics. The achievement of JEAN VANIER is of the practical order: the establishing of a worldwide network of communities where the mentally handicapped and their assistants share the work and life of a single community. But the soul of this achievement is the prophetic message of a personal theology which has led Vanier deep into the mystery of the Saviour's presence in the midst of the lives of these people, and opened up to countless others a new vision of what God has given to our broken world in Christ. Vanier had thought he would bring Christ to these people. Instead, he found Jesus waiting for him in their midst, to teach him the true wisdom of the gospel. In 1964, Vanier opened a small house for the handicapped at Trosly-Breuil, north of Paris. He tells us that he soon

> began to understand better the message of Jesus and his particular love for the poor in spirit and for the impoverished and weak ones of our society.... In a mysterious way, in their love they have revealed Jesus to me.... I have discovered also in a new way all those barriers in myself which cause me to despise and to reject others who are of different ways and opinions.[40]

In addresses throughout the world and in various publications, Vanier has shared the wisdom which has been given to him in the living out of this divinely simple program. In characteristic terms, Vanier speaks of the importance of the prophetic dimension in the life of the believing community:

> Whenever you meet someone (and each of us does at times) who has just encountered Jesus as Paul did on the road to Damascus, it is very important to ask: "What is he like, this Jesus that you met, and where did you meet him? What is he asking of you?" In the answers we will discover some of the designs of God and the Spirit for our times.[41]

Those who are familiar with Jean Vanier's writings will recognize that he makes a prophetic contribution to contemporary theology with an importance that could easily be overlooked. He makes it clear that humanity's need for salvation can provide a structuring principle for a theology which speaks powerfully to our time.

The saving aspect of the Christ-event has been given a striking expression in the "theologies of liberation" which have emerged in recent decades, particularly in Latin America. The theology of Jean Vanier is developed through a reflection upon the gospel message within a particular marginalized situation. Working on a much vaster canvas, the theologies of liberation have considered what this message has to say within historical situations of injustice and oppression.[42]

These theologies interpret what God has done for his people as a liberation which carries forward the very work of creation. In the scriptures, the creative act is linked, almost identified with, the act which freed Israel from slavery in Egypt; in the one through whom the world was made, the Christ-event brings forth a new creation. The decisive event of Israel's history, it is pointed out—the liberation from slavery in Egypt—was an action with profound political ramifications.[43] Social injustice is an offense to the creator, and the frustration of his designs for his people; and it follows that those who are God's people must take up the struggle for social justice if they are identified with his ways.

However, for GUSTAVO GUTIERREZ, one of the founders of this recent theological movement, the liberation which faith recognizes as Christ's achievement is not to be identified simply with liberating historical events. While it may occur in and through these events, the gospel truth of the liberation brought by Christ constitutes a prophetic challenge to the limitations and ambiguities of these events, calling them beyond themselves to their absolute fulfillment in that total communion which is realized only through the "kingdom" which Christ proclaims as the gift of God.

An important aspect of liberation theology is its critique of the tendency so often present in the public stance adopted by Christians, to limit the essential concerns of Christian faith to the strictly "religious" sphere, seeing them as touching the social order only indirectly or tangentially. A passage from Gutierrez' *A Theology of Liberation*[44] reproduced in the *Supplementary Texts* will give the reader a contact with the issues raised in this very significant development in contemporary theology.

Emancipation in all its forms is one of the deepest concerns of today's world. Liberation theology points to an oppression that is not difficult to recognize and which must be addressed by those who claim to interpret the relevance of the gospel truth to the struggles of humanity. There exist many other ways in which fundamental rights of the human person have been denied or restricted, as far as particular groups are concerned. One of the most important developments in contemporary theology derives from a recognition of the manner in which the patriarchal forms which have established themselves in the world's cultural traditions have affected the interpretation of the truth given to the world through the Christ-event. Feminist theology sets out to redress this imbalance. ROSEMARY RADFORD RUETHER, in a passage reproduced in the *Supplementary Texts,* discusses the radical nature of the distortions which must be acknowledged at the heart of Christian theology.[45]

The Christ-Event as Incarnation of the Eternal Word

Our reflections upon the incarnational aspect of the Christ-event in an earlier chapter began with the Johannine emphasis upon the Saviour's coming "in the flesh" (1 Jn. 4:2; cf. Jn. 1:14). We recognized, however, that the Son's "becoming flesh" is inseparable from the "story" in which his human existence was expressed. It must be acknowledged, nonetheless, that a view of the incarnation which did not give sufficient attention to the revelatory significance of the story of the historical Jesus has provided a structuring principle which has had enormous influence in the development of Christian theology until the recent past.[46]

In the Church of the Fathers, it was the school of Alexandria which championed this theological approach.[47] Reared in the Platonic tradition, the Alexandrians tended to emphasize the abstract rather than the concrete. The "words from heaven" model which this philosophical tradition fostered could not but become profoundly influenced by Christian faith's acknowledgement that the eternal Word himself "became flesh" (Jn. 1:14). When considering the Saviour, their vision centered itself instinctively on the Logos, of whose life and activity the incarnation was but an episode. Making the fourth Gospel their preferred text, they experienced little difficulty admitting that, in becoming incarnate, the Logos never ceased to be God. Paradoxically, although they took their stand upon the Johannine assertion that "the Word was made flesh," their principal shortcoming was a tendency to neglect the fact that the Saviour was fully man. In fact, the Johannine formula gave rise to a paradigm—*Logos-flesh*—which, while clearly affirming the Saviour's divine identity, tended to overlook the completeness of his manhood and the part played by his human interiority in the mission he had received from his Father.[48]

The thinking of Athanasius, which we have already considered, is developed in this perspective. One of the most influential exponents of the Alexandrian theology was CYRIL of ALEXANDRIA (†444). A passage from his writings illustrating the approach we have been describing is included in the *Supplementary Texts*.[49]

In the mid-twentieth century the same principle structured theological reflection associated with the emergence of a new sense of mission in the Church as it faced the challenges of the contemporary world. This new sense of mission found expression in the Catholic Action movement. Yves Congar, the great Dominican ecclesiologist, describes the "incarnational" outlook of this movement:

> They were enthusiastic young people, conscious of bearing the cause of evangelical witness in the milieu of working men. This consciousness fused with the theology of the Mystical Body as it could be found in popularized form...and this fusion led to an "incarnational" spirituality. Young workers continued the life of Christ the Worker, the life of the worker constituted a "continuation of the incarnation"—a theme which could lend itself to ambiguity but which Père Chenu helped us to interpret in terms of a realism of grace and the Word.[50]

Though this movement began among young blue-collar workers, its program of bringing Christ to all sections, or "milieux," of our contemporary world was taken up by other groups wrestling with the question of what it means for the Christian mystery to become a reality in the midst of their world. These groups sought a theology of the Christian life which pointed the way beyond an understanding of it as an owning of formalized codes of morality and worship; they sought the "transcendent" dimension which would bring a proper inspiration to their new-found "horizontal" involvement in the contemporary situation. All of these issues are raised, for example, in a small publication entitled *The Incarnation in the University: Studies in the University Apostolate.*[51] The interest this volume aroused among those concerned with the revitalization of Australian Catholicism indicated that the theology it expressed had a strong appeal for them on the eve of the Second Vatican Council. A similar climate prevailed in other parts of the world at that time.

The Second Vatican Council's Pastoral Constitution on the Church in the Modern World *(Gaudium et spes)* took up this "incarnational" theology and set it in the more adequate context provided by the theological vision which emerged in the course of the Council. Meanwhile, the ongoing work of renewed biblical scholarship has led to the recognition that the incarnation can be fully understood as the disclosure of who-God-is only when it is seen that the Christ-event speaks to us in the language of human life, in the story of Jesus of Nazareth.

The Christ-Event as Gift or Grace

Because it precedes any deserving or initiative on our part, all that is given to us in the Christ-event is utterly gratuitous. The Christ-event itself is a gesture of God's freedom, an expression of the manner in which God is absolutely and unconditionally "for us," prior to any merit or fault on our part. It is not surprising that this aspect of the Christ-event has captured the attention of some outstanding thinkers, becoming the structuring principle of the theological system they have elaborated.

One of these is ST. AUGUSTINE (†430), the North African scholar and bishop who has had an immense influence upon the theological development of the Western Church. A passage from Augustine's *Confessions,* illustrating some of the principal features of his theology, is reproduced in the *Supplementary Texts.*[52]

Augustine addresses God as truth itself (Ch. 26). His conversion came at the end of a long intellectual quest; and when he finally committed himself to the Christian faith, he did so within the framework of a philosophical awareness shaped by the Platonic tradition: this truth he has found is not something he contains, it contains him as it contains and enlightens all. The long struggle which has led to his conversion makes him very much aware, however, that it is only with difficulty that each person is open to the enlightenment which comes from the divine truth.

Having found the truth which is God, Augustine is overcome with the pathos of the sinner's foolishness (Ch. 27): the divine truth is so beautiful that it overwhelms those who find it, and they cannot but fall totally in love with it. He looks back upon his early life, recognizing the foolishness of allowing the beautiful things of this present world to keep him from the one who is their source. It was not Augustine's efforts which brought this about, however, but the generous and absolutely free initiative of God: "You called me...you broke my barrier of deafness...you put my blindness to flight."

But having fallen in love with the divine truth does not mean that Augustine's struggle is over: he does not cling to God with all his being, his life is not yet filled with God (Ch. 28). His pleasures are still sometimes unworthy, and his sorrows are symptomatic of an illness which is not completely cured, so that his existence in this life is "a long, unbroken period of trial." Here we see the somber side of Augustine's view of the human condition, a tendency to pessimism which was taken up by later theological movements—such as Calvinism and Jansenism, both of which acknowledged their indebtedness to Augustine—and which today provokes something of a reaction against his thought.

Augustine's concern in this text, however, is to acknowledge his continuing need of the divine "physician." God's generosity, or "grace" given in Christ, is concretized for Augustine (Ch. 29) in the manner in which God has led him and will continue to lead him from the burden he has just described to the true freedom which comes from falling in love completely with the divine truth and being drawn along the way this truth points out to him. To turn away from this truth is to begin to disintegrate, but to be led by God's grace is to find integrity and freedom.[53]

The other theologian whom we have chosen to illustrate the use of a structuring principle derived from the gratuitous favor of God shown to us in the Christ-event is KARL RAHNER (†1984). The text selected for inclusion in the *Supplementary Texts* serves as an introduction to Rahner's approach to the divine truth while at the same time showing him coming to grips with the issues raised by contemporary secularization.[54]

Rahner's theology aimed to maintain the essentials of the tradition which stems from Aquinas. He recognized, however, that to do this he must take account of the questions raised by later philosophical inquiry. The metaphysical approach which he adopted has been described as transcendental Thomism.[55] He saw every encounter with finite being as having intelligibility only through a reference to absolute being: the finite existent is known only against the horizon constituted by the beyond which is being as such, the divine transcendent. As Rahner points out in this passage, it must be recognized that this understanding of the transcendent implies that we cannot speak of God in a way which makes God part of a more comprehensive "system," or one of a series of existents. From this it seems to follow that every "objectification" of God made by the religious quest of humanity in its attempt to establish a relationship with God is an illusion: such an objectification would be different from God and infinitely removed from what God is.

The problem is particularly acute for the Christian faith, with its claim that phenomena in our world of experience are "definite and exclusive manifestations of God." In fact, Rahner observes, "the Christian claim could seem no more than a vulgar disturbance of the only attitude before the absolute mystery which is appropriate, a reverential agnostic silence." To unaided human wisdom, the objectification of God presents immense challenges—indeed, challenges such as those which we considered in the first chapter of the present work. Experience, however, indicates that an authentic immediacy to God is a possibility for the human person. If this takes place, it is not through the disappearance of the non-divine—something which religious and mystical traditions are tempted to postulate—but through the paradox of the non-divine's mediating of the divine immediacy: what is not God does not have to disappear when God draws near: "As God, he does not have to find a place by having something else which is not God make room." The real challenge of Christian faith is to acknowledge that this paradox is realized ultimately in the "self-communication of God" which takes place through a "salvation history" through "phenomena existing within our experience as definite and exclusive objectifications and manifestations of God."

This sovereignly free self-giving of the divine mystery, which constitutes the horizon of human awareness, is the cornerstone upon which Rahner goes on to build his whole theological synthesis. Thus Rahner's theological anthropology and his theology of grace are constructed upon an understanding which sees human nature, not as something which can be defined according to some self-contained intelligibility, but as something which can be defined only through its unlimited reference to the infinite fulness of the transcendent mystery— a question, as it were, to which God's mystery alone can provide the answer. Rahner's theology of grace explores the manner in which the answer has been given in a measureless generosity of self-giving. His theology of the incarnation is situated within the same perspective: a human nature such as we have described has so utterly surrendered itself to the divine mystery that it does not belong to itself but becomes at once the nature of the eternal Son himself, and an invitation to every man and woman to find the authenticity of their destiny by sharing in the Son's human response.[56]

The Christ-Event as
Establishing a New Covenant

In the world of early Hebrew experience, in which the spoken word was so important, the word which expressed an interpersonal agreement of covenant was invested with a ritual solemnity which, as it were, objectified it, placing it beyond being annulled or retracted, and promising dire consequences if the undertaking was betrayed. Treaties were made not only by equals but also by powerful protectors and their vassals. The solemnity of such undertakings made them second only to the bond of blood.

It is not surprising that from this experience the Israelites derived a notion which became central to their interpretation of the ongoing relationship which God had entered into with them. This notion became so fundamental to their interpretation of their sacred history that it established a perspective which dominated Old Testament theologies. The relationship interpreted through this theology was not, it is clear, one between equals. It depended upon God's free decision (Deut. 9:4); God had chosen this people out of all the world's peoples, not because of their greatness—they were "the fewest of all peoples"—but because of his love, and because of the word given by "the faithful God who keeps covenant and steadfast love with those who love him and keep his commandments to a thousand generations" (Deut. 7:6-9). This perspective was basic to two traditions of fundamental importance in Israel's theology, that of prophetic reflection and that of the chronicles which interpreted Israel's history.

The prophets' interpretation of the theme led them to a daring affirmation that the covenant which God had entered into with his people could be likened to an espousal.[57] The chronicles which interpreted Israel's history proposed an understanding based upon the covenant: God had fulfilled *his* word, but the infidelities of Israel had forced him to inflict upon them the threatened chastisements.

It was this same theme which was used as Israel looked forward to the fulfillment of its hopes, in a realization of God's purposes which transcended the existing order of things: God would give a "new covenant" in which Israel's fidelity would be realized through hearts imbued by the Lord with the undertaking they had made (Jer. 31:31-33): "I will take out of your flesh the heart of stone and give you a heart of flesh. And I will cause you to walk in my statutes and be careful to observe my ordinances" (Ez. 36:26-27).

It comes as no surprise that Jesus invokes this theme, so fundamental to the outlook of Israel, in the eucharistic gesture through which he identified himself with the "servant" whose vicarious sufferings brought life to the whole world. His words, "This is my blood of the covenant, which is poured out for the multitude" (Mk. 14:24), echo the most solemn moment of the establishing of the covenant of Sinai: "Moses took the blood and threw it upon the people, and said, 'Behold the blood of the covenant which the Lord has made with you in accordance with all these words' " (Ex. 24:8).

The structuring principle which we are considering has had an important place in the shaping of Christian thought. The world of medieval feudalism was not unlike that of the Old Testament experience we have described: it was the word of the liege lord and the vassal which provided for security and social stability. Within this context, ANSELM of CANTERBURY, as we have seen, proposed an interpretation of the Christ-event as a covenantal transaction. Through this transaction, the Saviour made a commensurate satisfaction for the offense offered to God by the sins of the world. Speaking as it did to those who lived in the social system of feudalism, Anselm's perspective was widely adopted, so that

> in the period which stretches from Anselm to Bonaventure and Aquinas, one finds compressed the development of a theology of redemptive satisfaction which aspires to comprehend all the aspects of Christ's suffering and death.[58]

This was, in fact, a narrowing of a rich perspective established by the early Christian centuries, which saw the Christ-event as God's victory over the forces of evil.[59] Although thinkers such as Aquinas maintained this broader understanding of the divine achievement in the Christ-event,[60] it was the narrower view which prevailed and which established the perspective largely taken for granted by both sides of the Reformation controversy of the sixteenth century. This perspective interpreted the Christ-event in terms of merit, propitiation and atonement.

The biblical notion of "justification," which was to prove so important in these controversies, served to accentuate this emphasis. It has been suggested that the decision made by the translators of the Old Testament into Greek, to use the Greek word *diatheke* for the Hebrew word for "covenant," *berith,* had important consequences in the development of New Testament thought. In the language of Hellenistic law, this term referred to legal disposition of an estate and the enactment of provisions one intends to effect. This choice laid the emphasis upon the divine transcendence and upon God's condescension in establishing the people of Israel and their law. It is these aspects of God's work for us in Christ that come to the fore in Paul's dramatic metaphor of "justification," portraying the Christ-event as the expression of a decision on our behalf prior to anything we had done.

We may now recognize that some of the confusion which bedeviled the sixteenth-century controversies arose from the fact that, whereas the theologians of the Reformation used the term "to justify" *(dikaioun)* in a sense which revived the predominant usage of the New Testament as meaning "to *declare* righteous," their Catholic opponents used it in the sense which it had acquired in patristic and medieval writings—"to *make* righteous." Beyond this confusion, as we have seen, the controversy involved a confrontation between a theology which sought to interpret the Christian faith in a way which was close to the language and rhetoric of the scriptural message, and a theology which interpreted the Christian mystery in terms of the analysis of medieval Scholasticism. Today, biblical and historical scholarship provides a common vantage point from which we can review the sixteenth-century controversy.[61]

This common view of the question implies the recognition that the perspective shaped by the covenant principle must not be adopted in a way which excludes aspects of the Christ-event that come to light in other perspectives. The document produced by the United States Lutheran-Roman Catholic dialogue group notes that, while the biblical concept of justification may be termed "forensic," or as portraying a divine decision on our behalf, this must not be taken to mean "that it gives exclusive primacy to one image for the saving action of God in Christ, over others."[62] Having made this qualification, the document goes on to note the importance of this biblical notion, an importance which we may acknowledge has often been neglected in Catholic theology:

> Particular images, however, are of special usefulness for
> particular purposes, and juridical or forensic ones are of
> prime importance when emphasizing the proclamatory
> character of justification. There are various ways of ex-
> pressing that God's promises are unconditional, but this is
> done with particular pointedness by saying that God de-
> clares or imputes an alien righteousness, that of Christ, to
> wholly undeserving sinners.[63]

Contemporary secularization challenges theology to
interpret the faith in a way that overcomes the tendency
to a complacent formalism which is present in sacralized
cultures. Taking up this challenge, some theologians
have revived a perspective which interprets the faith in an
interpersonal perspective. In twentieth-century philosophy, "existential" and interpersonal analysis has had a
similar objective, as it has sought to lead the Western intellectual tradition beyond the aridity of an impersonal
positivism and rationalism. These two movements
flowed together in the mid-twentieth century, calling
forth the theological perspective of existentialist
personalism. A theology which is carried out in this
perspective has inevitably been drawn to make the
interpersonal, or covenantal, relationship between God
and God's people a central focus of attention.[64]

Peter Fransen, a Belgian Catholic theologian who
contributed to this movement immediately prior to the
Second Vatican Council, pointed out that the approach he
adopted in his interpretation of the Christian mystery has
much in common with the "I-Thou" theme of the Jewish
philosopher Martin Buber, and with the existential
thought of the French thinker Gabriel Marcel. Looking
further afield, he saw antecedents for this approach in the
patristic period (Augustine and the Areopagite), in the
medieval mystics, and in modern thinkers such as John
Henry Newman and Dietrich von Hildebrand.[65]

The Christ-Event as the Assembling
of a People, with Mary as Model

This structuring principle has a recognizable affinity with that which we have just considered. It is through the covenant that God's people are gathered together in the midst of all the peoples, finding an identity through their relationship with God. The corporate destiny of the "people of God" displays to the world the mystery of God's ways and the generous plan which God has conceived for the whole of creation.

This theme had a fundamental place in the theological outlook of the patristic period. For the Fathers, the Christ-event was the climactic moment of the mystery whereby God was gathering humanity into a final unity in Christ.[66] The institutionalization of the Church's life which has taken place since the Middle Ages tended to obscure the identity which must be recognized by Christian faith, between the mystery realized by God through the Christ-event and the life of the Church.[67] But during the past century, as the Church has sought the ways to renewal, the reaffirmation of the mystery of the Church's life in Christ has absorbed the attention of some of the finest theological minds of our time. Among these, Yves Congar and Henri de Lubac have been outstanding, making a contribution to the work of the Second Vatican Council which can scarcely be exaggerated.

YVES CONGAR, who recognized the importance of today's movement towards Christian unity, saw that the recovery of a more adequate theology of the Church than has prevailed in recent centuries was necessary if this movement was to bear its full fruits. The text from Congar's work *Tradition and Traditions* which is reproduced in the *Supplementary Texts*[68] illustrates the rich theological synthesis Congar achieved in making use of this structuring principle.

The interpretation of the Christian mystery which emerges from Congar's study brings to light important themes which had been obscured by an unbalanced institutionalization of the Church's life. Congar's vast erudition puts his readers in touch with the thinkers who have given expression to these themes down through the ages. Appealing to authorities such as Origen, Hilary, Cyril of Jerusalem and Augustine, Congar sees "God's self-revelatory action" in the Christ-event as given to the believer through the mutuality of the Church and the scriptures: the Church is the "locus" in which the scriptures yield their authentic meaning. This subject, which is the recipient and the bearer of the message of God's Word, is the *catholica*, the worldwide believing community which, through the presence of the Spirit, is united by communion in the truth of God's Word in Christ.

This mutuality provides the basis of a theology of "tradition": the message of the scriptures which rules the Church must be authentically interpreted by the Church's living voice in every age and culture in a way which faithfully brings to light the immense implications of the Christ-event. This understanding of the manner in which the message and the reality of what God has done for the world in Christ is the very life of the Church, must help those in the Catholic tradition to recognize the manner in which a juridical mode of thought has impoverished theology: the "rule of faith" is far more than an ordinance of properly constituted canonical authority. It refers to a concrete reality to be found in the living faith of the Church.

Continuing this line of thought in the pages which follow, Congar notes that for the best thought of this tradition, this rule will be fully appropriated only by those who are spiritual, that is, open to the Spirit in the Pauline sense, whether individually or united in the Church's assemblies. All that the tradition which lives on in the Church has to communicate to our age will escape those whose legalistic understanding of the Church's authoritative teaching leaves them under the illusion that "the Church no longer has to strive for full fidelity, no longer has to strive to call down upon herself the visitation of the Spirit."

HENRI de LUBAC is another Catholic theologian of the present century who, adopting a similar approach, pointed the way towards the renewal of the Church undertaken by the Second Vatican Council. His concern looked to a broader canvas than that of Congar's ecumenical objectives. Exploring the tradition's understanding of the mystery of the Church, particularly in the early centuries, he has sought to shed light upon problems facing the contemporary Church. His theology shows that such an exploration can greatly enrich our understanding of the message of Christian faith. The paragraphs reproduced in the *Supplementary Texts* are taken from a work of de Lubac's entitled *Catholicism: A Study of Dogma in Relation to the Corporate Destiny of Mankind.*[69]

The problem he is taking up is that of the scandal of the exclusivism which seems to be implied by the belief that, through the Christ-event, God has assembled a people as his own in the midst of all the peoples of the world. If a narrow exclusivist interpretation has been a constant temptation for those who have been the recipients of God's call, the Christian tradition's interpretation of the message of the gospel points beyond such a view. In the first paragraph[70] de Lubac summarizes the view of the Church Fathers, who saw the visible Church as embodying a hope for the whole human race, in the implementation of a vast but mysterious plan which will finally assemble the whole of humanity to share in the astounding generosity of God's self-communication.

But, as de Lubac notes in the paragraphs then cited, this vision—which had been lost sight of when, to the eyes of medieval man, virtually the whole world had been absorbed into the visible Church—has been reappropriated only with difficulty by the theological interpreters of later centuries.

In the final paragraphs reproduced, he recapitulates this long theological discussion in terms of the axiom of Cyprian (†258): "Outside the Church there is no salvation." He suggests that ultimately the axiom may be understood in a positive sense which sums up the vision of the Fathers which he has described: "It is through the Church that salvation will come, that it is already coming to mankind."[71]

We have already indicated the passover mystery as providing a perspective which shaped the theological vision of the Second Vatican Council. The mystery of the Church, appreciated anew through the work of scholars such as Congar and de Lubac, provided another important structuring principle for the work of the Council. At the conclusion of the first session of the Council, Cardinal Garonne, a member of the Council's theological commission, summed up "the spirit and orientation of the Council" in these words:

> Not a study of a series of theological problems...but rather an effort to enable the Church to show her true countenance to the world.... The Church is not one of the themes of the Council, but the Council's whole concern.[72]

The newly elected Paul VI agreed: "The declarations of this Council are concerned, first and foremost, with the Church."[73] In fact, the two structuring principles we have pointed to interacted: the immediate concern of the Second Vatican Council was the renewal of the Church; the inherent logic of this task led to a deepened reflection upon the mystery of the Church within an understanding of the mystery of Christ as the passover event affecting the whole of creation.

Within the oldest expressions of the Catholic tradition, the theology of Mary is inseparable from that of the Church.[74] HUGO RAHNER, the brother of Karl Rahner, has presented this Marian view of the believing community's involvement in the Christ-event in a small volume entitled *Our Lady and the Church*.[75] As he points out with a wealth of illustration, the Catholic tradition has constantly been drawn to dwell upon the parallel between Mary and the Church, as it sought a deeper understanding of the one or the other. For example, in one chapter, entitled *"Mulier fortis,"*[76] he indicates the way in which documents of various periods, from the centuries of the Fathers until the early Middle Ages, have drawn a parallel between the calling of the pilgrim Church to participate in the mystery of Christ, and Mary's vocation. To follow the Saviour is to make a "toilsome journey." The Church must learn how to make this journey from the woman who first followed Jesus along this road, "shyly, distant and unnoticed...to the Easter festival of his death...the 'valiant woman,' standing at the foot of his cross."[77]

The title "valiant woman" echoes the Latin version of the first words of the poem in praise of the perfect wife found in the Book of Proverbs (31:10-31). Rahner's study of what the Church Fathers and the mystics of the early medieval period had to say upon this text leads him to judge that this tradition constitutes "one of the special treasures of the theology of Mary and the Church."[78] The moment of the incarnation in the heart of Mary is seen as the moment of her acceptance of the task of discipleship.

It was a moment in which she found a readiness to set out on the way which would lead to the cross. She showed herself the valiant woman who is an example to the Church, called to the discipleship which unites believers in the mystery of Christ:

> The symbol of the valiant woman is fulfilled also in the Church and her vocation on earth.... This acceptance of death, in which she follows Mary, is verified in her day-to-day history, her persecutions, and her daily cares.[79]

This same poem (Prov. 31:14) likens the valiant woman to a merchant's ship bringing bread from afar. The Fathers saw this as verified in Mary and the Church: through Christ (the Bread from Heaven, born in Bethlehem, the "House of Bread"), Mary, and—following her example—the Church, have changed the famine of sin into a feast of joy. As they respond to their calling, "the destitute world becomes rich, and starving mankind is fed lavishly."[80]

Mary's acceptance of the motherhood of the Saviour meant not only the ultimate acceptance of his death, it meant also the acceptance of the daily trials of the long journey that lay ahead of her. From her the Church must learn the faith and courage needed in a continuing fidelity to its mission:

> Her whole history is a meeting with death, she is forced into retirement, despised and forgotten, and yet has an ever-present anxiety about her heart's beloved child: in a word, she is a true mother.[81]

In fact, Mary represents for the Church a call to continuing fidelity: "It rests with us, her children, her members...whether this Marian mystery of the valiant woman is verified in the world or not."[82]

The Christ-Event as
Source of a Sacramental Economy

Paul points to this approach as he takes up a theme which was central to the apocalyptic literature of the period: the plan which God has made for the final achievement of the divine purposes is at present hidden; later it will be dramatically revealed (cf. Dan. 2:28).[83] Paul declares that he has been called

> to make the word of God fully known, the mystery hidden for ages and generations but now made manifest...the riches of the glory of this mystery, which is Christ in you, the hope of glory (Col. 1:25-27; cf. Eph. 3:5-9; Rom. 11:33; 16:25-26).[84]

In the sacred history God has shared with the chosen people, coming to its climax in the Christ-event, this hidden plan is already revealed in a mysterious way recognizable to faith. For Paul, the Christ-event is an ever-present reality, shown to the world through the sacramental rites in which the believing community is caught up in what God has done for his "servant" in the Christ-event (cf. Rom. 6:3-6; 1 Cor. 10:16-17; 11:26).

But it is John who is outstanding among the theologians of the New Testament in his development of this theme. He sees the sacramental pattern of the Christian mystery as bringing to light an extension of the economy of the incarnation and its revelation of God's hidden purposes. While he has few direct references to the sacramental rites of the believing community, his whole Gospel is conceived within a sacramental perspective.

None of the "signs" which he portrays are so meaningful as those that point to the sacramental life of the Church:

> The wine of Cana that replaces the Jewish water of purification (2:1-11); the life-giving water that comes from Christ (3:5-7; 4:10-14; 7:37-38); the heavenly bread that is his flesh (6:51)—all these signify the sacraments that are efficacious in virtue of his redemptive work, bestowing the Holy Spirit that is the life of the Church (19:34; 1 Jn. 5:6,8).[85]

Tradition has seen this sacramental theology—which presents the life of the believing community as a sharing in the realization of God's hidden purpose in the Christ-event—as coming to its climax in John's solemn reference to the blood and water flowing from the pierced side of Christ:

> Many of the Fathers, not without good reason, interpret the water and blood as symbols of baptism and the Eucharist, and these two sacraments as signifying the Church which is born like a second Eve from the side of another Adam.[86]

The patristic culture of the early Christian centuries was strongly influenced by a Platonic outlook which saw the contingent and mutable world of immediate experience as a kind of reflection of the transcendent world of eternal realities. It is not surprising that this climate disposed the theologians of the patristic period to interpret the Christ-event and its presence in the Church's life in sacramental terms. Augustine, for instance, takes this perspective for granted. For him, this sacramental economy of the Church's life in the mystery of Christ is so all-embracing that those who have been raised in an awareness of "the seven sacraments," highlighted in Christian consciousness since the Middle Ages, will find his approach disconcerting. "They are called sacraments," he preached to his people, "because in them one thing is seen and another is understood. That which is seen has a bodily appearance; that which is understood has a spiritual fruitfulness."[87] And on the basis of this understanding he nominates some ninety elements of the Church's life as "sacraments," including such things as the sign of the cross and the Lord's Prayer.[88]

The *Supplementary Texts* include a passage from the *Apologia pro vita sua* of JOHN HENRY NEWMAN[89] which makes quite clear the influence of what he calls "the sacramental principle" in his theological development. Newman's earliest Christian awareness made it inevitable that the Platonic outlook of the Church Fathers should have a profound appeal for him.[90]

In the passage which has been reproduced, Newman notes that it was the thought of the Fathers which helped to clarify for him the doctrinal positions which brought him beyond the uncertainties of "liberalism." The school of Alexandria, and the Platonic tradition which its great thinkers made use of in the elaboration of their theology, captured his attention: for them, "the exterior world, physical and historical, was but the outward manifestation of realities greater than itself." They saw the Christian faith as providing the key which brought to light the hidden mysteries pointed to by the visible world:

> The visible world still remains without its divine interpretation; Holy Church in her sacraments and her hierarchical appointments, will remain even to the end of the world only a symbol of those heavenly facts which fill eternity.[91]

This theological perspective has something important to contribute to the life of the Church. We have had occasion in an earlier chapter to point to the importance of the sacramental dimension in the Church's life, sharing with the Word the function of rendering present to successive ages the truth in the Christ-event. It has been pointed out that a sacramental event—involving, as it does, a meeting of divine and human activities—"has meaning and consequences beyond what we can understand and measure," and, as a result, enables a "recovery of a sense of the mystery of God's action and the mystery of our own sinfulness." This recovery has importance for the believing community as it renews its life of worship and seeks a greater fidelity to the gospel by taking up today's challenges of social action:

> Every attempt either to fashion liturgy or to formulate public policy would be conditioned by the modesty associated with mystery, i.e., with the realization that we can never fully grasp and express God's will and action, that no design for worship or for social programs will fully capture our ideals or the dimensions of mystery.[92]

The Christ-Event as Expression of God's Universal Plan

This perspective takes up what must obviously be one of the essential concerns of a theology which interprets the significance of the Christ-event to an age with a growing awareness of human solidarity. The message of Christian faith speaks in a powerful way to this situation. What God has done in Christ is directed to the benefit of the whole human race, not merely to some privileged section of humanity: "God our Saviour...desires all men to be saved and to come to the knowledge of the truth" (1 Tim. 2:4). The words of Christ spoken as he enacted the eucharistic gesture with which he bade farewell to his followers—echoing the Isaian "servant" theme—refer to the universal scope of his atoning death: "This is my blood of the covenant which is poured out for the multitude" (Mk. 14:24). The election spoken of so frequently in the scriptures is not a call to be set apart from the rest, but a call to a special role for the sake of the others: election is "not a privilege of the elected but the call to live for others."[93]

What we have seen of the work of de Lubac earlier in this chapter makes it clear that the history of doctrinal development warns us against neglecting this perspective. But it must be acknowledged that, while the issues it raises have not been ignored by contemporary theologians, they have often remained peripheral. One exception to this generalization is DIETRICH BONHOEFFER (†1945). This brilliant German theologian had already established his place in contemporary theology when he died at a relatively early age at the hands of a Gestapo hangman.[94]

During the final months of his life, Bonhoeffer gave himself to reflection upon the challenge faced by contemporary theology as it endeavors to relate the tragic reality of a contemporary secularized world to the purposes of God revealed in the gospel. He was one of the first theologians to meet the challenge of secularization head on. By describing today's cultural situation as that of a "world come of age," Bonhoeffer had no intention of implying that it had become wiser or better. He was referring, rather, to contemporary disenchantment with traditional religious forms, projecting an image of God which did not meet the existential needs of struggling humanity in our time. The solution, Bonhoeffer was convinced, was not the abandonment of any part of the Church's traditional faith—that, he saw, was the "weakness of liberal theology"[95]—but the reexpression of the full gospel message in "non-religious" terms.

Bonhoeffer would be gravely misrepresented if it were suggested that the demise of religion meant that, for him, God was no longer at the very center of human existence. But he thought that, with the demise of religiosity, many honorable people would shape their lives with an "unconscious Christianity," whereby they identified with the ways of God without finding a conscious relationship with God. Those who are confessing Christians may have to revive the *arcana*, the discipline of the early Church, according to which the Christian mystery was disclosed only to those who were ready to receive it in faith.

If Bonhoeffer anticipated the complete disappearance of religion from our culture, most today would disagree with him. However, if one distinguishes various forms of religious expression, it is difficult, as we have seen, to disagree with the view that Christians today face a crisis brought on by the fact that many traditional forms no longer meet the needs of contemporary men and women. These issues are discussed in the passage which has been reproduced in the *Supplementary Texts*.[96]

In this passage, made up of excerpts from letters written from prison, he takes up the problem of communicating the message of Christian faith—"who Christ really is for us today"—to those living in a secularized culture. This communication has depended upon the religious *a priori* of previous cultures; today, in a world which is becoming "radically religionless," this task takes on a completely new form: How must a "religionless" Christianity express itself? "How can Christ become the Lord of the religionless as well?" Though he is still struggling to clarify his ideas, he envisages a new Christian consciousness which would learn from Christ, "belonging wholly to the world," finding God anew, not in the comforts of "religion," "not on the boundaries but at the center, not in weakness but in strength; and therefore not in death and guilt but in man's life and goodness," for "God is beyond in the midst of our life."

In passing, as we have seen, he comments upon the shortcomings of the responses proposed by Karl Barth on the one hand and Rudolf Bultmann on the other. He admires Barth's criticism of religion, to which he is clearly indebted, but finds that he has not succeeded in meeting the challenge which this criticism presents. Bultmann's "demythologizing" he sees as "abridging the gospel," removing embarrassing elements; on the other hand, he sees the real task as one of translating the *whole* of the scriptural message into a non-religious idiom.

The Christ-Event as Realized in the One Who Came Among Us as Servant

---

In the previous section we considered a theological perspective which, while it possesses obvious importance for the contemporary believer, has yet to be fully developed. Mention may well be made in this context of a perspective which is almost completely undeveloped but which, in the end, may come to be recognized as of fundamental importance if the essential message of the gospel truth is to be interpreted to the world.

In their bringing of this message to the broader world, Christians have usually adopted the attitude of being in a superior and privileged position in their relationship to the ongoing struggles of humanity.[97] It was a stance which scarcely identified them with the one whose disciples they professed to be. Have interpreters of the Christian faith given adequate consideration to this aspect of the Christ-event and what it has to say to every age, especially our own? When the ways of God found expression among us, it was through the one who—identifying utterly with the ways of the Father—"came not to be served but to serve" (Mt. 20:28); the one who, when he "knew that his hour had come to depart out of this world to the Father, having loved his own who were in the world, he loved them to the end. And during the supper...laid aside his garment, girded himself with a towel...and began to wash his disciples' feet, and to wipe them with the towel with which he was girded" (Jn. 13:1-5; cf. Lk. 12:37); the one who "emptied himself, taking the form of a servant" (Phil. 2:7).[98]

This emphasis takes us to the heart of the divine truth embodied in the Christ-event. It brings us face to face with the final significance of the new commandment to which Jesus calls his disciples: "Love one another as I have loved you" (Jn. 13:34). It has been suggested that this New Testament theme has implications which today come to light as never before, since we are capable of a critical reflection upon the nature of service which was impossible in the first century.[99]

Understandings of service which were taken for granted in other ages show up their inadequacy today. These understandings presupposed a fundamental condition of inequality between persons, and took for granted that the servant must serve the master in a way which expressed and reinforced his own condition of inequality. More recently, the altruistic service of modern times has reversed this situation. The one who serves recognizes the need of the one who is served and is in a position to alleviate that need. Such a relationship is still one expressing inequality, and, if it is not transcended, may well prove to be little more than a subtle but powerful form of domination. The divine truth given to the world in the Christ-event is not only the revelation of God and his ways, it is also the affirmation of what it means to be authentically human. The one who makes the Father known to us by becoming a servant in our midst is not merely giving us a lesson in humility, he is revealing the astounding ways of God, ways which give the lie to the foolishness which has made a world far removed from God's truth.

The ways of God affirm the ultimate truth of all personhood and of the relationships with others which are the essential expression of all personhood. It is an expression which challenges the depths of our personhood, as, with Peter, we draw back from such a gesture. This divine truth does not deny the existence of personal differentiation: he who washes the disciples' feet unhesitatingly declares himself their "Lord and Teacher" (Jn. 13:14). But it makes clear that differentiation—even that which exists between the Lord and the disciples—must never serve as a basis for domination or manipulation of any kind: according to the ways of God revealed in the Christ-event, the form that all personal relationships should have is that of friendship.[100]

An interpretation of the Christ-event tracing it back to the Old Testament antecedents of the Isaian "servant" theme and following out its full implications for human existence would constitute a presentation of the message of faith which simultaneously would lead us into the depths of the ways of the living God and offer a critique of unredeemed human existence astounding in its depth and simplicity.

The Christ-Event as
Realization of the *Eschaton*,
God's Final Achievement

God's intervention on behalf of his people in the Christ-event is the realization of the final reality (*eschaton* in Greek) towards which the whole plan of creation has been directed. This final purpose of God—a taking possession of the whole of creation, so that God is "all in all" (Eph. 1:23), which Jesus called the "kingdom"—was the central content of his proclamation. His risen glory, whereby he is one with the Father in the fulness of the divine name, is at once the manifestation of this final achievement to the world and an invitation to the whole of humanity to share in that glory as their final destiny.

We have here, therefore, an emphasis which is so fundamental to Christian faith that one is surprised to find that theology has, for the most part, seriously neglected it. As Hans Urs von Balthasar has pointed out, the rediscovery of this dimension of Christian faith had an important place in the vigorous contributions towards the renewal of theology made by Protestant scholars during the twentieth century: first, Albert Schweitzer and, later, Karl Barth and Rudolf Bultmann.[101] He observed that if, at the time he was writing, this rediscovery had provoked a "plowing up of theology," it still had to produce its real fruits. He cites the Protestant theologian Emil Brunner:

> If we ask what this theology, my own included...has contributed to the formulation of eschatology, we must confess with shame and amazement that only a great void has

been uncovered. And hardly anything of greater significance has been done.[102]

Von Balthasar goes on to acknowledge the formative influence this aspect of the Christ-event should have on
theological development:

> It is not without significance that a whole generation of
> theologians learns, in the face of an *opening* horizon in
> eschatology, to engage in genuine theological work, only
> then becoming aware of the whole form-giving character
> of the Last Things for theological thought.[103]

The intellectual climate of our times called for this
new outlook. Today's awareness of social and historical
change, undergoing acceleration in an unprecedented
fashion, invites a consideration of the future. Whereas
the order established in the beginning has been taken by
previous cultures as the measure of present reality, today
we look to future, more perfect forms of things as our
measure. It is ironic that the interpreters of Christian faith
had become so insensitive to the eschatological thrust of
the gospel message that they failed to recognize the immense importance of this fact for theology. Challenged
by this new awareness, secular thought did begin to
wrestle with the question of interpreting the movement of
history.

In the words of the Catholic ecclesiologist Yves
Congar:

> It seems that the presentation of religion primarily as wor-
> ship and moral obligations, the classic heritage bequeathed
> by the seventeenth century, deprived us in some ways of
> the realization that Christianity presents a *hope*, a total
> hope, even for the material world. This religion of reason
> allowed eschatology to be laicized. In fact, at a time when
> Christians were neglecting this aspect of their message,
> philosophies of history were coming into being (Vico,

Montesquieu) that were the preparation for the great modern interpretations of the history of the world without God and without Christ (Hegel, Marx). Confronted by religion without a world, men formulated the idea of a world without religion. We are now emerging from this wretched situation; the People of God is rediscovering once again that it possesses a messianic character and that it bears the hope of a fulfillment of the world in Jesus Christ.[104]

Jürgen Moltmann's *Theology of Hope*[105] was one of the most remarkable products of this rediscovery within contemporary theology. We have already had occasion to mention this work and its relationship to Moltmann's later study of the theology of the cross. In his brief Preface to *Theology of Hope*, Moltmann stresses the point that the eschatological question should be more than one department of theology, more than a "separate doctrine" among other Christian doctrines; it should restore a fundamental but neglected orientation to the whole of theological interpretation. His "aim is to show how theology can set out from hope and begin to consider its theme in an eschatological light."[106]

The passage reproduced in the *Supplementary Texts* to illustrate the use of this structuring principle is from the writings of WOLFHART PANNENBERG.[107] Pannenberg's theology has been directed towards the resolution of some of the problems created by contemporary European philosophy. The meaning of history has a central place in his theological enterprise.[108] As he explains in the Foreword to this two-volume collection:

To say that the revelation of God is not a supernatural event which breaks into history perpendicularly from above and, rather, that it is the theme of history itself, the power that moves it in its deepest dimension, is to say something about God and his relation to the world. Furthermore, if it is true that only with reference to the *total-ity* of reality can one speak meaningfully about a revelation of God as the world's creator and Lord, and that reality (understood as historical) is first constituted as the totality of a simple history by the end of all occurrences, then eschatology acquires constitutive significance not only for the question of knowledge, but also for that of the reality of God.[109]

This passage illustrates the way in which the eschatological thrust of the truth given to the world in the Christ-event affects the whole gamut of theological issues. To begin with, Pannenberg takes up the fundamental question which has preoccupied contemporary Western philosophy: whether human language can speak of "God" at all. Can God be spoken of as *something*? Is it not contradictory to speak of the infinite, transcendent one as a "being" constituting with other beings a totality which would encompass God and the rest—and therefore be greater than God? Pannenberg notes that the best theological thought has reflected upon this problem in a self-critical fashion.[110] Taking up the challenge, he seeks a new way of speaking of God along the lines being explored by Marxist philosopher Ernst Bloch and his reflection upon the ultimate significance of hope as an existential constant of human experience. He interprets Bloch's "atheism" as a rejection of the understanding of God all too common in a superficial theism which has neglected the problem to which he has referred and pretended to define the transcendent.

Taking up Bloch's lead, he judges that our understanding of God must derive from a historical understanding of human existence in terms of the *end* towards which history if directed. This approach, he points out, is in harmony with the gospel preached by Jesus, which characterized God as the God of the eschatological kingdom, as the God whose ways and Lordship will be fully known only through what God does for us in the end.

Such an understanding confronts the believer with the mystery of God: that achievement through which God is proved to be God for us belongs to the future; the God who is "the power of the future" cannot be captured by language or concept, yet is shown to be present, determining what will emerge from the present; as "the power of the future," God offers us the possibility of being freed to participate in this future—contradicting the present, it releases forces to overcome it. Thus, God as "the power of the future" is the object of Christian hope.

This notion of God transforms our understanding of creation. If the "primeval event" of the beginning has tended to shape our understanding of creation, this new faith awareness understands creation in its relation to its "eschatological future." How, Pannenberg asks, does this notion of God relate to the "eternity" which has been traditionally attributed to God? God as "the power of the future," he would reply, has been as truly present to the most distant past as to every present moment.

Within Catholic theology, Edward Schillebeeckx, also acknowledging his indebtedness to Bloch, has adopted an approach similar to that of Pannenberg, in his efforts to find a theological idiom which is accessible to the contemporary European mind.

The theological writings of TEILHARD de CHARDIN, the French Jesuit who became a renowned paleontologist, had a great impact upon the intellectual life of Catholicism in the mid-twentieth century. Although he did not see himself as a theologian, and his reflections came from a very different background from that of Pannenberg, he sought to formulate a theological synthesis within an evolutionary world view. It had much in common with Pannenberg's point of view.[111]

Teilhard feared that the scientific project of the contemporary world was in danger of losing its way unless it was provided with a unified vision and a hope which was intelligible to the scientific mind. He saw the cosmic Christ proclaimed in the New Testament—characterized by Teilhard as the "omega point"—as providing a unifying principle for the evolutionary understanding of the physical universe which has emerged in our times. The extracts from Teilhard's writings[112] which have been included in the *Supplementary Texts* are from one of his very early works, *La vie cosmique,* of 1916, showing that the eschatological perspective which sought to integrate the findings of modern science with the vision of Christian faith was present in his thought early in its development.

CHAPTER TWELVE

The Variety of Investigative Principles Employed by Different Theologies

The structuring principles which we have considered in the preceding chapter have often been called forth by the needs of the personal and historical situation of those engaged in the task of interpreting the Christian faith to God's people; ultimately, however, they derive from the nature of the Christ-event and its many aspects as the embodiment of the divine truth. The formative principles which we must now review come from the human resources which are brought into play in the theologian's work of interpretation. Something of what is discussed in this chapter has already been touched upon in earlier chapters, but it seems worthwhile setting out this material in a systematic fashion.

Traditionally, philosophy has been the principal resource used in theology's interpretation of Christian truth. Today, however, it is being recognized that many other disciplines must contribute to theology's project through the light they shed upon the human situation and through the understanding they bring to different aspects of human existence. This is so because, while the gospel truth shows its meaningfulness for us by interpreting our existential situation, by the same token, our human situation helps us to appreciate the full import of the gospel truth. As the Second Vatican Council declared: "The truth is that only in the mystery of the incarnate Word does the mystery of humanity begin to show itself clearly."[1] By helping us to understand the human situation, therefore, many disciplines can make important contributions to the project of theology and bring to light the significance the Christ-event should have for us.

Historical studies, through the understanding they afford of the ongoing story of humanity and the issues this story has grappled with in different ways, can bring to light the truth concerning existence-in-authenticity addressed to every human situation by the God who comes to us in the Christ-event.

Anthropological, sociological and comparative cultural studies, through their exploration of the worlds which different cultures have constructed for themselves, serve in a similar way. Contemporary psychology's new insights into the subtle needs and dynamisms at work in our lives may also make an important contribution.

Technical and Non-Technical Philosophies

We may define philosophy as understanding become conscious of itself and seeking to explore the ultimate dimensions of intelligibility. We usually associate the name with the intellectual project of an academic discipline, though, as we shall see, the concept can have a broader reference.

It is clear that these resources, whatever their form, will be of genuine service to theology only when they are, in principle, open to the recognition of the transcendent dimension essential to the truth given to the world in the Christ-event. We say "in principle" because a system of thought as developed by its exponents may be apparently closed or even actually closed to this reference, even though the insights and principles upon which it is grounded are in fact open to such reference when properly developed.

As we have seen, the work of Aquinas illustrates this point. His achievement made it clear that the philosophy of Aristotle could be used with profit by Christian theology—even though to many of the contemporaries of St. Thomas it seemed closed to a satisfactory transcendent reference, and its introduction was bitterly opposed.[2] Today the same issue arises with regard to the philosophies of such thinkers as existentialist Martin Heidegger and Marxist Ernst Bloch. Many Christian theologies would argue that the essential genius of their philosophies can be disentangled from the limits imposed upon them by their authors.

There are many examples of the use of philosophy derived from an academic tradition by Christian theology. The early Christian centuries relied heavily upon the philosophical tradition which derived from Plato. We have seen that it had a profound appeal for John Henry Newman. This Platonic approach, backed by the authority of Augustine, dominated theological awareness in the West until the thirteenth century. At that time Aquinas, following the lead of his teacher, Albert the Great, initiated a revolutionary change by making the philosophy of Aristotle the principal resource of his theological investigations.

If the monastic system, which had been the formative influence of Western civilization for many centuries, found congenial the Platonic outlook with its concentration upon the unseen world of eternal realities, the thirteenth century—experiencing the first stirrings of modernity as feudalism began to be replaced by a new social order—was in need of another philosophical perspective, one which took more seriously the world of experience. As secular reality became aware of its own autonomy, the message of the gospel was called upon to enter into a new dialogue with this reality. The mendicant friars, who established their communities, not in monastic solitude, but in the center of the developing towns, were part of an immense movement in which gospel "brotherhoods" throughout Europe entered into this dialogue. M.-D. Chenu has suggested that Aquinas' decision to turn to the Aristotelian tradition reflects these developments and the emerging recognition of the proper autonomy of secular reality which they entailed.[3]

If the philosophical tradition deriving from Plato concentrated attention upon the invisible world of eternity, Aristotle, a pioneer of scientific observation, concentrated his attention upon the realities which belong to this present world of experience. Though he was indebted to his teacher, Plato, for the way he had brought the most profound of philosophical issues to light, Aristotle rejected Plato's assumption that the real world which should absorb the philosopher's attention was a realm of eternal ideas, subsistent in themselves, and he sought to bring to light the intelligibility of the individual realities which make up the world of immediate experience.[4]

It should be noted that in opting for the Aristotelian tradition Aquinas did not completely turn his back on Platonism. His philosophical synthesis carried him beyond what had been achieved by Aristotle. Among other things, he saw that the Platonic tradition's recognition of the relationship between mundane realities and the transcendent could be integrated into a philosophical system which was essentially Aristotelian. He achieved this integration through his doctrine of "participation" and "analogy."[5]

The philosophical movement which derives from Aquinas has had a wide variety of forms within the Catholic tradition. Its official promotion by ecclesiastical authority in the twentieth century, as we have seen, was an ambiguous benefit, giving rise more often than not to a superficial formalism which had more of the character of an ideology than of a genuine philosophical movement.[6] In the hands of its best exponents, however, it has proved itself a theological resource of lasting worth. It was contributed substantially to the work of leading Catholic theologians of this century, such as Karl Rahner and Bernard Lonergan. Building upon the work of J. Maréchal, "transcendental Thomism" has sought to accommodate the enduring worth of Aquinas' principles to the philosophical context of post-Kantian European thought.

The problems raised by developments in Western philosophy since the seventeenth century have constituted a considerable challenge for theologians. Some, like Karl Barth, have turned away from the traditional assumption that metaphysical principles provide an essential resource for theology. Others have taken up the challenge. Within the Catholic tradition, as we have noted, thinkers such as Rahner and Lonergan have addressed the problems of post-Kantian thought. Within the Protestant tradition, theologians such as Tillich and Pannenberg have done the same. The philosophical tradition of existentialism deriving from Soren Kierkegaard and Martin Heidegger has played an important part in the theologies of scholars such as Rudolf Bultmann and Karl Rahner. The thinking of G.W.F. Hegel has influenced the work of many European theologians.[7]

Karl Marx's social analysis has contributed to the work of a number of twentieth-century theologians in their reflections upon the implications of a meeting between the gospel message and the social and political situations of contemporary humanity. Several theologians of our day, as we have seen, have made use of the philosophy of hope developed by the Marxist thinker Ernst Bloch.

Some thinkers and traditions have drawn upon a personal "philosophy" which was not developed in the technical way we associate with philosophy as an academic discipline. It was in this way that Tertullian utilized Stoic thought, so influential in the world view of the second century.[8] John Henry Newman, to cite another example, never considered himself a philosopher and was almost bashful when making reference to metaphysics. But there is a sense in which—being in touch with the deep currents of thought of his own time, yet never in danger of being imprisoned within the limitations of that thought—he developed an original and profound personal "philosophy" in which there was a meeting of the two great movements that contributed so much to contemporary Western culture: the Enlightenment and Romanticism.[9]

It is not difficult to recognize that the establishing of a truly local theology in the great variety of cultural traditions existing in the world today—one of the urgent tasks of the contemporary Church—calls for a discerning use of the wisdom of these cultures, many of which may not have developed philosophy as an academic discipline. The wisdom which shapes their basic approach to human existence and to the issues fundamental to existence, is obviously indispensable to the task of interpreting Christian truth in their situations.

The history of theology proves that it would be wrong to expect that theologies which have made use of such non-academic resources as we have described are necessarily inferior to those making use of philosophies deriving from academic traditions.

Resources Provided by Other Disciplines

Turning to the non-philosophical resources we have already indicated, we may note that these resources, too, may have a technical or a non-technical form. This we see exemplified among the theologies we met in the previous chapter.

Henri Nouwen, a clinical psychologist, for instance, is one of a number of Christian thinkers who are utilizing the "third force" in contemporary psychology[10] to explore the Christian mystery. By way of contrast, Jean Vanier, whom we have also quoted, employs psychological and anthropological insights deriving, not from academic sources, but from his personal experience of sharing life with the intellectually handicapped.

Developments within historical disciplines have an unmistakable contribution to make to the work of the theologian, not only in the obvious benefits these disciplines provide in the interpretation of the documents of the scriptures and the Church's long tradition, but also in opening up the comparative point of view to which we have referred more than once in the course of our discussions. We have seen how scholars such as Congar and de Lubac have used this comparative view to interpret the Christian tradition—and, in doing so, to clarify important issues facing the contemporary believing community.

In a similar fashion, the political theology of the first world finds that the message of the gospel takes on a new meaningfulness when considered within the context of the social developments of our century. If philosophy has explored the essential issues of human existence, the history of the twentieth century has been a dramatic acting out of these issues. Modernity, as we have seen, is associated with the recognition of the autonomy of the secular order, and of human responsibility for history. The twentieth century has been convulsed by the extreme responses called forth by the invitation contained in this situation. Its history confronts the theologian with many of the radical issues raised by human responsibility and the hopes that register the full dimension of human existence. Theologians such as Harvey Cox in the Protestant tradition and J.B. Metz in the Catholic tradition have taken up this challenge, recognizing that contemporary theology would be seriously deficient if it failed to consider these momentous issues in the light of the gospel truth. They have made an initial contribution to a chapter of Christian theology which has just begun.

CHAPTER THIRTEEN

Conclusion

The theological developments which we have met in the course of the present study leave one in no doubt that today Christian theology is in the midst of an unprecedented crisis. This situation should be viewed positively. A "crisis" is a moment of decision. If the crisis in contemporary theology involves the setting aside of long-established ways, we have been able to recognize that this was made necessary by the impact of modernity and secularization upon Western culture. This crisis has initiated a new era in theology of which we have seen only the beginnings: the interpreters of Christian truth are exploring in new ways the points of contact between the implications of that truth and the existential concerns of humanity which have come to light as mundane reality finds its proper autonomy in a moment which is without precedent.

If we are to reap the benefits of this moment wisely, and carry forward the work which it has initiated, some principles need to be clarified.

In the first place, the analysis we have made of the theological task, and the historical development we have surveyed, should put us on our guard against a theological parochialism which looks to one particular theological tradition or school, whether of the past or of the present, to provide all the needs of the believing community. All traditions of theology have something of value to contribute to the theological project as a whole as it interprets the truth given to the world in Christ. If one were to become imprisoned in one particular system, one would deprive oneself of insights and achievements which must have their place in the total theological project.

If this is so, however, how are we to avoid a shallow eclecticism, which recognizes that many important contributions have been made to the project of theology, but has not found a point of reference, a position from which to assess these contributions?

In the course of the discussion carried on in the chapters of the present work, it should have become clear that the standard of reference against which this assessment must be made is not some system of theological interpretation. Those who fail to appreciate this will fall once more into a subtle form of theological parochialism. The Christ-event itself, as the embodiment of the gospel message of God's goodness towards his people, must provide the point of reference to which we always refer. All must be evaluated in the light of a living faith in this divine truth, a faith which must judge whether or not the interpretations offered by particular theologians and theological traditions lead the believer deeper into that truth and its implications for struggling humanity or not. We are left in no doubt about the importance of prayer and spiritual discernment in the life of the theologian.

Besides this first principle of evaluation, other principles have emerged in the course of our discussion which will help in the evaluation of the many theologies which are coming to flourish in the contemporary Church. The nature and quality of the contribution made by particular theologies will be gauged in terms of the three orders of principle we have identified: 1) the particular context of existential concerns which have been addressed; 2) the structuring principles or aspects of the Christ-event, which have influenced the creation of interpretative perspectives; and 3) the investigative principles, or intellectual resources, which have been employed in the interpretation of the divine truth. Clearly, each of these orders of principle is capable of imposing limitations upon the theology it produces.

This is especially true of the investigative principles used. Investigative resources are capable only of leading the inquirer to an answer to the questions they are capable of raising. A proper appreciation of this principle is liberating rather than constricting, because it enables the theological inquirer to recognize that the achievements of those who employ different resources—whether philosophical, historical, political or psychological—should be seen, not as competing with one another for acceptance to the exclusion of others, but as complementing one another in theology's total project of interpretation.

Too often in recent centuries theology has been viewed as an academic pursuit carried on as a personal career. The renewal of the Church in our time calls us to recognize that of its nature it is a public task, a ministry within the believing community, which must be carried out first and foremost in a spirit of service towards the broader community of believers, so that their faith may be sustained and nourished:

> Now there are varieties of gifts, but the same Spirit;
> and there are varieties of service, but the same Lord....
> To each is given the manifestation of the Spirit
>   for the common good.
> To one is given through the Spirit the utterance of wisdom,
> to another the utterance of knowledge
>   according to the same Spirit....
> All these are inspired by one and the same Spirit,
> who apportions to each one individually as he wills.
>
>   (1 Cor. 12:4-11)

SUPPLEMENTARY TEXTS

THOMAS AQUINAS[1]

It was necessary for man's salvation that there should be a knowledge revealed by God, besides philosophical science built up by human reason. Firstly, indeed, because man is directed to God, as to an end that surpasses the grasp of his reason: *The eye hath not seen, O God, besides Thee, what things Thou hast prepared for them that wait for Thee* (Isa. lxiv. 4). But the end must first be known by men who are to direct their thoughts and actions to the end. Hence it was necessary for the salvation of man that certain truths which exceed human reason should be made known to him by divine revelation. Even as regards those truths about God which human reason could have discovered, it was necessary that man should be taught by a divine revelation; because the truth about God such as reason could discover, would only be known by a few, and that after a long time, and with the admixture of many errors. Whereas man's whole salvation, which is in God, depends upon the knowledge of this truth. Therefore, in order that the salvation of men might be brought about more fitly and more surely, it was necessary that they should be taught divine truths by divine revelation. It was therefore necessary that, besides philosophical science built up by reason, there should be a sacred science learnt through revelation.

(Part I, q.1, art.1)

The notion of mission includes two things: the habitude of the one sent to the sender; and that of the one sent to the end whereto he is sent. Anyone being sent implies a certain kind of procession of the one sent from the sender: either according to command, as the master sends the servant; or according to counsel, as an adviser may be said to send the king to battle; or according to origin, as a tree sends forth its flower. The habitude to the term to which he is sent is also shown, so that in some way he begins to be present there: either because in no way was he present before in the place

[1]Thomas Aquinas, *Summa Theologiae,* five volumes, (Westminster, Maryland: Christian Classics) 1981.

whereto he is sent, or because he begins to be there in some way in which he was not there hitherto. Thus the mission of a divine person is a fitting thing, as meaning in one way the procession of origin from the sender, and as meaning a new way of existing in another; thus the Son is said to be sent by the Father into the world, inasmuch as He began to exist visibly in the world by taking our nature; whereas *He was* previously *in the world* (Jo. i. 1).

(Part I, q.43, art.1)

It was fitting that Christ should not commit His doctrine to writing. First, on account of His dignity: for the more excellent the teacher, the more excellent should be his manner of teaching. Consequently it was fitting that Christ, as the most excellent of teachers, should adopt that manner of teaching whereby His doctrine is imprinted on the hearts of His hearers; wherefore it is written (Matth. vii. 29) that *He was teaching them as one having power.* And so it was that among the Gentiles, Pythagoras and Socrates, who were teachers of great excellence, were unwilling to write anything. For writings are ordained, as to an end, unto the imprinting of doctrine in the hearts of hearers.

Secondly, on account of the excellence of Christ's doctrine, which cannot be expressed in writing; according to Jo. xxi. 25: *There are also many other things which Jesus did: which, if they were written everyone, the world itself, I think, would not be able to contain the books that should be written.* Which Augustine explains by saying: *We are not to believe that in respect of space the world could not contain them:...but that by the capacity of the readers they could not be comprehended.* And if Christ had committed His doctrine to writing, men would have had no deeper thought of His doctrine than that which appears on the surface of the writing.

Thirdly, that His doctrine might reach all in an orderly manner: Himself teaching His disciples immediately, and they subsequently teaching others, by preaching and writing: whereas if He Himself had written, His doctrine would have reached all immediately.

(Part III, q.42, art.4)

KARL BARTH[1]

'SCRIPTURE AS THE WORD OF GOD'

In the statement: we believe that the Bible is the Word of God, we must first emphasize and consider the word 'believe'. Believing does, of course, involve recognizing and knowing. Believing is not an obscure and indeterminate feeling. It is a clear hearing, apperceiving, thinking and then speaking and doing. Believing is also a free human act, i.e., one which is not destroyed or disturbed by any magic; but, of course, a free act which as such is conditioned and determined by an encounter, a challenge, an act of lordship which confronts man, which man cannot bring about himself, which exists either as an event or not at all. Therefore believing is not something arbitrary. It does not control its object. It is a recognizing, knowing, hearing, apperceiving, thinking, speaking and doing which is overmastered by its object. Belief that the Bible is the Word of God presupposes, therefore, that this over-mastering has already taken place, that the Bible has already proved itself to be the Word of God, so that we can and must recognize it to be such. But when and where there is this proof, it must be a matter of the Word of God itself. We must say at once, that of itself the mere presence of the Bible and our own presence with our capacities for knowing an object does not mean and never will mean the reality or even the possibility of the proof that the Bible is the Word of God. On the contrary, we have to recognize that this situation as such, i.e., apart from faith, only means the impossibility of this proof. We have to recognize that faith as an irruption into this reality and possibility means the removing of a barrier in which we can only see and again and again see a miracle. And it is a miracle which we cannot explain apart from faith, or rather apart from the Word of God in which faith believes. Therefore the reality and possibility of it cannot be maintained or defended at all apart from faith and the

---

[1]K. Barth, *Church Dogmatics,* Vol. 1/2 (Edinburgh: T. and T. Clark) 1963, pp. 506-8, 512-514.

Word. Nor can there be any assurances of it apart from faith and the Word. It is not only that we cannot attribute to ourselves any capacity or instrument for recognizing the Word of God either in the Bible or elsewhere. It is also that if we are serious about the true humanity of the Bible, we obviously cannot attribute to the Bible as such the capacity—and in this it is distinguished, as we have seen, from the exalted and glorified humanity of Jesus Christ—in such a way to reveal God to us that by its very presence, by the fact that we can read it, it gives us a hearty faith in the Word of God spoken in it. It is there and always there as a sign, as a human and temporal word—and therefore also as a word which is conditioned and limited. It witnesses to God's revelation, but that does not mean that God's revelation is now before us in any kind of divine revealedness. The Bible is not a book of oracles; it is not an instrument of direct impartation. It is genuine witness. And how can it be witness of divine revelation, if the actual purpose, act and decision of God in His only-begotten Son, as seen and heard by the prophets and apostles in that Son, is dissolved in the Bible into a sum total of truths abstracted from that decision—and those truths are then propounded to us as truths of faith, salvation and revelation? If it tries to be more than witness, to be direct impartation, will it not keep from us the best, the one real thing, which God intends to tell and give us and which we ourselves need? But if it does not try to do this, if it is really witness, we must understand clearly what it means and involves that in itself it is only witness. It means the existence of those barriers which can be broken down only by miracle. The men whom we hear as witnesses speak as fallible, erring men like ourselves. What they say, and what we read as their word, can of itself lay claim to be the Word of God, but never sustain that claim. We can read and try to assess their word as a purely human word. It can be subjected to all kinds of immanent criticism, not only in respect of its philosophical, historical, and ethical content, but even of its religious and theological. We can establish lacunae, inconsistencies and over-emphases. We may be alienated by a figure like that of Moses. We may quarrel with James or with Paul. We may have to admit that we can make little or nothing of large tracts of the Bible, as is often the case with the records of other men. We can take offence at the Bible. And in the light of the claim or the assertion that the Bible is the Word of God—granting that the miracle of faith and the Word does not intervene—we are bound to take offence at it. But this is a miracle which we cannot presuppose. We can remember it. We can wait for it. But we cannot set it up like one chessman with others, which we can 'move' at the right moment. Therefore we are bound to take offence at the Bible in the light of that claim. If we do not, we have not yet realized the importance of that claim. Only the miracle of faith and the Word can genuinely and seriously prevent us from taking offence at the Bible. But the *theopneustia* [the fact of the Bible being *inspired by God*] of the Bible, the attitude of obedience in which it is written, the compelling fact that in it true men speak to us in the name of the true God: this—and here is the miracle of it—is not simply before us because the Bible is before us and we read the Bible. The *theopneustia* is the act of revelation in which the prophets and apostles in their humanity became what they were, and in which alone in their humanity they can become to us what they are...

...But now in order to see the full acuteness of the problem, we must also emphasize and consider the concept 'Word of God' in the statement: We believe that the Bible is the Word of God. What we have said so far cannot mean that the miracle just mentioned consists in our having to believe in a sort of enthusiastic rapture which penetrates the barriers of offence by which the Bible is surrounded. Of course, the whole mystery of this statement rests on the fact that faith is not for everybody, and that even if we have it, it is a small and weak and inadequate because not a true faith. Therefore the miracle which has to take place if the Bible is to rise up and speak to us as the Word of God has always to consist in an awakening and strengthening of our faith. But the real difficulty of the statement does not rest in the side which concerns us men, but in that which concerns God Himself. It does not rest, therefore, in the severity of the offences caused by the humanity of the Bible. Although the question of faith of which we have just been speaking is central, it is only the secondary form of the question which has to be decided at this centre. Faith can in fact only be obedience and cling to the Word as a free human decision. And it can do so only because the Word has come to it and made and introduced it as faith. Therefore faith cannot simply grasp at the Bible, as though by the energy of its grasping, perhaps that highest energy which may even rise to enthusiasm, the Word of God would come to it in spite of all the offences (which are therefore overcome by the enthusiasm). Rather, the energy of this grasping itself rests on the prior coming of the Word of God. Faith does not live by its own energy and therefore not even by its arousing and strengthening by the Word of God. It lives by the energy of the movement in which the Word of God in Holy Scripture has come to us in spite of all the offences which we might take at it, and has first created our faith. Whether this has happened or not is the objective mystery which confronts and precedes the question of faith, the mystery of the statement that 'the Bible is the Word of God.' In the statement that 'the Bible is the Word of God,' we cannot suddenly mean a lesser, less potent, less ineffable and majestic Word of God, than that which has occupied us in the doctrine of the Trinity and in the doctrine of Christ and of the Holy Spirit. There is only one Word of God and that is the eternal Word of the Father which for our reconciliation became flesh like us and has now returned to the Father, to be present to His Church by the Holy Spirit. In Holy Scripture, too, in the human word of His witnesses, it is a matter of this Word and its presence. That means that in this equation it is a matter of the miracle of the divine Majesty in its condescension and mercy. If we take this equation on our lips, it can only be as an appeal to the promise in virtue of which this miracle was real in Jesus Christ and will again be real in the word of His witnesses. In this equation we have to do with the free grace and the gracious freedom of God. That the Bible is the Word of God cannot mean that with other attributes the Bible has the attribute of being the Word of God. To say that would be to violate the Word of God which is God Himself—to violate the freedom and the sovereignty of God. God is not an attribute of something else, even if this something else is the Bible. God is the subject, God is Lord. He is Lord even over the Bible and in the Bible. The statement that the Bible is the Word of God cannot therefore say that the Word of God is tied to the Bible. On the contrary, what it must say is that the Bible is tied to the Word of God. But that means that in this statement we contemplate a free decision of God—not in uncertainty but in certainty, not without basis but on the basis of the promise which the Bible itself proclaims and which we receive in and with the Church. But its content is always a free decision of God, which we cannot anticipate by grasping at the Bible—even if we do it with the greatest faith of which we are capable, but the freedom of which we will have to recognize when we grasp at the Bible in the right way. The Bible is not the Word of God on earth in the same way as Jesus Christ, very God and very man, is that Word in heaven. The being of Jesus Christ as the Word of God even in His humanity requires neither promise nor faith. The act in which He became the Word of God in His humanity requires neither repetition nor confirmation. But in His eternal presence as the Word of God He is concealed from us who now live on earth and in time. He is revealed only in the sign of His humanity, and especially in the witness of His prophets and apostles. But by nature these signs are not heavenly-human, but earthly- and temporal-human. Therefore the act of their institution as signs requires repetition and confirmation. Their being as the Word of God requires promise and faith—just because they are signs of the eternal presence of Christ. For if they are to act as signs, if the eternal presence of Christ is to be revealed to us in time, there is a constant need of that continuing work of the Holy Spirit in the Church and to its members which is always taking place in new acts. If the Church lives by the Bible because it is the Word of God, that means that it lives by the fact that Christ is revealed in the Bible by the work of the Holy Spirit. That means that it has no power or control over this work. It can grasp at the Bible. It can honour it. It can accept its promise. It can be ready and open to read and understand and expound it. All these things it can and should do. The human side of the life of the Church with the Bible rightly consists in all these things. But apart from these things, the human side of its life with the Bible can consist only in the fact that it prays that the Bible may be the Word of God here and now, that there may take place that work of the Holy Spirit, and therefore a free applying of the free grace of God. Over and above that: the fulfilment of this prayer, that the Bible is the Word of God here and now in virtue of the eternal, hidden, heavenly presence of Christ—that is the divine side of the life of the Church. Its reality cannot be doubted: the fulness of the reality of the life of the Church with the Bible lies in this its divine aspect. Also the certainty of the perception of it cannot be doubted: it is mediated to us in the promise, it can be grasped in faith. But the very fact that this happens, that the promise speaks to us and that we are obedient in faith, is always before us as the question which has to be answered again and again by the work of the Holy Spirit. This is the event we look to, if—here on earth in the Church non-triumphant, but militant—we confess that the Bible is

God's Word. For in doing so we acknowledge God and His grace, and the freedom of His grace.

MARTIN LUTHER[1]

from his defense of his theses at Heidelberg

XVIII

It is certain that man ought utterly to despair of himself so that he may become fit to receive the grace of Christ.

The purpose of the law is that a man should despair of himself as it leads him to hell and humbles him, showing him that he is a sinner in all his works, as the Apostle does in Rom. 2 and 3: "We have all been proved to be under sin" (Rom. 3:9). However, he who does "what in him lies" and believes that he is doing something good, is not making himself absolutely nothing, nor is he despairing of his own powers. On the contrary, he is presuming to such an extent that he is striving after grace on his own strength.

XIX

He is not worth calling a theologian who seeks to interpret the invisible things of God on the basis of the things that have been created.

This is clear from those who were theologians of such a kind, who were in fact described as fools by the Apostle in Rom. 1:22: "Professing themselves to be wise they were made fools." Furthermore the invisible things of God are his strength, his divinity, wisdom, righteousness, goodness and the like. Knowledge of all these things does not make a man worthy or wise.

---

[1]Martin Luther, *Early Theological Works* (London: SCM, Library of Christian Classics) 1962, pp. 290-294.

XX

*But he is worth calling a theologian who understands
the visible and hinder parts of God to mean the pas-
sion and the cross.*

The visible and hinder parts of God are set over against those
which are visible. These invisible parts mean the humanity of God,
his weakness, his foolishness. Paul calls these "the weakness and
foolishness of God" (I Cor. 1:25). For because men put to wrong
use their knowledge of God which they had gained from his works
God determined on the contrary to be known from sufferings. He
sought to condemn that sort of knowledge of the things invisible
which was based on a wisdom from things visible. So that in this
way those who did not worship God as made known in his works
might worship him hidden behind his sufferings. For thus he says
in I Cor. 1:21: "For seeing that in the wisdom of God the world did
not know God by means of its wisdom, it was God's good pleasure
to save those who believe by the foolishness of the preaching" so
that from now on it could never be enough for a man, nor could it
benefit him to know God in his glory and majesty unless he knows
him at the same time in the humility and shame of the cross. In
this way he destroys the wisdom of the wise and brings to nought
the understanding of the prudent. As Isaiah says, "Verily thou art a
hidden God" (Isa. 45:15).

Thus in John 14 when Philip asks in the spirit of the theology
of glory, "Show us the Father," Christ immediately pulled him up
sharp. He took him with his high-flying ideas of seeking God
somewhere else and led Philip right back to himself, saying,
"Philip, whosoever sees me sees my Father as well." Therefore in
Christ crucified is the true theology and the knowledge of God. He
says elsewhere also, "No man comes to the Father except through
me" (John 14:6). And again, "I am the door: by me if any man enter in, he shall be saved" (John 10:9).

XXI

*The theologian of glory says bad is good and good is
bad. The theologian of the cross calls them by their
proper name.*

This is really quite clear, for as long as a man does not know
Christ he does not know God as hidden in sufferings. Such a man,
therefore, prefers works to sufferings, and glory to a cross: he
prefers powers to weakness, wisdom to foolishness, and at all
times good for evil. These are they the Apostle calls enemies of the
cross of Christ. Quite clearly, because they hate the cross and sufferings they certainly love works and the glory that goes with
them. And thus they say that the good of the cross is evil, and call
the evil of works good. But God is not to be found except in sufferings and in the cross as has been stated already. Thus the friends of
the cross say that the cross is good and that works are evil, because
through the cross works are destroyed and the old Adam, who is
rather inclined to be made stronger by good works, is crucified. For
it is impossible for a man not to be inflated by his own good
works unless the experience of suffering and evil, having previously taken all the spirit out of him and broken him, has taught
him that he is nothing and his works are not his own but God's.

XXII

*The sort of wisdom which sees the invisible things of
God in known good works simply inflates a man, and
renders him both blind and hard.*

This has been said already. For since it is clear that they know
nothing about the cross and even hate it, then of necessity they
love the opposite, that is wisdom, glory, power and the like.
Therefore by such a love they become more and more blind and
hardened. For it is impossible for cupidity to be satisfied with the
things it desires when it has acquired them. For just as the love of
money grows as fast as the wealth increases, so it is with the thirst
of the soul, the more it drinks the more it thirsts. As the poet said,
"The more the waters are drunk the more they dry up." The book of

Ecclesiastes says the same: "The eye is never satisfied with what it sees nor the ear with what it hears" (Eccl. 1:8). The same is true of all longings and desires.

For the same reason, too, the curiosity of knowing is not satisfied with wisdom when it has been acquired, but it is more and more aroused. Thus the desire for glory is not satisfied by glory when it has been achieved. Nor is the desire to conquer satisfied by the power and might gained. Nor is the desire for praise satisfied with the praise given. And so we could go on. Christ gave expression to the same thought, too, "He who drinks of this water shall thirst again" (John 4:13).

The remedy remains the same. It is not cured by satisfying it but by destroying it. That is, that he who wishes to become wise should not go forward and seek wisdom but should become a fool, go back and seek foolishness. Thus, he who wants to become powerful and famous, to have a good time and enjoy all the good things of life, let him flee from power, fame, enjoyment and a sufficiency of everything and not seek after them. This is the wisdom we are talking about, the wisdom which is foolishness to the world.

XXIII

The law works wrath: it kills, curses, makes guilty,
judges and damns every one who is not in Christ.

Thus in Gal. 3:13: "Christ has freed us from the curse of the law," and similarly in Gal. 3:10:"As many as are of the works of the law are under the curse." Rom. 4:15, also: "The law works wrath." And Rom. 7:10: "What was intended to bring to life was found to bring me to death." Rom. 2:12, also: "As many as have sinned in the law shall be judged by the law." Therefore, whosoever glories in the law as being wise and learned glories in his own shame: he is glorying in being cursed, he is glorying in the wrath of God, he is glorying in death. He is like those Jews Paul addressed in Rom. 2:23: "Thou who boasteth in the law, dishonoureth thou God in breaking the law?"

XXIV

*Yet it is not that this wisdom is evil, nor that we
should flee the law, but that the man who has not
learnt the theology of the cross puts the finest things
to their worst possible use.*

For the law is holy (Rom. 7:12) and every gift of God is good
(I Tim. 4:4). All creation is perfectly good (Gen. 1:31). But as was
said earlier, he who has not yet been broken and brought to nothing
through the cross and suffering assigns to himself works and de-
vises his own idea of wisdom. But these works are not the works
God wants nor is the wisdom God's. In this way such a man
abuses the gifts of God and renders them odious.

The truth of the matter is that whosoever has been brought to
nought by sufferings does not thereby do good works. On the contrary he simply knows that God is working in him and effecting
everything. Therefore whether he is doing good works or whether
he is not doing good works is all the same to him: he neither
boasts if he does a good work nor is he ashamed when God is not
working anything in him. Thus he knows that it is enough if he
suffers and is broken through the cross, nay rather is utterly
brought to nought. But this is exactly what Christ says in John
3:7: "Ye must be born again." If we are to be born again we must
first die and be exalted with the Son of Man. I said, "Die," and that
means to find death ever present in all experiences.

XXV

*The righteous man is not the man who does very
much in the way of good works, but it is he who
apart from any works believes very much in Christ.*

Because the righteousness of God is not acquired by acts frequently repeated, as Aristotle taught, but is infused by faith. For
the righteous man lives by faith (Rom. 1:17), and as it says in
Rom. 10:10: "With the heart man believeth unto righteousness."
Wherefore I want that phrase "apart from works" to be understood
in the following way: not that the righteous man does no good

work, but rather that the good works he does do not create his righteousness. Or still better, that his righteousness is effecting the good works. For without any work of ours grace and righteousness are infused, and when they are infused the works follow at once. Thus it says, in Rom 3:20: "By the works of the law shall no man be justified in his sight." And Rom. 3:28: "We conclude therefore, that a man is justified by faith apart from the works of the law." That means, quite simply, that works do absolutely nothing towards salvation. Then because a man knows that the good works he is doing are the outcome of such a faith and are not his own at all but God's, he therefore does not seek to be justified or glorified by these. On the contrary, he seeks God: the righteousness which comes from faith in Christ is sufficient for him. Christ is his wisdom, his righteousness and all, as it says in I Cor. 1:30; the justified man is surely the work and instrument of Christ.

XXVI

The law says "Do this," but it is never done. Grace says: "Believe in him," and everything is done already.

The first statement is clear from the many references in the Apostle and in his interpreter, Augustine. Further, it is clearly established earlier in the Disputation (Thesis XXIII) that the law rather works wrath and holds everybody under its curse.

The second statement is also clear on the same authorities, Paul and Augustine, because it is faith that justifies. As Augustine says: "The law commands what faith achieves." In such a way is Christ in us by faith. Nay rather than in us he is one with us. Now Christ is righteous and fulfils all the commands of God, therefore we also through him fulfil all things when he is made ours through faith.

JÜRGEN MOLTMANN[1]

But what kind of theology of the cross does him justice, and is necessary today? There is a good deal of support in tradition for the theology of the cross, but it was never much loved. It begins with Paul, to whom its foundation is rightly attributed, and then leaps forward to Luther, in whom it is given explicit expression, and is present today in the persecuted churches of the poor and the oppressed. It returned to life in a distinctive way in Zinzendorf. It left its mark on the better side of early dialectical theology and on the Luther renaissance of the 1920s. In a famous lecture in 1912, Martin Kähler described the cross of Christ as the 'basis and standard of christology', but unfortunately did not cling to this principle himself. In all the cases we have mentioned, the theology of the cross was relevant only within the framework of human misery and of salvation, even though attempts have been made to take it further.

To return today to the theology of the Cross means avoiding one-sided presentations of it in tradition, and comprehending the crucified Christ in the light and context of his resurrection, and therefore of freedom and hope.

To take up the theology of the cross today is to go beyond the limits of the doctrine of salvation and to inquire into the revolution needed in the concept of God. Who is God in the cross of the Christ who is abandoned by God?

To take the theology of the cross further at the present day means to go beyond a concern for personal salvation, and to inquire about the liberation of man and his new relationship to the reality of the demonic crisis in his society. Who is the true man in the sight of the Son of Man who was rejected and rose again in the freedom of God?

Finally, to realize the theology of the cross at the present day is to take seriously the claims of Reformation theology to criticize

[1]Jürgen Moltmann, *The Crucified God* (London: SCM) 1974, pp. 3-5.

and reform, and to develop it beyond a criticism of the church into a criticism of society. What does it mean to recall the God who was crucified in a society whose official creed is optimism, and which is knee-deep in blood?

The final issue, however, is that of the radical orientation of theology and the church on Christ. Jesus died crying out to God, 'My God, why hast thou forsaken me?' All Christian theology and all Christian life is basically an answer to the question which Jesus asked as he died. The atheism of protests and of metaphysical rebellions against God are also answers to this question. Either Jesus who was abandoned by God is the end of all theology or he is the beginning of a specifically Christian, and therefore critical and liberating, theology and life. The more the 'cross of reality' is taken seriously, the more the crucified Christ becomes the general criterion of theology. The issue is not that of an abstract theology of the cross and of suffering, but of a theology of the crucified Christ.

I may be asked why I have turned from 'theology of hope' to the theology of the cross. I have given some reasons for this. But is it in itself a step backwards? 'Why,' asked Wolf-Dieter Marsch with approval, 'has Moltmann come back from the all too strident music of Bloch, step by step to the more subdued *eschatologia crucis*?' For me, however, this is not a step back from the trumpets of Easter to the lamentations of Good Friday. As I intend to show, the theology of the cross is none other than the reverse side of the Christian theology of hope, if the starting point of the latter lies in the resurrection of the *crucified* Christ. As I said in *Theology of Hope,* that theology was itself worked out as an *eschatologia crucis.* This book, then, cannot be regarded as a step back. *Theology of Hope* began with the *resurrection* of the crucified Christ, and I am now turning to look at the *cross* of the risen Christ. I was concerned then with the remembrance of Christ in the form of the *hope* of his future, and now I am concerned with hope in the form of the *remembrance* of his death. The dominant theme then was that of *anticipations* of the future of God in the form of promises and hopes; here it is the understanding of the *incarnation* of that future, by way of the sufferings of Christ, in the world's sufferings.

GUSTAVO GUTIERREZ[1]

The liberation from Egypt—both a historical fact and at the same time a fertile Biblical theme—enriches this vision and is moreover its true source. The creative act is linked, almost identified with, the act which freed Israel from slavery in Egypt. Second Isaiah, who writes in exile, is likewise the best witness to this idea: "Awake, awake, put on your strength, O arm of the Lord, awake as you did long ago, in days gone by. Was it not you who hacked the Rahab in pieces and ran the dragon through? Was it not you who dried up the sea, the waters of the great abyss, and made the ocean depths a path for the ransomed?" (51:9-10) The words and images refer simultaneously to two events: creation and liberation from Egypt. Rahab, which for Isaiah symbolizes Egypt (cf. 30:7; cf. also Ps. 87:4), likewise symbolizes the chaos Yahweh had to overcome to create the world (cf. Pss. 74:14; 89:11). The "waters of the great abyss" are those which enveloped the world and from which creation arose, but they are also the Red Sea which the Jews crossed to begin the Exodus. Creation and liberation from Egypt are but one salvific act. It is significant, furthermore, that the technical term *bara*, designating the original creation, was used for the first time by Second Isaiah (43:1, 15; cf. Deut. 32:6) to refer to the creation of Israel. Yahweh's historical actions on behalf of his people are considered creative (41:20; 43:7; 45:8; 48:7). The God who frees Israel is the Creator of the world.

The liberation of Israel is a political action. It is the breaking away from a situation of despoliation and misery and the beginning of the construction of a just and fraternal society. It is the suppression of disorder and the creation of a new order. The initial chapters of Exodus describe the oppression in which the Jewish people lived in Egypt, in that "land of slavery" (13:3; 20:2; Deut. 5:6): repression (1:10-11), alienated work (5:6-14), humiliations (1:13-14), enforced birth control policy (1:15-22). Yahweh then awakens the vo-

[1]Gustavo Gutierrez, *A Theology of Liberation* (New York: Orbis) 1973, pp. 155-157.

cation of a liberator: Moses. "I have indeed seen the misery of my people in Egypt. I have heard their outcry against their slave-masters. I have taken heed of their sufferings, and have come down to rescue them from the power of Egypt.... I have seen the brutality of the Egyptians towards them. Come now; I will send you to Pharaoh and you shall bring my people Israel out of Egypt" (3:7-10).

Sent by Yahweh, Moses began a long, hard struggle for the liberation of his people. The alienation of the children of Israel was such that at first "they did not listen to him; they had become impatient because of their cruel slavery" (6:9). And even after they had left Egypt, when they were threatened by Pharaoh's armies, they complained to Moses: "Were there no graves in Egypt, that you should have brought us here to die in the wilderness? See what you have done to us by bringing us out of Egypt! Is not this just what we meant when we said in Egypt, 'Leave us alone; let us be slaves to the Egyptians'? We would rather be slaves to the Egyptians than die here in the wilderness" (14:11-12). And in the midst of the desert, faced with the first difficulties, they told him that they preferred the security of slavery—whose cruelty they were beginning to forget—to the uncertainties of a liberation in process: "If only we had died at the Lord's hand in Egypt, where we sat round the fleshpots and had plenty of bread to eat!" (16:3). A gradual pedagogy of successes and failures would be necessary for the Jewish people to become aware of the roots of their oppression, to struggle against it, and to perceive the profound sense of the liberation to which they were called. The Creator of the world is the Creator and Liberator of Israel, to whom he entrusts the mission of establishing justice: "Thus speaks the Lord who is God, he who created the skies,...who fashioned the earth.... I, the Lord, have called you with righteous purpose and taken you by the hand; I have formed you, and appointed you...to open eyes that are blind, to bring captives out of prison, out of the dungeons where they lie in darkness" (Isa. 42:5-7).

Creation, as we have mentioned above, is regarded in terms of the Exodus, a historical-salvific fact which structures the faith of Israel. And this fact is a political liberation through which Yahweh expresses his love for his people and the gift of total liberation is received.

CYRIL of ALEXANDRIA[1]

Incarnation and Eucharist

[Nestorius: 'I will quote the words of his which gave offence. The Lord Christ was talking with them about his flesh. "Unless you eat the flesh of the Son of Man," he said, "and drink his blood, you will not have life in you." His hearers could not take in the sublimity of what he said. They thought, in their folly, that he was suggesting cannibalism.']

Well then, how is it that this is not a matter of cannibalism? In what way is this mystery sublime, unless we say that it was the very Word of the Father who was sent, and acknowledge the fashion of his sending to be his becoming man. Then we shall see that the flesh united with him has life-giving power; it is not alien flesh, but flesh which belonged to him who can give life to all things. Fire, in this world of the senses, can transmit the power of its natural energy to any materials with which it comes in contact; so that it can change even water, which is in its own nature a cold substance, to an unnatural condition of heat. This being so, is it strange or in any way incredible that the very Word from God the Father, who is in his own nature life, should give to the flesh united to himself this life-giving property? For this flesh belongs to the Word; it does not belong to some other being than himself who may be thought of separately as another member of the human race. If you remove the life-giving Word of God from this mystical and real union with the body, if you completely set him apart, how are you to show that body as still life-giving? Who was it who said, 'He who eats my flesh, and drinks my blood, remains in me, and I remain in him'? If it was a man who was born in his own separate nature; if the Word of God did not come to be in our condition; then indeed what is performed is an act of cannibalism, and

---

[1]Cyril of Alexandria, *Against Nestorius*. As translated in J. Bettenson, *The Later Christian Fathers*. By permission of Oxford University Press, 1974, pp. 257-258.

participation in it is of no value at all. I hear Christ himself saying, 'The flesh is of no value; it is the spirit that gives life'...

The rays of light sent from the sun may be said to be radiant on account of their sender or rather on account of their source; but it is not from participation that they have the power to give light. It is by a kind of natural nobility of origin that they convey the excellence of the sender, or rather of the source that flashed them out. In the same way, I suppose, and on the same principle, even if the Son said that he lives 'because of the Father' he would be claiming for himself the nobility which he derives from the Father; he will not be acknowledging that he has life in no distinctive way from that of created things in general, a life conferred from outside.

M.-D. CHENU[1]

Religion as such emanates from man. Its aim is to satisfy the needs he experiences in his thought and in his actions, the full meaning of which he recognizes—although in a prereflexive way— by basing them on the lived acknowledgement of a divine Being. In referring them to God, he sacralizes these needs and hopes. For that reason, he surrounds them with "signs" and rites that withdraw these terrestrial realities from current usage, and also from the investigation of reason.

These needs proliferate in great variety and differ according to time and place, person and environment. Among their manifestations various types can be distinguished which differ greatly in object as well as in the value of their sacralization. The sociologists of religion speak of a "useful" religion, aimed at reaching mysterious forces, a religion of "fear," aimed at alleviating our fears and guaranteeing a measure of security, a religion of "homage," based on a feeling deep within that reflects a divine absolute, and a religion of "communion," which is the highest because the absolute comes to fulfill man's aspirations and raise him above himself.

The common denominator of these needs and religions is the fact that they ascend from man to the divinity. They are represented, one might say, by vertical images; one looks "up to heaven," as the supreme source of our satisfaction. The sense of what lies beyond death, with its fears and hopes, underlies our feelings, our imagination, our acts, and our cults. In brief, religion is made by man in this ascension. The unbeliever will say that the consciousness of God is a projection of consciousness of self. The Marxist systematizes this interpretation and calls it "alienation."

Whatever it is, this religion springs from the nature of man— from his instincts, whether reasonable or not, and from his aspira-

---

[1]M.-D. Chenu, "The Need for a Theology of the World," in *The Great Ideas Today* (1967), edited by R. Hutchin and M. Adler (Chicago: Britannica) 1967, pp. 57-59.

tions, whether consistent or not. It is a natural religion, inscribed on the intelligence and heart of man. It remains so despite its subsequent expressions and the deviations, degradations, or alienations of which the history books are full and which extend from the animistic religions of the primitive peoples down to the civilized "deism" of the eighteenth century, and beyond.

Faith, as such, proceeds in exactly the opposite way. Considered phenomenologically, the act of a believer has a totally different inspiration from the religious act just described. The Gospel itself suggests this to the Christian. The New Testament rarely speaks of "religion" and then seemingly only with great caution. The early Christians were sharply aware of the difference that the Christian faith had introduced into the world of "religion."

Faith is not the action of a man ascending toward the Divine. It is the act of response to and of communion with a personal God, who on his own initiative enters into conversation with men and establishes a communion in love. In accord with the logic of love, this God enters into the life of the "other" and makes himself man in order to bring this act to its full reality. Divinization thus comes by means of a humanization. All this may seem to the unbeliever nothing but myth or illusion, but it is the very object of faith and governs its design and structure.

In faith we are dealing with an event. We are no longer in nature but in history. One day, God became man and entered into the history of men. History becomes the proper dimension for this act, and not nature with its needs. God is not conceived or called for because of his usefulness. Love is freely bestowed, on my side as well as his, through my free response. To be a Christian is to be in relation to a fact—the fact of Christ—to a history, and not to a morality, a law, a theory, or a cult.

Because of this divine immersion, divinization comes through the community of men, over and above the individuals and their good will. Humanity on the march is the subject of this plan, or "economy," as the Greek fathers called it. The Man-God sums up all values, whatever their source. He achieves the realization of a fraternal humanity in the ontological plenitude of a collective consciousness—in what Paul calls the divine "pleroma." By faith, the personal history of the believer is inserted into a "sacred history," and he becomes a collaborator in bringing the creator's design to its fulfillment. Whereas the man of *religion* gropes for the link between transcendence and immanence, the man of *faith* escapes the uncertainty of both false transcendence and false immanence.

It has been said that Christianity is not a religion. This statement is paradoxical by current standards. Yet it forcibly expresses the irreducible originality of Christianity in comparison with other religious phenomena. If I approach God through a sacralization of natural forces whose mystery troubles me and goes beyond my understanding, I will contribute to acts of worship which express a religion. But these acts as such have nothing to do with the "witness" of the Word of God, in communion with the mystery of the dead and risen Christ. It is just here, in the very midst of authentic grandeurs, that I run the risk of yielding to dehumanizing transfers, to improper lures, to magical acts, to clerical castes, and to all the forms of alienation.

This distinction between the two virtues, this disjoining faith and religion, is made today in the midst of the desacralization of the world. Under the pressure of this fact, we must undertake a new criticism of the sacred and of religion as a rite, a cult, a representation and explanation of the world, and as a belief that is socially transmitted. We must revise the sacral foundations of the faith.

AUGUSTINE[1]

26

Where, then, did I find you so that I could learn of you? For you were not in my memory before I learned of you. Where else, then, did I find you, to learn of you, unless it was in yourself, above me? Whether we approach you or depart from you, you are not confined in any place. You are Truth, and you are everywhere present where all seek counsel of you. You reply to all at once, though the counsel each seeks is different. The answer you give is clear, but not all hear it clearly. All ask you whatever they wish to ask, but the answer they receive is not always what they want to hear. The man who serves you best is the one who is less intent on hearing from you what he wills to hear than on shaping his will according to what he hears from you.

27

I have learnt to love you late, Beauty at once so ancient and so new! I have learnt to love you late! You were within me, and I was in the world outside myself. I searched for you outside myself and, disfigured as I was, I fell upon the lovely things of your creation. You were with me, but I was not with you. The beautiful things of this world kept me far from you and yet, if they had not been in you, they would have had no being at all. You called me; you cried aloud to me; you broke my barrier of deafness. You shone upon me; your radiance enveloped me; you put my blindness to flight. You shed your fragrance about me; I drew breath and now I gasp for your sweet odour. I tasted you, and now I hunger and thirst for you. You touched me, and I am inflamed with love of your peace.

[1] Augustine, *Confessions*, translated by R.S. Pine-Coffin, (Penguin Edition) 1971, pp. 231-233 (Book 10).

28

When at last I cling to you with all my being, for me there will be no more sorrow, no more toil. Then at last I shall be alive with true life, for my life will be wholly filled by you. You raise up and sustain all whose lives you fill, but my life is not yet filled by you and I am a burden to myself. The pleasures I find in the world, which should be cause for tears, are at strife with its sorrows, in which I should rejoice, and I cannot tell to which the victory will fall. Have pity on me, O Lord, in my misery! My sorrows are evil and they are at strife with joys that are good, and I cannot tell which will gain the victory. Have pity on me, O Lord, in my misery! I do not hide my wounds from you. I am sick, and you are the physician. You are merciful: I have need of your mercy. Is not our life on earth a period of trial? For who would wish for hardship and difficulty? You command us to endure these troubles, not to love them. No one loves what he endures, even though he may be glad to endure it. For though he may rejoice in his power of endurance, he would prefer that there should be nothing for him to endure. When I am in trouble I long for good fortune, but when I have good fortune I fear to lose it. Is there any middle state between prosperity and adversity, some state in which human life is not a trial? In prosperity as the world knows it there is twofold cause for grief, for there is grief in the fear of adversity and grief in joy that does not last. And in what the world knows as adversity the causes of grief are threefold, for not only is it hard to bear, but it also causes us to long for prosperous times and to fear that our powers of endurance may break. Is not man's life on earth a long, unbroken period of trial?

29

There can be no hope for me except in your great mercy. Give me the grace to do as you command, and command me to do what you will! You command us to control our bodily desires. And, as we are told, when I knew that no man can *be master of himself, except of God's bounty, I was wise enough already to know whence the gift came.* Truly it is by continence that we are made as one and regain that unity of self which we lost by falling apart in the search for a variety of pleasures. For a man loves you so much the less if, besides you, he also loves something else which he does not love for your sake. O Love ever burning, never quenched! O Charity, my God, set me on fire with your love! You command me to be continent. Give me the grace to do as you command, and command me to do what you will!

KARL RAHNER[1]

THE TENSION BETWEEN A TRANSCENDENTAL STARTING POINT AND HISTORICAL RELIGION

The question about finding God and his activity with us in our concrete, historical experience in the world creates special difficulties today. We have been considering God up to now as the creative ground of everything which can encounter us within the ultimate horizon which he himself is and which he alone forms. As he who cannot be incorporated along with what is grounded into a system which encompasses them both, we saw him as always transcendent, as the presupposition of everything which exists, and therefore as someone who cannot be thought of as one of these existents, that is, as someone comprehended or comprehensible by us. But this seems to have as its consequence the very thing which constitutes perhaps the basic difficulty which people have today with the concrete practice of religion.

As ineffable and incomprehensible presupposition, as ground and abyss, as ineffable mystery, God cannot be found in his world. He does not seem to be able to enter into the world with which we have to do because he would thereby become what he is not: an individual existent alongside of which there are others which he is not. If he wanted to appear in his world, he apparently would immediately cease to be himself: the ground of everything which appears but which itself does not appear. By definition God does not seem able to be within the world. If someone says too quickly that he does not need to, that he is always to be thought of as beyond the world, he has probably not yet felt this really radical difficulty. The difficulty consists in the fact that by definition God does not seem to be able to be where by definition we are. Every objectification of God, as localized in time and space, as definable in the here

---

[1] From *Foundations of Christian Faith* by Karl Rahner. English translation © 1978 by The Crossroad Publishing Company. Reprinted by permission of the publisher.

and now, seems by its very nature not to be God, but something which we have to derive as a phenomenon from other phenomena in the world which can be specified or must be postulated.

But religion as we know it, as a religion of prayer for God's intervention, as a religion of miracles, as a religion with a salvation history differentiated from other history, as a religion in which there are supposed to be certain subjects with the fullness of divine power as distinguished from other subjects, as a religion with an inspired book which comes from God, as a religion with a particular word which is supposed to be God's word as distinguished from other words, as a religion with definite prophets and bearers of revelation authorized by God, as a religion with a Pope who is called vicar of Jesus Christ (and the term "Jesus Christ" functions here more or less the same as the term "God"), all religion of this kind declares phenomena existing within our experience as definite and exclusive objectifications and manifestations of God. Consequently, in this way God as it were appears within the world of our categorical experience at quite definite points as distinguished from other points.

Such a religion seems incompatible with our transcendental starting point, which, on the other hand, we cannot abandon if we want to talk about God at all today. As it is practiced by people in the concrete, religion always and inevitably seems to say: "God is here and not there," or "This is in accordance with his will and not that," or "He has revealed himself here and not there." As practiced in the concrete, religion seems neither willing nor able to avoid making God a categorical object. Religion which does avoid this seems to evaporate into a mist which perhaps does exist, but in practice it cannot be the source of religious life. Conversely, our basic starting point seems to say that God is everywhere insofar as he grounds everything, and he is nowhere insofar as everything that is grounded is created, and everything which appears in this way within the world of our experience is different from God, separated by an absolute chasm between God and what is not God.

Although we have expressed it in very formal terms, here perhaps lies the basic difficulty for all of us today. All of us, even the atheist who is troubled and terrified by the agonizing nothingness of his existence, seem to be able to be religious in the sense that we reverence the ineffable in silence, knowing that there is such a thing. It strikes us only too easily as an irreligious indiscretion, almost as bad taste vis-à-vis this silent and religious reverence before the absolute mystery when we not only talk about the ineffable, but when beyond that we point our finger as it were at this or that particular thing among the usual pieties within the world of our experience and say: there is God. It is obvious that the historical, revealed religion which Christianity is experiences its most fundamental and universal threat from this difficulty. To do justice to this difficulty we must proceed carefully and in several steps.

IMMEDIACY TO GOD AS MEDIATED IMMEDIACY

It is easy to see that however it is to be understood more exactly, either there can be no immediacy to God in his own self at all, or it cannot be impossible just because of the fact that it is mediated in some sense. If there is any immediacy to God at all, that is, if we really can have something to do with God in his own self, this immediacy cannot depend on the fact that the non-divine absolutely disappears. There can, of course, be a religious fervor which almost lives by the basic sentiment that God appears by the fact that the creature disappears. This feeling that one must vanish, as it were, if God is to become manifest is a completely understandable sentiment which is attested to repeatedly in the Old Testament. The naively religious person who imagines God in a categorical way has no difficulty with this, of course, no more than he sees a difficulty in the fact that he has freedom although he is a creature of God even in his freedom, both as faculty and as act. But the moment we experience that we come radically from God, that we are dependent on him to the last fiber of our being, then the realization that we also have freedom vis-à-vis God is truly something which is not all that self-evident.

If immediacy to God is not to be an absolute contradiction right from the start, it cannot depend on the fact that what is not God absolutely disappears when God draws near. As God he does not have to find a place by having something else which is not him make room. For at least the presence of God as the transcendental ground and horizon of everything which exists and everything which knows (and this is a presence of God, an immediacy to him) takes place precisely in and through the presence of the finite existent.

Mediation and immediacy are not simply contradictory. There is a genuine mediation of immediacy with regard to God. And when according to the understanding of Christian faith the most radical and absolutely immediate self-communication of God in his very own being is given to us, namely, in the immediate vision of God as the fulfillment of the finite spirit in grace, this most radical immediacy is still mediated in a certain sense by the finite subject experiencing it, and thereby also experiencing itself. The finite subject does not disappear in this mot immediate manifestation of God and is not suppressed, but rather it reaches its fulfillment and hence its fullest autonomy as subject. This autonomy is at once both the presupposition and the consequence of this absolute immediacy to God and from God.

Something finite as such, insofar as it appears as a definite, individual thing within our transcendental horizon, cannot represent God in such a way that, by the very fact that it is given, the very self of God is also present in a way which goes beyond the possibility of mediation in our transcendental experience. Prescinding from the fact that transcendental experience and its orientation to God can be mediated by every categorical existent, we must insist that a definite, individual thing within our transcendental horizon cannot mediate God in such a way that, simply by the fact that *it* is given, this presence of God over and beyond his transcendentality could have the kind of character which we seem to presuppose in a popular interpretation of religious phenomena. This is precluded simply by the absolute difference which necessarily obtains between the holy mystery as the ground, and everything which is grounded. The individual existent in its categorical individuality and limitations can mediate God to the extent that in the experience of it the transcendental experience of God takes place. But it is admittedly still not clear why and to what extent this kind of mediation should belong to one particular categorical existent rather than to another. And not until we can explain this can there be something like a concrete religion which is practiced in the concrete with its categorical religious realities.

YVES CONGAR[1]

The "locus" of God's self-revelatory action, and of his communication of the understanding of the Word, is the Church, made up of men who have been converted to Christ.

The unanimous thought of the Fathers, and of theologians of all times, goes on further to affirm that Scripture can be authentically preserved and its true meaning fully understood only in the Church. St. Irenaeus sees the Church as the "place" where the reading of Scripture is authentic, because it is the place of the divine charisms, and these charisms are found in particular among the presbyters, who have the apostolic succession. The same assertion is found in Origen and—we only mention this text, after Franzelin, as witnessing to the common doctrine of the third century—in the pseudo-Clementine *Recognitiones*. "Those who are outside the Church", said St. Hilary, "cannot have any understanding of God's Word." (*PL* 9, 933.) "We cannot", continues St. Cyril of Jerusalem, "learn and profess the faith except in receiving it as transmitted by the Church, and protected by the texts of holy Scripture." (*PG* 33, 520f.) Commenting on the verse of the psalm: "He has stretched out the heavens like a tent", St. Augustine interprets it figuratively, seeing this heaven as Scripture, and he adds: "God has placed this authority first of all in his Church." (*PL* 37, 1341.) For St. Augustine, Scripture and the Church are two instances, each with some degree of immediacy incorporating the divine authority. They are interdependent, and the faithful can submit properly to one only in submitting to the other. It is for this reason that we can gather from St. Augustine, sometimes texts primarily referring to Scripture and then to the Church, as to an additional authority, and sometimes texts placing the rule of faith in the living consciousness and teaching of the Church. In any case, we must follow Scripture as it has been transmitted to us from the time of Christ and the apostles by a succession of bishops and as it has

[1]*Theologians Today: Yves M.-J. Congar*, edited by M. Redfern (London: Sheed and Ward) 1972, pp. 62-70.

come down to us, preserved, recommended and explained by the *Catholica*. We have seen already what Vincent of Lerins thought.

This traditional position remains that of the Middle Ages, often also with a more precise insistence on the canonical and institutional structures of the Church. It remains that of modern Catholic theology too. Though Tradition, as far as dogma is concerned, consists principally in the integral interpretation of Scripture from the christological, soteriological, ecclesiological and eschatological viewpoints, this Tradition expresses itself in the teaching of the Church.

This teaching of the Church is the rule of faith. This expression, "rule of faith", refers, in the Fathers, not to a formal regulative principle, but to the concrete rule found in the Church's faith preserved by the succession, which the catechumen accepts and in the profession of which he is baptized. Our faith is concretely conditioned by the structures in which God has conveyed his revelation and which he has given to his covenant. Thus, St. Thomas Aquinas, whose astonishing sense of the wholly theological character of the act of faith is almost without parallel in other theologians, could nevertheless define its determining motive in these terms: "The adherence of faith is given to all the articles of faith because of...the first Truth as it is proposed to us in Scripture, properly understood according to the Church's teaching." (*ST* II-II, 2.5, a.3, ad 2.)

One must always return to the Church's faith and the Church's teaching, and one starts from these in judging. Where this teaching has not yet been formally expressed, it nevertheless exists in some virtual or latent manner, in the *sensus ecclesiasticus,* the *phronema ekkesiastikon* which Eusebius speaks of in citing St. Hippolytus, so happy an expression that it was taken up by all the theologians of Tradition in the nineteenth century. Other expressions have approximately the same meaning: that Christian sense, that feeling of the *ecclesia* about the real content of its belief. The New Testament spoke of *dianoia,* the active faculty of understanding (I Jn. 2:20-27; Jn. 6:45), and the Latin Fathers of *sensus, intelligentia, intellectus.* We have spoken about this Catholic sense already under its subjective aspect of a spiritual instinct, and its objective aspect as communion or unanimity: both are made active by the influence of the Holy Spirit. We shall return later to the *consensus Patrum.*

The Fathers and the medievals understand by "Church" not only, as we have seen, the whole Christian community, but a fundamentally spiritual reality. It is true that beginning with the Gregorian Reform (last third of the eleventh century) a juridical mode of thought slowly infiltrated into ecclesiological ideas and ended by an invasion of the modern treatises *De Ecclesia*. The rediscovery of Tradition was only made in the nineteenth century with Möhler and the Tübingen school and the influence of this on Passaglia, Franzelin, Scheeben, with Newman also, and then in the twentieth century.

When the Fathers and the medieval writers, not yet influenced by a legalistic view of things, speak of Tradition, whether they use the word or not, as an ecclesial understanding of revelation, of which the canonical Scriptures are, as it were, the real presence, they understand by the "Church" less a hierarchical charism, juridically assured and exercised, than the mystery of the Bride, unceasingly turning from sinfulness to purity, striving to live a life of perfect fidelity towards the Spouse, and of openness to his Spirit. They understand it as the totality of men who are converted to Jesus Christ, and in whom the Spirit is at work. From Origen to St. Gregory, including St. Augustine, the Fathers inform us that *gnosis* or understanding is given to the souls who are converted to Jesus Christ: "The veil is lifted from the eyes of a Church which has been converted to the Lord," said Origen. (*GCS,* 204f.) "If we do not look to Jesus Christ, the Scriptures become tasteless; if we taste the Saviour there, all is light and understanding, all is reason," says St. Augustine, who recalls the change of attitude in the disciples at Emmaus: their doubt and disillusion before their recognition of Christ ("We had hoped..."), then the warmth and joyful certainty of their souls when they have recognized him and their hearts are opened: "Were not our hearts burning within us?" (*PL* 35, 1459.) Elsewhere, Augustine writes that when the Church is converted and turns to Christ, the veil is lifted from its eyes and it receives the interior grace of justification. (*PL* 44, 219.) Origen's remarks on the Transfiguration were in the same vein: when Moses bears witness to Christ, the veil which covered his face falls, and his face becomes completely luminous. In the Middle Ages we sometimes find the same idea in the depiction of Christ with one hand crowning the Church, whilst with the other he removes the bandage covering the eyes of the Synagogue: *Quod Moyses velat,*

Christi doctrina revelat ("what was veiled in Moses is now revealed in the teaching of Christ"). This profound idea, according to which we *see* the true meaning of a text when we turn and come to Christ, so as to find him everywhere in it, is at the basis of typological exegesis (or "allegorical" exegesis, in the early meaning of the word).

HENRI de LUBAC[1]

Thus we always come back to the Church without ever being able to consider her mystic reality apart from her visible existence in time. She is both at the beginning and at the end, and all that lies between is full of her foreshadowings and her expansion. Seen by the eye of faith the whole religious history of mankind stands out illuminated, its several parts fall naturally into place, and what many were tempted to consider the irremediable conflict between belief in a world-wide call to salvation and belief in the Church as necessary for this same salvation is seen to be resolved.

The problem of the "salvation of unbelievers" has confronted the Christian conscience in tragic guise as a consequence of successive discoveries in geography, history and pre-history which, while they immeasurably increase the sum of human achievement, seem to diminish in proportion the achievement of Christ. But gradually this problem has been solved by most theologians in the only true Catholic sense. "Not one single drop of grace falls on the pagans", exclaimed Saint-Cyran with a sort of holy enthusiasm. Such a narrow solution has been rejected and condemned, like that of certain Jansenists who, with their idea of a God like to the meanest of men, feared that the "grace of God would be degraded if it were used lavishly". So too has been rejected, as quite inadequate, the solution that has recourse to miracles, for it is of the nature of a miracle that it should be of rare occurrence. How can it be believed that God, contrary to the designs of his providence, will multiply private revelations? So, lastly, has been rejected the expedient of a natural salvation by which the greater part of humanity, though all of it is made in the image of God, should be cast into the twilight of Limbo. This thesis, which was taught in the seventeenth century by Trithemius and Archbishop Claude Seyssel, was taken up again by many apologists in the eighteenth and nineteenth centuries to meet the objections of Jean-Jacques Rousseau; but it was

---

[1] Henri de Lubac, *Catholicism* (London: Burns and Oates) 1950, pp. 93, 107, 117-118.

too much opposed to the best-established tradition to have any chance of prevailing.

.   .   .

Surely we can find the required explanation, at least in embryo, in the traditional principles that the preceding chapters have tried to reproduce. The human race is one. By our fundamental nature and still more in virtue of our common destiny we are members of the same body. Now the life of the members comes from the life of the body. How, then, can there be salvation for the members if, *per impossibile*, the body itself were not saved? But salvation for this body, for humanity, consists in its receiving the form of Christ, and that is possible only through the Catholic Church. For is she not the only complete, authoritative interpreter of Christian revelation? Is it not through her that the practice of the evangelical virtues is spread throughout the world? And, lastly, is she not responsible for realizing the spiritual unity of men in so far as they will lend themselves to it? Thus this Church, which as the invisible Body of Christ is identified with final salvation, as a visible and historical institution is the providential means of this salvation. "In her alone mankind is re-fashioned and re-created."

.   .   .

We are now in a position to understand the full force of that rigorous and at the same time comforting axiom which, from Origen and Cyprian right down to Pius XI's encyclical *Mortalium animos,* has ever been the expression of orthodox doctrine on the subject we are treating: outside the Church, no salvation. Obviously it cannot mean that no one is ever saved who does not belong exteriorly to the Church, and it is significant that the texts in which it occurs, when they are not addressed simply to schismatics, contain also the immediate qualifying statement which we should expect, excepting the case of invincible ignorance in pagans of good will. But the explanation for which a formula has been found during the last few centuries in the distinction between the body and soul of the Church is neither sufficient nor entirely exact; for the axiom refers, more often than not, not to the soul but to the body of the Church, her social visible body. Following Innocent III's example

Pius IX is still more explicit: he speaks of the Roman Church. The explanation taken from Suarez also appears to us incomplete: according to this in order to be saved it is necessary to belong, at least in heart and by implicit desire, to the Catholic communion, *voto saltem ac desiderio*. Whereas these explanations take on again their true force and can be used without danger once it is recognized, by interpreting them collectively, that, for humanity taken as a whole, there can be no salvation outside the Church, that this is an absolute necessity, and a necessary means to which there can be no exception.

In this way the problem of the "salvation of unbelievers" receives a solution on the widest scale and at the same time no opening is left for compromising laxity. There is no encouragement to indifference. We see now how the Church can, in the words of a theologian, "be merciful to paganism without diminishing her proper character of being the only vehicle of salvation for souls"; and if it is thought that in spite of all these considerations the formula "outside the Church, no salvation" has still an ugly sound, there is no reason why it should not be put in a positive form and read, appealing to all men of good will, not "outside the Church you are damned", but "it is by the Church and by the Church alone that you will be saved". For it is through the Church that salvation will come, that it is already coming to mankind.

JOHN HENRY NEWMAN[1]

There is one remaining source of my opinions to be mentioned, and that far from the least important. In proportion as I moved out of the shadow of liberalism which had hung over my course, my early devotion towards the Fathers returned; and in the Long Vacation of 1828 I set about to read them chronologically, beginning with St. Ignatius and St. Justin. About 1830 a proposal was made to me by Mr. Hugh Rose, who with Mr. Lyall (afterwards Dean of Canterbury) was providing writers for a Theological Library, to furnish them with a History of the Principal Councils. I accepted it, and at once set to work on the Council of Nicæa. It was launching myself on an ocean with currents innumerable; and I was drifted back first to the ante-Nicene history, and then to the Church of Alexandria. The work at last appeared under the title of "The Arians of the Fourth Century"; and of its 422 pages, the first 117 consisted of introductory matter, and the Council of Nicæa did not appear till the 254th, and then occupied at most twenty pages.

I do not know when I first learnt to consider that Antiquity was the true exponent of the doctrines of Christianity and the basis of the Church of England; but I take it for granted that Bishop Bull, whose works at this time I read, was my chief introduction to this principle. The course of reading which I pursued in the composition of my work was directly adapted to develop it in my mind. What principally attracted me in the ante-Nicene period was the great Church of Alexandria, the historical centre of teaching in those times. Of Rome for some centuries comparatively little is known. The Battle of Arianism was first fought in Alexandria; Athanasius, the champion of the truth, was Bishop of Alexandria; and in his writings he refers to the great religious names of an earlier date, to Origen, Dionysius, and others who were the glory of its see, or of its school. The broad philosophy of Clement and

---

[1]John Henry Newman, *Apologia* (London: Collins, Fount Paperback) 1977, pp. 114-116.

Origen carried me away; the philosophy, not the theological doctrine; and I have drawn out some features of it in my volume, with the zeal and freshness, but with the partiality of a neophyte. Some portions of their teaching, magnificent in themselves, came like music to my inward ear, as if the response to ideas, which, with little external to encourage them, I had cherished so long. These were based on the mystical or sacramental principle, and spoke of the various Economies or Dispensations of the Eternal. I understood them to mean that the exterior world, physical and historical, was but an outward manifestation of realities greater than itself. Nature was a parable: Scripture was an allegory: pagan literature, philosophy, and mythology, properly understood, were but a preparation for the Gospel. The Greek poets and sages were in a certain sense prophets; for "thoughts beyond their thought to those high bards were given." There had been a divine dispensation granted to the Jews; there had been in some sense a dispensation carried on in favour of the Gentiles. He who had taken the seed of Jacob for His elect people, had not therefore cast the rest of mankind out of His sight. In the fulness of time both Judaism and Paganism had come to nought; the outward framework, which concealed yet suggested the Living Truth, had never been intended to last, and it was dissolving under the beams of the Sun of Justice behind it and through it. The process of change had been slow; it had been done not rashly, but by rule and measure, "at sundry times and in divers manners," first one disclosure and then another, till the whole was brought into full manifestation. And thus room was made for the anticipation of further and deeper disclosures, of truths still under the veil of the letter, and in their season to be revealed. The visible world still remains without its divine interpretation; Holy Church in her sacraments and her hierarchical appointments, will remain even to the end of the world, only a symbol of those heavenly facts which fill eternity. Her mysteries are but the expressions in human language of truths to which the human mind is unequal. It is evident how much there was in all this in correspondence with the thoughts which had attracted me when I was young, and with the doctrine which I have already connected with the Analogy and the Christian Year.

DIETRICH BONHOEFFER[1]

...What is bothering me incessantly is the question what Christianity really is, or indeed who Christ really is, for us today. The time when people could be told everything by means of words, whether theological or pious, is over, and so is the time of inwardness and conscience—and that means the time of religion in general. We are moving towards a completely religionless time; people as they are now simply cannot be religious any more. Even those who honestly describe themselves as 'religious' do not in the least act up to it, and so they presumably mean something quite different by 'religious'.

Our whole nineteen-hundred-year-old Christian preaching and theology rest on the 'religious *a priori*' of mankind. 'Christianity' has always been a form—perhaps the true form—of 'religion'. But if one day it becomes clear that this *a priori* does not exist at all, but was a historically conditioned and transient form of human self-expression, and if therefore man becomes radically religionless— and I think that that is already more or less the case (else how is it, for example, that this war, in contrast to all previous ones, is not calling forth any 'religious' reaction?)—what does that mean for 'Christianity'? It means that the foundation is taken away from the whole of what has up to now been our 'Christianity', and that there remain only a few 'last survivors of the age of chivalry', or a few intellectually dishonest people, on whom we can descend as 'religious'. Are they to be the chosen few? Is it on this dubious group of people that we are to pounce in fervour, pique, or indignation, in order to sell them our goods? Are we to fall upon a few unfortunate people in their hour of need and exercise a sort of religious compulsion on them? If we don't want to do all that, if our final judgment must be that the Western form of Christianity, too, was only a preliminary stage to a complete absence of religion, what kind of situation emerges for us, for the Church? How can

---

[1]D. Bonhoeffer, *Modern Theology: No. 5 Dietrich Bonhoeffer*, edited by E. Tirsley (London: Epworth) 1973, pp. 77-80.

Christ become the Lord of the religionless as well? Are there religionless Christians? If religion is only a garment of Christianity—and even this garment has looked very different at different times—then what is a religionless Christianity?

Barth, who is the only one to have started along this line of thought, did not carry it to completion, but arrived at a positivism of revelation, which in the last analysis is essentially a restoration. For the religionless working man (or any other man) nothing decisive is gained here. The questions to be answered would surely be: What do a church, a community, a sermon, a liturgy, a Christian life mean in a religionless world? How do we speak of God—without religion, i.e., without the temporally conditioned presupposition of metaphysics, inwardness, and so on? How do we speak (or perhaps we cannot now even 'speak' as we used to) in a 'secular' way about 'God'? In what way are we 'religionless-secular' Christians, in what way are we the *ek-klesia,* those who are called forth, not regarding ourselves from a religious point of view as specially favoured, but rather as belonging wholly to the world? In that case Christ is no longer an object of religion, but something quite different, really the Lord of the world. But what does that mean? What is the place of worship and prayer in a religionless situation? Does the secret discipline, or alternatively the difference (which I have suggested to you before) between penultimate and ultimate, take on a new importance here?...

...The Pauline question whether [circumcision] is a condition of justification seems to me in present-day terms to be whether religion is a condition of salvation. Freedom from [circumcision] is also freedom from religion. I often ask myself why a 'Christian instinct' often draws me more to the religionless people than to the religious, by which I don't in the least mean with any evangelizing intention, but, I might almost say, 'in brotherhood'. While I'm often reluctant to mention God by name to religious people—because that name somehow seems to me here not to ring true, and I feel myself to be slightly dishonest (it's particularly bad when others start to talk in religious jargon; I then dry up almost completely and feel awkward and uncomfortable)—to people with no religion I can on occasion mention him by name quite calmly and as a matter of course. Religious people speak of God when human knowledge (perhaps simply because they are too lazy to think) has come to an end, or when human resources fail—in fact it is always the *deus ex machina* that they bring on to the scene, either for the apparent solution of insoluble problems, or as strength in human failure—always, that is to say, exploiting human weakness or human boundaries. Of necessity, that can go on only till people can by their own strength push these boundaries somewhat further out, so that God becomes superfluous as a *deus ex machina*. I've come to be doubtful of talking about any human boundaries (is even death, which people now hardly fear, and is sin, which they now hardly understand, still a genuine boundary today?). It always seems to me that we are trying anxiously in this way to reserve some space for God; I should like to speak of God not on the boundaries but at the centre, not in weaknesses but in strength; and therefore not in death and guilt but in man's life and goodness. As to the boundaries, it seems to me better to be silent and leave the insoluble unsolved. Belief in the resurrection is *not* the 'solution' of the problem of death. God's 'beyond' is not the beyond of our cognitive faculties. The transcendence of epistemological theory has nothing to do with the transcendence of God. God is beyond in the midst of our life. The Church stands, not at the boundaries where human powers give out, but in the middle of the village. That is how it is in the Old Testament, and in this sense we still read the New Testament far too little in the light of the Old. How this religionless Christianity looks, what form it takes, is something that I'm thinking about a great deal.

A few more words about 'religionlessness'. I expect you remember Bultmann's essay on the 'demythologizing' of the New Testament? My view of it today would be, not that he went 'too far', as most people thought, but that he didn't go far enough. It's not only the 'mythological' concepts, such as miracle, ascension, and so on (which are not in principle separable from the concepts of God, faith, etc.), but 'religious' concepts generally, which are problematic. You can't, as Bultmann supposes, separate God and miracle, but you must be able to interpret and proclaim *both* in a 'non-religious' sense. Bultmann's approach is fundamentally still a liberal one (i.e., abridging the gospel), whereas I'm trying to think theologically.

WOLFHART PANNENBERG[1]

The question now arises as to what the word "God" can still mean in this context. The criticism of the ordinary way of thinking of the "transcendent" God as a self-contained being alongside other beings still stands. A God conceived as a thing at hand, even as a thingified person, or a "reified hypostasis," is no longer credible. One may ask, however, whether such a characterization does full justice to the intention of the traditional philosophico-theological doctrines of God in the transcending, self-critical movement of their reflections upon the inadequacy of their own statements. Whatever the case may be, an absolute in the mode of being present at hand [*Vorhandenheit*] is no longer thinkable. For everything that already exists, all beings, can be fundamentally called into question and superseded. Therefore we must agree with Bloch that he has transposed the question of the most perfect being [*ens perfectissimum*] into a temporal mode, and turned it into "the highest utopian problem, that of the end." In this sense, his atheism is to be accepted. But the question of God arises once again insofar as the end must be conceived as being numinous in itself. In this connection, however, the question must now be concerned exclusively with the possibility of a God "with futurity as a quality of being," and therefore a return to the God of theism must be ruled out at this stage.

The idea of the future as a mode of God's being is still undeveloped in theology despite the intimate connection between God and the coming reign of God in the eschatological message of Jesus. What is the meaning of this intimate connection? For instance, is the future of his lordship, the kingdom of God, inessential to his deity, something merely appended to it? Is not God God only in the accomplishment of his lordship over the world? This is why his deity will be revealed only when the kingdom comes, since only then will his lordship be visible. But are God's revela-

---

[1] Reprinted from *Basic Questions in Theology*, Volume 2 by Wolfhart Pannenberg, copyright © 1971 Fortress Press. Used by permission of Augsburg Fortress.

tion of his deity and his deity itself separable from each other? The God of the Bible is God only in that he proves himself as God. He would not be the God of the world if he did not prove himself to be its Lord. But just this proof is still a matter of the future, according to the expectations of Israel and the New Testament. Does this not mean that God is not yet, but is yet to be? In any case, he exists only in the way in which the future is powerful over the present, because the future decides what will emerge out of what exists in the present. As the power of the future, God is no thing, no object presently at hand, which man could detach himself from and pass over. He appears neither as one being among others, nor as the quiescent background of all beings, the timeless being underlying all objects. Yet, is being itself perhaps to be understood as in truth the power of the future? As the power of the future, the God of the Bible always remains ahead of all speech about him, and has already outdistanced every concept of God. Above all, the power of the future does not rob man of his freedom to transcend every present state of affairs. A being presently at hand, and equipped with omnipotence, would destroy such freedom by virtue of his overpowering might. But the power of the future is distinguished by the fact that it frees man from his ties to what presently exists in order to liberate him for *his* future, to give him his freedom.

The power of the future and it alone can be the object of hope and trust. For the future is powerful in the present. It is the power of contradiction to the present, and releases forces to overcome it. Just for this reason is it alone able to rescue and preserve. Since the future has been powerful in the same way in every past time over what existed then, so everything that has come to pass, even in times long gone, has come about and also been changed once again through this same power of the future which decides over the present just as it has brought it forth. Thus, reflection upon the power of the future over the present leads to a new idea of creation, oriented not toward a primeval event in the past but toward the eschatological future. Ernst Bloch believed he must reject the idea of a creator-God in favour of the kingdom, as the still unrealized consummation, because the former appears to him to be the expression of a "mythology of an opulent past." Certainly one cannot deny the strong influence of such mythological conceptions of the primordial age upon the thinking of the biblical accounts of the creation. But the God of the coming kingdom had to become the occasion for an eschatological reversal of the idea of creation as soon as he was recognized—as happened in the message of Jesus—as the one who by the future of his lordship is alone powerful over the present world and decisive for its meaning, its essence. In the message of Jesus, creation and the eschatological future belong together most intimately. To be sure, theology has not yet recognized the task involved in this fact because its doctrine of creation remains within the confines of a thinking oriented toward the mythical origin of the primordial age, in contrast to the eschatological character of the message and history of Jesus.

This does not mean that the futurity of God excludes every possible idea of his eternity. For is the future not only of our present but also of every past age? Nor has he been this in the action-less distance of something remote and receding ever further from the historical process; rather, in accord with what has just been said, he has been this in such a way that he has allowed every event and age to participate in his immediate historical future, which through its realization has ceased to be future. In this way, God, through the realization of the historical future at a given time, pushed this away from himself as power of the ultimate future and in this way mediated himself to it in his own eschatological futurity. If God is to be thought of in this way as the future of even the most distant past, then he existed before our present and before every present, although he will definitively demonstrate his deity only in the future of his kingdom. He existed as the future that has been powerful in every present. Thus, the futurity of God implies his eternity. But it is one thing to conceive eternity as timelessness or as the endless endurance of something that existed since the beginning of time, and quite another to think of it as the power of the future over every present.

TEILHARD de CHARDIN[1]

Incapable of being mingled or confounded with the participating being whom He sustains, inspires and links with Himself, God is at the birth, the growth and the ultimate end of all things...

The unique business of the world is the physical incorporation of the faithful in Christ, who is of God. This major task is pursued with *the rigour and harmony of a natural process of evolution...*

At its inception an operation of a transcendent order was required, grafting—in accordance with mysterious but physically regulated conditions—the Person of a Deity on to the Human Cosmos...

Et Verbum caro factum est. That was the Incarnation. By this first and fundamental contact of God with our kind, by virtue of the penetration of the Divine into our nature, a new life was born, an unexpected enlargement and 'obediential' prolongation of our natural capacities: Grace. Grace is the unique sap passing from a single trunk into the branches, blood flowing into the veins from the pumping of a single heart, nervous impulses reaching the limbs at the bidding of a single head; and the radiant Head, the powerful Heart, the fruitful Trunk, these are inevitably Christ...

The Incarnation is a renewal and a restoration of all the forces and powers of the universe; Christ is the instrument, the centre, the end of all animate and material Creation; by Him all things are created, sanctified, made alive. This is the constant and customary teaching of St. John and St. Paul (the most 'cosmic' of the sacred writers), the teaching conveyed by the most solemn sentences of the Liturgy...but which we repeat, and which future generations will repeat to the end, though they cannot master or measure its mysterious and profound significance: it is bound up with the comprehension of the Universe.

From the commencement of things an Advent of ploughing and harvesting began, in the course of which, gently and lovingly,

[1]Teilhard de Chardin, *The Future of Man* (London: Collins, 1964) pp. 304-305.

the determinisms reached out and moved towards the growing of a Fruit that was beyond hope and yet awaited. So harmoniously adapted and arranged that the Supreme Transcendent might seem to be engendered wholly of their immanence, the energies and substances of the world concentrated and purified themselves in the stem of Jesse, composing of their distilled and accumulated riches the sparkling jewel of Matter, the pearl of the Cosmos and its link with the personal, incarnate Absolute: the blessed Virgin Mary, Queen and Mother of all things, the true Demeter. And when the day of the Virgin dawned, the profound and gratuitous finality of the Universe was suddenly revealed: from the day when the first breath of individualisation, passing over the burgeoning supreme lower Centre, caused the first monads within it to smile, everything moved towards the Child born of the Woman.

And since the time when Jesus was born, when He finished growing and died and rose again, *everything has continued to move because Christ has not yet completed His own forming.* He has not yet gathered in to Himself the last folds of the Garment of flesh and love which His disciples are making for him. *The mystical Christ has not yet attained His full growth.* In the pursuance of this engendering is situated the ultimate spring of all created activity...Christ is the Fulfilment even of the natural evolution of beings.

ROSEMARY RADFORD RUETHER[1]

The doctrine of Christ should be the most comprehensive way that Christians express their belief in redemption from all sin and evil in human life, the doctrine that embraces the authentic humanity and fulfilled hopes of all persons. The theological categories adopted by early Christianity to define the doctrine of Christ—early Christology, in other words—would seem to be inclusive of women. And yet, of all Christian doctrine, it has been the doctrine of Christ that has been most frequently used to exclude women from full participation in the Christian Church. How is this possible?

Early Christianity used the word 'logos' to define that presence of God which has become incarnate in Jesus Christ. This term drew on a long tradition of religious philosophy. In Greek and Hellenistic Jewish philosophy, the divine Logos was the means by which the transcendent God came forth in the beginning to create the world. The Logos was simultaneously the immanence of God and the ground of creation. Through the Logos God created the world, guided it, was revealed to it and reconciled the world to God.

The Logos was particularly related to the rational principle in each human soul. By linking the term Christ, the Messiah, through which God redeemed the world, to the Logos, early Christianity prevented a split between creation and redemption threatened by early gnosticism. The God revealed in Christ was the same God who created the world in the beginning, the authentic ground of creation manifest in fulfilled form over against the alientatino of creation from its true being. The term Logos as the divine identity for Christ should have been a term that pointed all humans to the foundations of their true humanity.

---

[1]"The Liberation of Christology from Patriarchy", by Rosemary Radford Ruether, reprinted from *Feminist Theology,* edited by Ann Loades. First published in Great Britain and the U.S.A., 1990. Reprinted by permission of Westminster/John Knox Press.

Yet the Greek and Hellenistic Jewish tradition was shaped in a patriarchal culture which gave the terms Logos and Christ an androcentric bias. Since rationality was presumed tby these patriarchal cultures to be normatively male, all the theological reference points for defining Christ were defined androcentrically. Essential humanity, the image of God in humanity and the Logos of God were interrelated in androcentric definitions. These definitions re-enforced the assumption that God was male and that Christ must therefore be male in order to reveal the male God.

Although Christianity has never said that God was literally a male, it has assumed that God represents pre-eminently the qualities of rationality and sovereignty. Since men are presumed to have these qualities and women not to have them, the male metaphor has been seen as appropriate for God, while female metaphors have been regarded as inappropriate. The Logos or Word which reveals the 'Father' therefore also have been presumed to be properly imaged as a male. The title 'Son of God', an inadequate metaphor for divine immanence, imagined as something like a parent begetting an offspring, has also been taken literally and seen as further indication that the Logos is male. These notions of the maleness of God, in turn, affected the Christian interpretation of the *imago dei*.

Genesis 1, 27-28 says, 'So God created man in his own image; in the image of God he created him; male and female he created tham.' This passage leaves open the possibility that the term man (Adam) is to be understood generically and that Genesis 1, 27b teaches that this image of God is possessed equally by both sexes (which would also mean that women share in the sovereignty of 'man' over the earth referred to in Genesis 1. 26). But practically the whole patristic and medieval tradition rejected the possibility that women were equally theomorphic. It split the concept of *imago dei* from gender difference. This might also suggest that the *imago dei* was asexual or spiritual and therefore was neither male nor female. Gregory of Nyssa reads the text this way. But most of the Church Fathers concluded that it was the male who possessed the image of God normatively, whereas women in themselves did not possess theimaeg of God, but rather were the image of the body, or the lower creation, which man was given to rule over.

NOTES

CHAPTER ONE

1   *Religion and Culture* (London, 1949), p. 50.
2   The precise nature of this development is not easy to define. Indeed, one sociologist is cited by historian Owen Chadwick—*The Secularization of the European Mind in the Nineteenth Century* (Cambridge, 1975), p. 2—as judging that all reference to secularization should be erased from the sociological dictionary "because it only exists in the minds of those who wish it to occur." Chadwick thinks the warning is salutary because one is dealing with "a subject infested with the doctrinaire" *(loc. cit.)*. He judges, however, that secularization is an undeniable fact of contemporary Western culture. He points to a historical parallel: "The historian has often to use words to describe large processes.... [If] he finds it hard to say precisely what the Renaissance was...it does not follow that the umbrella-word is misused" *(loc. cit.)*. The complexity of the issues involved in this development becomes clear when one reviews the writings of sociologists and theologians on the subject. See, for instance: C. Dawson, "The Secularization of Western Culture," ch. 8 of *Progress and Religion* (London, 1945); J. Coleman, "The Situation of Modern Faith," *Theological Studies*, 39 (1978):601-622; B. Wilson, "Secularization," *Encyclopedia of Religion*, ed. by M. Eliade, 13:159-165; A. Keller, "Secularization," *Concise Sacramentum Mundi* (New York, 1975), pp. 1554-1561; J. Childress, "Secularization," *A New Dictionary of Christian Ethics*, ed. by Macquarrie *et al.*, pp. 568-569; J. Brothers, "On Secularization," *Concilium* (1973), pp. 46-57; C. O'Grady, "The Secular City," *Doctrine and Life*, 20 (1970):523-538; J.B. Metz, "Theology in the Modern Age and Before Its End," *Concilium* (1984), pp. 13-17; K. Rahner, "Theological Considerations on Secularization and Atheism," *Theological Investigations*, 11:166-184—see also 14:254-259 and 10:318-348; K. Lehmann, "Prolegomena to the Secularization Problem," *Theology Digest*, 21 (1973):224-228; F. Barry, *The Secular and the Supernatural* (London, 1969); C. Williams, *Faith in a Secular Age* (London, 1962); G. O'Collins, *The Theology of Secularity*

(Dublin, 1974). *Concilium* has published two volumes of essays containing much pertinent comment: *Sacralization and Secularization in the History of the Church* (1969) and *Indifference to Religion* (1983).

3 See W.K.C. Guthrie, *The Greeks and Their Gods* (London, 1968), pp. 27-35, 49-52.

4 Guthrie has described the emergence among the Greeks of properly philosophical reflection within the cultural context of an established mythological interpretation of the cosmos and the human situation (*op. cit.,* chs. 3 and 5). This development was paralleled in the Hindu tradition of the Indian sub-continent (see R.C. Zaehner, *Hindu Scriptures* [London, 1966], Introduction).

5 *The Sacred and the Profane* (New York, 1961), p. 11. See also Eliade's *Patterns in Comparative Religion* (London, 1958); *The Quest: History and Meaning in Religion* (Chicago, 1969); *A History of Religious Ideas* (Chicago, vol. 1 1978, vol. 2 1982); *Symbolism, the Sacred and the Arts* (New York, 1985).

6 Eliade, *The Sacred and the Profane,* pp. 63, 65.

7 *Ibid.,* p. 94.

8 *Ibid.,* p. 95.

9 *Ibid.,* p. 100.

10 *Ibid.,* pp. 116-117.

11 *Ibid.,* pp. 118, 126, 129, 135-136.

12 *Patterns in Comparative Religion,* pp. 31-32.

13 In Eliade's judgment, therefore, the sacred "is not...another world alongside the 'real world' of experience. The sacred world is the world of real events and things residing within the experienced world. The desire of the religious man to live 'in the sacred' is but a 'desire to live in tune with real events' and 'not according to phoney or deceiving experiences' "—J. Bettis, *Phenomenology of Religion* (London, 1960), p. 203, summarizing Eliade.

14 "The Need for a Theology of the World," *The Great Ideas Today,* ed. by R. Hutchins and M. Adler (Chicago, 1967), p. 57. An excerpt from this important essay (pp. 57-59) is reproduced in the *Supplementary Texts.* See also G. Baum, "Definitions of Religion in Sociology," *Concilium* (1980), pp. 25-32.

15　The writer was told by Ivan Illich, in 1975, that Latin-American churchmen showed a singular lack of interest in the serious studies of the nature and forms of popular religion in their region which were being prepared by his center in Cuernavaca, Mexico.

16　See *The God Question and Modern Man* (New York, 1967; German ed. 1958), pp. 13-14. See also John Macquarrie's Introduction to this volume, especially pp. xiii-xv.

17　*The God Question*, p. 100.

18　*Ibid.,* p. 101.

19　*The Symbolism of Evil,* trans. by E. Buchanan (Boston, 1969), p. 5. See the Introduction.

20　See *Theology of the World* (New York, 1971; German ed. 1968), pp. 58-60. Citations which follow are from these pages.

21　*Theology of the World,* pp. 58-59.

22　*Ibid.,* pp. 59-60. Developments in contemporary science may well indicate that the statement quoted should be qualified: see Fritjof Capra, *The Turning Point.*

23　*Theology of the World,* p. 34. See H. Schürmann, "N.T. Notes of the Question of 'Desacralization': The Point of Contact for the Sacral within the Context of the N.T. Revelation," *Theology Digest,* 17 (1969):62-67.

24　*Theology of the World,* p. 34.

25　*Loc. cit.*

26　*Ibid.,* p. 35.

27　*Ibid.,* p. 34.

28　See J. Thornhill, *Sign and Promise: A Theology of the Church for a Changing World* (London, 1988), p. 60; *The Person and the Group* (Milwaukee, 1967), pp. 7-9.

29　Metz, *Theology of the World,* p. 35.

30　Von Balthasar writes: " 'Secularization' is a process which Christians normally feel to be ruin and defection, a 'becoming worldly' in the sense of being profaned. Yet, even from the Christian point of view, it has a definitely positive aspect: it means that the Christian way of thought is accepted outside the sphere of the Church, that Christian postulates are recognized as true" (*The God Question*, p. 78). One must acknowledge, as von Balthasar points out, that secularization can assume a form which is indeed a "defection" and displays "a clearly anti-Christian bias" (*ibid.,* p. 79). H. Schürmann notes that today's loss of sensitivity for "the God-revealing aspect of the world in general" must be judged with Paul as a "suppression of the truth" ("N.T. Notes on the Question of 'Desacralization,' " *Theology Digest,* 17 [1969]:67). In making this judgment, we will do well to ponder the qualification introduced by the text of Wisdom, ch. 13, to which Paul is referring: those who, "from the good things that are seen, have not been able to discover him-who-is" (v. 1) are certainly at fault, but the blame which must be attributed to them is "small" (v. 6) because, "living among his works, they...fall victim to appearances, seeing so much beauty" (v. 7).

31 J.A.T. Robinson, *Honest to God* (London, 1963).

32 *The Meaning of Modern Atheism* (Dublin, 1965), p. 14.

33 *The Problem of God* (New Haven, Yale University Press, 1964), p. 119. Murray notes that the biblical revelation speaks at this same existential level, and he finds a parallel between the option against God made by some of our contemporaries and that made by the irreligious person of the Bible.

34 See *The Joyful Wisdom,* section 125.

35 See James Collins, "Nietzsche and the Evangel of God's Death," *God in Modern Philosophy* (London, 1960), pp. 257-268.

36 *Ibid.,* p. 259.

37 *Ibid.,* pp. 259-260.

38 *Ibid.,* p. 261.

39 *The Problem of God,* pp. 107-112. The lines which follow summarize Murray's analysis.

40 *Ibid.,* p. 108.

41 *Ibid.,* p. 109.

42 *Ibid.,* p. 110.

43 *Loc. cit.*

44 *Ibid.,* p. 111.

45 *Ibid.,* p. 113.

46 *Loc. cit.*

47 See G. Baum, "Definitions of Religion in Sociology," *Concilium* (1980), p. 31.

48   *Gaudium et spes,* no. 19. This was no doubt due, in part, to our failure to undertake an adequate criticism of the effect of the sacralization process upon the life and outlook of the believing community.

49   *The Secularization of the European Mind,* p. 2.

50   *Theories of Comparative Religion* (Oxford, 1965), pp. 4-5; see also Eliade, *Patterns in Comparative Religion,* pp. 30-31. Evans-Pritchard criticized the simplistic evolutionary *a priori* of these interpretations (p. 11); the anti-religious bias reflecting a prevailing rationalism (p. 15); their neglect of any profound study of Christianity and the other world religions (pp. 16-17, 112-113); and their inconsistent methodological assumptions.

51   *Theories of Comparative Religion,* p. 113.

52   See G. Baum, "The Survival of the Sacred," *Concilium* (1973), pp. 11-22; "Definitions of the Sacred," *Concilium* (1980), pp. 25-32; A. Greeley, *The Persistence of Religion* (London, 1973); "The Myths of Secularity," ch. 1 of *The World in the Church,* ed. by J. Aumann (Chicago, 1969); J. Coleman, "The Situation for Modern Faith," *Theological Studies,* 39 (1978):601-632.

53   "The Myths of Secularity," p. 21.

54   *The God Question,* pp. 142-143. Cf. Martin Buber's "third presence."

55   *Theology of the World,* p. 70.

56   *Ibid.,* pp. 22-23. Together with other contemporary Christian theologians, Metz is indebted for this point of view to the philosophy of hope developed by the Marxist thinker Ernst Bloch.

57   *A Rumour of Angels: Modern Society and the Rediscovery of the Supernatural* (Penguin, 1973), p. 70.

58   *Ibid.,* p. 71.

59   *Ibid.,* p. 76.

60   *Ibid.,* p. 79.

61   *Ibid.,* p. 79.

62   *Ibid.,* p. 83.

63   *Ibid.,* p. 84.

64   *Ibid.,* p. 90.

65   *Loc. cit.*

66 "Some Religious Stuff I Know About Australia," *The Shape of Belief*, ed. by D. Harris *et al.* (Homebush West, 1982), pp. 13-27. Secularization takes on very different forms in various parts of the Western world. Europe faces an acute problem by reason of the omnipresence of the symbols produced by long centuries of sacralized culture which established the very identity of Europe. For these traditions, disengagement from the sacralization of their past is a painful and at times bitter experience. In the English-speaking world, North America's cultural identity is profoundly linked with the religious stand taken by the founding fathers—a factor which profoundly modifies the manner in which secularization has emerged. The Australian culture, on the other hand, possessing no such heritage, has demonstrated the characteristics of secularization in a striking form in recent decades.

67 "Some Religious Stuff," p. 13.

68 *Ibid.*, p. 26. Citations which follow are from this passage.

69 *Ibid.*, pp. 14-15.

70 *Ibid.*, p. 16.

71 *Ibid.*, pp. 16-17.

72 *Ibid.*, p. 17.

73 *Ibid.*, pp. 18-19.

74 *Ibid.*, p. 20.

75 *Ibid.*, p. 21.

76 *Loc. cit.*

77 *Loc. cit.*

CHAPTER TWO

1   "The Need for a Theology of the World," p. 58.
2   *Loc. cit.*
3   *The Art of Biblical Narrative* (New York, 1981).
4   Alter cites H. Schneidau's description of this other literature: "A cosmology of hierarchical continuities, as in mythological thought, exhibits strong metaphorical tendencies. The enmeshing and interlocking of structures are coherently expressed in poetic evocation of transferable, substitutable qualities and names. In this world, movement tends to round itself into totalization, impelled by the principle of closure" (*The Art of Biblical Narrative*, p. 26).
5   *Ibid.*, p. 32.
6   *Ibid.*, see p. 33: "What the Bible offers us is an uneven continuum and a constant interweaving of factual historical detail (especially, but by no means exclusively, for the later periods) with purely legendary 'history'; occasionally enigmatic vestiges of mythological lore; etiological stories; archetypal fictions of the founding fathers of the nation; folktales of heroes and wonder-working men of God; verisimilar inventions of wholly fictional personages attached to the progress of national history; and fictionalized versions of known historical figures. All of these narratives are presented as history, that is, as things that really happened and that have some significant consequence for human or Israelite destiny."
7   *Ibid.*, p. 33. The implications concerning the unity of the faith belonging to the New Testament with that of the Old Testament should be noted.
8   *Ibid.*
9   *Old Testament Theology*, 2:320; see pp. 319-321, from which the quotations which follow are taken.
10 The New Testament expressed this conviction by declaring that what had happened in Christ was "according to the scriptures" (1 Cor. 15:3-5). See C.H. Dodd, *According to the Scriptures* (London, 1965); C.F.D. Moule, *The Birth of the*

New Testament (London, 1966), ch. 4; *The Origin of Christology* (Cambridge, 1980); C. Westermann, *The Old Testament and Jesus Christ* (Minneapolis, n.d.; German ed. 1968); G. von Rad, *Old Testament Theology*, 2:319-335, 357-387; P. Grelot, "Relations Between Old and New Testaments in Jesus Christ," ch. 4 of *Problems and Perspectives of Fundamental Theology*, ed. by R. Latourelle and G. O'Collins (New York, 1982); L. Sabourin, *The Bible and Christ* (New York, 1980); A.M. Ramsey, *The Resurrection of Christ* (London, 1961), pp. 25-30.

11 See J. Thornhill, "Sinful Man Before the Living God: Has Our Teaching Done Justice to the Message of the Scriptures?" in *Australasian Catholic Record*, 60 (1983):252-273.

12 *The Crucified God* (London, 1979), p. 190. One is reminded of the often cited words of Blaise Pascal in the "memorial" in which he recorded a profound conversion experience: "God of Abraham, God of Isaac, God of Jacob, not of philosophers and scholars...God of Jesus Christ.... He can only be found by the ways taught in the Gospels" (*Pensées*, ed. by Krailsheimer [Penguin, 1975], p. 309). The implications of the absolutely fundamental point made by Pascal and Moltmann will be misunderstood if a distinction is not made among philosophical achievements. It is true that many philosophers have arrived at an understanding of God which is inadequate. See the comments of Metz on the Greek understanding of God already cited *(Theology of the World*, p. 34). Pascal and Moltmann are right in declaring that faith must judge these notions, not *vice versa*. On the other hand, the opposition between faith and philosophy is not so absolute that one must deem philosophy incapable of a balanced understanding of the transcendent mystery of the divinity. Whatever one may think of his followers, the *"theologia negativa"* of Aquinas is completely open to a meeting with the mystery of the divine transcendence in the Christ-event. See John C. Murray, *The Problem of God*, pp. 70-71; *Theological Studies*, 23 (1962):14-16.

13 See W. Kasper, *Jesus the Christ* (London, 1976), p. 70; J. Thornhill, *Sign and Promise* (London, 1988), pp. 74-76.

14 *The Problem of God*, pp. 10-11.

15 See Aquinas, *Summa theol.*, II-II, q. 1, art. 2, *corpus* and *ad* 2.

16 *Jesus the Christ*, pp. 81-82.

17 *The Spiritual Journey of St. Paul* (New York, 1972), pp. 124-125.

18 Schürmann, "New Testament Notes on the Question of 'Desacralization,' " *Theological Digest*, 17 (1969):64.

19 See E. Schillebeeckx, *Interim Report on the Books "Jesus" and "Christ"* (London, 1980), p. 61. Schillebeeckx continues: "It is not necessary to be an exegete in order to be a good Christian, however necessary this specialist function is and however much it benefits the community. The idea that the deepest meaning of human existence, which is interpreted through the life and death of Jesus, can only be experienced in a context of critical thought, rests on an over-intellectual misunderstanding of the reality of faith. We are required only to keep our eyes and ears open for family relationship between Jesus' words and deeds, his life and death, and our own experience of existence. The same problems of life are in question in both instances. Jesus' life and death can disclose to us our own experience of existence and express it critically in such a way that we can recognize in it authentic possibilities for human life."

20 *The Prophetic Imagination* (Philadelphia, 1983), pp. 16-18.

21 *Ibid.*, p. 16.

22 *Loc. cit.*

23 Chenu makes the same point: "Whereas...*religion* gropes for the link between transcendence and immanence...*faith* escapes the uncertainty of both false transcendence and false immanence" ("The Need for a Theology of the World," p. 59).

24 *The Prophetic Imagination*, p. 25.

25 "The Need for a Theology of the World," p. 66.

26 *Loc. cit.*

27 *Loc. cit.* See p. 59: "If I approach God through a sacralization of natural forces whose mystery troubles me and goes beyond my understanding, I will contribute to acts of worship which express a religion. But these acts as such have nothing to do with the 'witness' of the Word of God, in communion with the mystery of the dead and risen Christ. It is just here, in the midst of authentic grandeurs, that I run the risk of yielding to

dehumanizing transfers, to improper lures, to magical acts, to clerical castes, and to all the forms of alienation."

28   On the position taken by Luther, Barth and Bonhoeffer, see J. Thornhill, "Is Religion the Enemy of Faith?" in *Theological Studies,* 45 (1984):254-274. C.H. Talbert writes: "Recent scholars, e.g., Hans Conzelmann *(An Outline of the Theology of the New Testament* [New York: Harper and Row, 1969], p. 46) and Ferdinand Hahn *(The Worship of the Early Church* [Philadelphia: Fortress Press, 1973], pp. 35, 38-39); R. Bultmann *(Theology of the New Testament* [New York: Scribner's, 1951] 1:121, takes exactly the same position as that taken by Hahn and Conzelman) are hostile to any use of the term 'cult' for early Christianity's worship. The reason seems to be that today the word is identified with the sacralization of a special defined area (place, time, personnel). Hostility towards the use of 'cult' for early Christianity is, therefore, linked to the rejection of a distinction between the realms of the sacred and the secular. In the sense of a sacred order separate from the secular, Christianity, it is argued, knows no cult at all" *(What Is a Gospel?* [Philadelphia, 1977], p. 92).

29   See my article just cited (n. 28), pp. 245-255.

30   Karl Barth, commenting on the Second Vatican Council's undertaking to renew the liturgy, observed: "Catholic worship is too florid, too loaded. And our worship...has become too reminiscent of the synagogue. One might say that the great temptation of Protestantism is Judaism, whereas the great temptation of the Catholic Church would be paganism" *(The Tablet* [London, March 2, 1963], p. 236).

31   This term, suggested by Bonhoeffer *(Letters from Prison,* ed. by E. Bethge [New York, 1972], p. 285), seems a useful one in differentiating the degenerations of religion from religion as such.

32   "The Ambiguity of Religion: A Biblical Account," ch. 6 of *Religion and Alienation: A Theological Reading of Sociology* (New York, 1975).

33   See my article already cited, "Is Religion the Enemy of Faith?" pp. 271-274. When writing this article I was not aware of H. Schurmann's "N.T. Notes on the Question of

'Desacralization,' " already referred to, which takes up a similar concern and arrives at similar conclusions.

34 Schürmann, "N.T. Notes," pp. 63-64. Schürmann points to the Eucharist as providing a normative New Testament model.

35 *Ibid.*, p. 67.

CHAPTER THREE

1   "The Need for a Theology of the World," p. 58.

2   Anselm of Canterbury's definition (*Proslogion,* Proemium).

3   As reported in *Syndey Morning Herald,* Sept. 2, 1972.

4   *Aspects of Biblical Inspiration* (Chicago, 1965), pp. 21-22. This volume contains versions of two articles by Benoit: "Les analogies de l'inspiration," published in *Sacra Pagina: Miscellanea Biblica Congressus Interationalis Catholici de Re Biblica,* ed. by J. Coppens *et al.* (1959), and "Révélation et inspiration selon la bible chez saint Thomas et dans les discussions modernes," *Revue Biblique,* 70 (1963):321-370. For a discussion of aspects of this question as it concerns the universe of awareness in which Christ lived, see J. Thornhill, "Christ's Prophetic Anointing by the Spirit," *Pacifica,* 1 (1988):68-84.

5   Benoit, *Aspects of Biblical Inspiration,* p. 62.

6   *Dogma unter dem Wort Gottes* (Mainz, 1965), pp. 58-96.

7   *Aspects of Biblical Inspiration,* p. 67.

8   "History and Truth," ch. 6 of *Problems and Perspectives of Fundamental Theology,* ed. by R. Latourelle and G. O'Collins (New York, 1982), p. 87.

9   *Loc. cit.*

10   The principal issues in the so-called "Modernist" crisis in the Catholic Church early in the twentieth century had to do with this question.

11   See Henri Marrou, *The Meaning of History,* trans. by R. Olsen (Baltimore, 1966).

12   Cited by Ignace de la Potterie, "History and Truth," p. 92.

13   *An Introduction to Christian Faith* (New York, 1980), p. 155, introducing a chapter entitled "The Historical Nature of Faith." Kasper notes that Ernst Troeltsch's prediction—that "the encounter between theology and history would...raise far greater problems than the encounter between theology and natural science"—has been proved right *(loc. cit.).*

14   *Ibid.,* p. 159.

15   *Loc. cit.*

16 *Ibid.*, p. 156.
17 *Ibid.*, p. 160.
18 *Loc. cit.*
19 *Loc. cit.*
20 *Ibid.*, p. 161.
21 *Loc. cit.*
22 *Loc. cit.*
23 *Ibid.*, pp. 163-164.
24 *Ibid.*, p. 162.
25 "History and Truth," p. 88.
26 *Ibid.*, p. 90.
27 De la Potterie quotes Hegel: "The truth is the whole. The whole, however, is merely the essential nature reaching its completeness through the process of its own development" ("History and Truth," p. 93).
28 As de la Potterie observes, "When radicalized, these two forms of thought lead to a completely secularized concept of truth, in which there is no longer any room for any kind of openness to God on the part of truth" (*ibid.*, p. 94).
29 *Ibid.*, p. 97.
30 De la Potterie lists the names given to it in Christian tradition: "The mystery of truth, revealed truth, the truth of the gospel, the light of truth, Christian truth, the rule of truth, the doctrine of truth, the way of truth, and others" (*ibid.*, p. 98).
31 *Loc. cit.*
32 *Loc. cit.*
33 *Ibid.*, p. 99.
34 De la Potterie judges that it is to Hegel's credit that "in contrast to certain positivist or excessively notional conceptions of truth, he saw truth as always subject to the action of the Spirit and as open to the end state." He criticizes the fact that Hegel "disregards excessively the historical objectivity and uniqueness of the Christ-event and therefore the value of the fact of Jesus' life as *sign* and *revelation*. Nor does he respect adequately the mystery and transcendence of Jesus who calls himself *the* Truth" (*ibid.*, p. 102).
35 De la Potterie points to Kierkegaard's view in this regard. He notes, however, that Kierkegaard's understanding of "truth as interiority" has an ambiguity which must be removed if it is

to be faithful to the message of Christian revelation, which refers rather to an "interiorization of truth" (*ibid.*, pp. 102-103).

36 *Ibid.*, p. 103.
37 *Ibid.*, p. 156.

CHAPTER FOUR

1   Some readers may be puzzled by the term "Christ-event." Through this expression, contemporary theology points *at once* to the unity of the Saviour's earthly destiny (the cause, or "mission," which gave meaning to his conduct and teaching during his mortal life, the drama of his death, and its victorious aftermath) *and* to the fact that this destiny of Christ's constitutes God's definitive intervention on behalf of the world in fulfillment of Israel's hopes—hopes which had their basis in the great things God had done; this event is the consummation of Israel's history.

2   See Bruce Vawter's commentary on this verse in *The Jerome Biblical Commentary*, 63:45, citing J.A.T. Robinson.

3   S. Moore, "The Secular Implications of the Liturgy," *The Christian Priesthood*, ed. by N. Lash and J. Rhymer (London, 1970), p. 218.

4   It may be noted that the most authentic traditions of Buddhism do not fall under this criticism. Indeed, this Buddhism is remarkable in that, acknowledging the ambiguity of the products of sacralization, it seeks a living acknowledgment of the Absolute as the final dimension of all being beyond all conceptualization and symbolism.

5   *Does Jesus Know Us? Do We Know Him?* (San Francisco, 1983), pp. 83-84.

6   *Interim Report on the Books "Jesus" and "Christ"* (London, 1980), p. 30.

7   *Ibid.,* p. 33.

8   The German scholar Martin Kaehler long ago pointed to the distinction made by Schillebeeckx: he distinguished between what is *historisch* (historical, in the sense of belonging to the events of the past) and *geschichtlich* (historic, in the sense of being an event which possesses abiding significance); see J. Jeremias, *The Problem of the Historical Jesus* (Philadelphia, 1964), pp. 6-7. On the question of the accessibility of the historical Jesus, see Jeremias, *op. cit.,* pp. 12-15; E. Trocme, *Jesus as Seen by His Contemporaries* (Philadelphia, 1973);

I.H. Marshall, *I Believe in the Historical Jesus* (London, 1977); B. Vawter, *This Man Jesus* (New York, 1975), pp. 28-29. Jeremias and Trocme survey the development of scholarship which has led to Schillebeeckx's conclusion.

9   *Church Dogmatics,* IV/3:55, 83-84.

10   Shea's *Stories of God: An Unauthorized Biography* (Chicago, 1978) contains brilliant and original insights—particularly concerning "world-making" stories. He employs the term "myth" for these stories, thereby extending the meaning we have met in earlier pages (cf. especially pp. 42 and 52). Tilley has built upon Shea's work in *Story Theology* (Wilmington, 1985). He distinguishes (ch. 3) "myths" (stories which set up worlds), "parables" (stories which upset worlds—as opposed to "counter-myths," which demolish existing worlds) and "actions" (stories which are set within and explore established worlds).

11   Chenu, "The Need for a Theology of the World," p. 58.

12   New York, 1980. Cf. Chs. 8 and 12.

CHAPTER FIVE

1   See J. Thornhill, *Sign and Promise*, pp. 96-97, 87-89.
2   *An Introduction to Christian Faith*, p. 161. See Kasper's definition of the "faith" called for by Jesus, in *Jesus the Christ*, pp. 81-82, referred to in ch. 2.
3   *Method in Theology* (London, 1972).
4   In Lonergan's words: "the indirect discourse that sets forth the conviction and opinions of others" (p. 267).
5   "...to the direct discourse that states what is so" *(loc. cit.).*
6   *Ibid.,* p. 268.
7   *Loc. cit.*
8   *Ibid.,* pp. 267-268.
9   *Ibid.,* p. 269. He continues: "They do not advert to the multiplicity of horizons. They do not exercise their vertical liberty by migration from the one they have inherited to another they have discovered to be better."
10 *Ibid.,* p. 338.
11 *Ibid.,* pp. 267-268.
12 *Ibid.,* pp. 240-241. Lonergan continues: "For Christians it is God's love flooding our hearts through the Holy Spirit given to us. It is the gift of grace, and, since the days of Augustine, a distinction has been drawn between operative and cooperative grace. Operative grace is the replacement of the heart of stone by a heart of flesh, a replacement beyond the horizon of the heart of stone. Cooperative grace is the heart of flesh becoming effective in good works through human freedom. Operative grace is religious conversion. Cooperative grace is the effectiveness of conversion, the gradual movement towards a full and complete transformation of the whole of one's living and feeling, one's thoughts, words, deeds and omissions." One may ask whether what Lonergan has to say would be further clarified if the distinction which we have emphasized in early chapters, between "religion" and "faith," had been more developed.
13 *"Gratiae gratum facientes"* and *"gratiae gratis datae."* They are often set in contrast, but this can be misleading. The latter

"charisms" (to employ a more contemporary term), since their
function is the manifestation of the mystery shared in by the
former gifts, and since they are for the building up of the
whole Christian community, should normally, in the first
place, build up the recipient.

14   See J. Thornhill, "Is Religion the Enemy of Faith?" in
Theological Studies, 45 (1984):266-267.

15   The most fundamental distinction Aquinas points to among
"virtues" arises from the fact that their qualitative
intentionality may be directed, on the one hand, towards a
good which "does not exceed the connatural capacity of man"
or, on the other hand, towards a good which is "supernatural."
The former are "natural" virtues; the latter are "supernatural"
insofar as their qualitative intentionality "cannot be acquired
by human acts but is 'infused' by God" (*Summa theol.*, I-II,
q. 65, art. 2; see *Quaest. disp. de virt.*, art. 10).

16   *Summa theol.*, I-II, q. 68 *passim.*

17   *Ibid.*, I-II, q. 68, art. 4, ad 3. For more on this and related
questions, see J. Thornhill, "The Spirit in the Life of God's
People," *Austr. Cath. Record*, 61 (1984):385-395.

18   See *The Jerome Biblical Commentary*, 2:606-607, 616, 618.

19   Literally, "fuller sense." On the emergence of this term in
contemporary discussion, see R. Brown, *Jerome Bibl.
Comm.*, 71:9, 57-70.

20   "Biblical Exegesis—Spiritual Exegesis," *Concise
Sacramentum Mundi* (New York, 1974), pp. 126-133. See
Henri de Lubac, *L'Ecriture dans la tradition* (Paris, 1966);
Ignace de la Potterie, "Reading Scripture in the Spirit,"
Communio (1986).

21   "Biblical Exegesis—Spiritual Exegesis," pp. 128-129.

22   See S. Schneiders, "The Foot Washing (Jn. 13:1-20): An
Experiment in Hermeneutics," *Cath. Bibl. Quart.*, 43 (1981):
80-88.

CHAPTER SIX

1   See J. Thornhill, *Sign and Promise*, pp. 89-91.
2   *Ibid.*, p. 99.
3   On the important implications of this Pauline figure, see *Sign and Promise*, pp. 24-35. This New Testament teaching is grounded in and fulfills the faith of Israel. Much of the lore of humanity's religious quest, as we have seen, has been mythological (attempting to break out of the framework of time and history, to pierce "the beyond" and find the transcendent order which explains the enigmas of the human situation). The faith of Israel, as we have noted, was radically at odds with such mythologies. To interpret its present situation, Israel did not rely upon such projections of the human spirit, whatever the wisdom they may contain. Israel's understanding of its present situation and destiny was grounded in its recalling of the "great works" God had done for his people—works which were the revelation of his ways and constituted a promise that he would continue to be present in their future: because the God who acted on behalf of their fathers is a living God, ever faithful to the covenant commitment he had made to his people, they saw themselves as benefitting from his great acts of the past in a way which went beyond what is achieved in a man-made memorial. See B. Childs, *Memory and Tradition in Israel* (London, 1962); K. O'Shea, *The Christ-Life: Its Idealism and Its Realism* (Homebush, 1970), pp. 143-144. It was within this perspective that Jesus gave his disciples the eucharistic "memorial" which was the transcendent fulfillment of Israel's hopes. In it the final act of God achieved in Christ's self-giving to the Father for the sake of the world, is made accessible to us.
4   See Second Vatican Council, *Dei verbum*, nos. 7-12.
5   Which may be rendered: "A norm which is not subjected to any [superior] norm." See W. Kasper, *The Methods of Dogmatic Theology* (New York, 1969), pp. 26-29; J. Thornhill, *Sign and Promise*, pp. 85-93. The Second Vatican

Council declares: "In composing the sacred books, God chose men and, while employed by him, they made use of their powers and abilities, so that, with him acting in them and through them, they, as true actors, consigned to writing everything and only those things which he wanted" (*Dei verbum*, no. 11). This use of human agency by God's Spirit involved not only individuals but also the community of the Church.

6   *The Methods of Dogmatic Theology*, p. 28.

7   Kasper *(loc. cit.)* writes: "If we accept the notion that Scripture must be the 'soul' of theology, we shall have to emend the dogmatic approach which developed over the last two hundred years...and return to the tradition of the Church Fathers and the early Middle Ages."

8   *Ibid.*, p. 26. See *The Final Report* of the Anglican-Roman Catholic International Commission (London, 1982), p. 70: "Since the Scriptures are the uniquely inspired witness to divine revelation, the Church's expression of that revelation must be tested by its consonance with Scripture. This does not mean simply repeating the words of Scripture, but also both delving into their deeper significance and unravelling their implications for Christian belief and practice.... This combination of permanence in the revealed truth and continuous exploration of its meaning is what is meant by Christian tradition."

9   See Second Vatican Council, Constitution on the Church, *Lumen gentium*, no. 8; Decree on Ecumenism, *Unitatis redintegratio*, nos. 3 and 6.

10 See J. Thornhill, *Sign and Promise*, pp. 207-209.

11 See Walter Kasper's commentary on *Lumen gentium*, no. 12, in *An Introduction to Christian Faith*, pp. 144-147, to which the following pages are indebted.

12 Refer to what has been said concerning this "connaturality" in the previous chapter. *Lumen gentium* declares: "The body of the faithful as a whole, anointed as they are by the Holy One (cf. Jn. 2:20, 27), cannot err in matters of belief. Thanks to a supernatural sense of the faith which characterizes the people as a whole, it manifests this unerring quality when, 'from the bishops down to the last member of the laity' (Augustine), it shows universal agreement in matters of faith and morals."

13   See Kasper, *An Introduction to Christian Faith,* pp. 109 and 163; Y. Congar, *Tradition and Traditions,* p. 239 and note.

14   On these, consult theological dictionaries.

15   In recent centuries, the hierarchical emphasis which has dominated Catholic understanding of the Church has obscured this important truth; see J. Thornhill, *Sign and Promise,* pp. 56-64. The relationship between the believing community, the norms provided by the scriptures and the witness of past ages, and the Church's pastoral authority, is well summed up by the Second Vatican Council: "Sacred tradition and sacred Scripture form one sacred deposit of the Word of God, which is committed to the Church. Holding fast to this deposit, the entire holy people united with their pastors remain always steadfast in the teaching of the apostles, in the common life, in the breaking of bread, and in prayers (cf. Acts 2:42, Greek text), so that in holding to, practicing and professing the heritage of the faith, there results on the part of the bishops and faithful a remarkable common effort" *(Dei verbum,* no. 10). This text is all the more significant in that, as a result of the conciliar debates, it replaced a text shaped by a hierarchical perspective.

16   To be found in *Civiltà Cattolica* (1973), vol. 2. The International Theological Commission discussed this question again in 1975 ("Theses on the Relationship Between the Ecclesiastical Magisterium and Theology"). This document is discussed at length by F. Sullivan, *Magisterium* (New York, 1983), ch. 8.

17   See Kasper, *An Introduction to Christian Faith,* pp. 169-173.

18   Sometimes called "authentic teaching"—a term which refers to the fact that the pronouncement is authorized by the Church's authority and is not merely an expression of the opinion of particular individuals or groups within the believing community. Clearly, this latter term is open to misunderstanding if its significance is not understood. See *Lumen gentium,* no. 25: "Bishops...are authentic teachers; that is, teachers endowed with the authority of Christ."

19   See J. Thornhill, *Sign and Promise,* p. 119.

20   See *Lumen gentium,* no. 25.

CHAPTER SEVEN

1   It has been pointed out that a parallel exists between, on the one hand, the emerging choice, within Greek philosophy, of the God of *logos* (or critical awareness) in preference to the God of the mythologies, and, on the other hand, Israel's rejection of the conceptions of the ancient religions in their understanding of the living God who had become present to them in the events of a history. This history, in fact, culminated in the incarnation of the *Logos* in a manner Greek philosophy could never have anticipated.

2   See J.C. Murray, *The Problem of God*, p. 47; B. Lonergan, "The Dehellenization of Dogma," *Theol. Studies*, 28 (1967): 336-351.

3   See Anglican-Roman Catholic International Commission's *The Final Report*, p. 70, already cited.

4   See J.C. Murray, *The Problem of God*, pp. 70-71; *Theol. Studies*, 23 (1962):14-16; B. Mondin, *The Principle of Analogy in Protestant and Catholic Theology* (The Hague, 1963), chs. 1-4; "Analogy, Theological Use of," *New Cath. Encyc.*; G. Klubertanz, "Analogy," *New Cath. Encyc.*; J. Crehan, "Analogy of Being," *A Cath. Dict. of Theol.*, ed. by H. Davis *et al.*

5   It would be wrong to judge that Aquinas' *Summa theologiae* is an example of this misunderstanding. His normal manner of teaching was from the "sacred page" of the scriptures; the *Summa* was intended as a systematic handbook making available to the student the Scholastic treatment of basic questions. See M.-D. Chenu, *Introduction à l'étude de saint Thomas d'Aquin* (Paris, 1950), pp. 59-60, 264-265, 269-271. This work is also available in an English version: *Toward Understanding St. Thomas* (Chicago, 1964).

6   Kasper, *An Introduction to Christian Faith*, p. 155.

7   *Ibid.*, p. 165.

8   *Ibid.*, p. 166; see also pp. 166-169.

9   *Ibid.*, p. 169. He continues: "It can promise human being definitive meaning." We have already seen that Kasper looks

to Hegel to provide at least part of the solution to the problem: the truth of which the Church is the bearer is an eschatological truth which is in process of self-affirmation.

10 See *Interim Report on the Books "Jesus" and "Christ"* (London, 1980), pp. 3-19.

11 *Ibid.*, pp. 6-8.

12 *Ibid.*, p. 143. When Schillebeeckx writes, "There is...no such thing as the saving significance of Jesus 'in itself,' as a kind of timeless, supra-historical, abstract datum.... [On the other hand, however,] as Christians we cannot just make what we like of Jesus, or simply see him as a cipher for our own human experiences. What we are concerned with is rather a mutually critical correlation in which we attune our belief and action within the world in which we live, here and now, to what is expressed in the biblical tradition" (*op. cit.*, p. 50), his response to the question we are asking seems to become so esoteric as to be beyond the grasp of the ordinary believer.

13 "They may be found 'good' or 'bad,' 'effective' or 'ineffective'...but not 'true' or 'false' " (*Story Theology*, [Wilmington, 1985], p. 178).

14 *Loc. cit.*

15 If we must, today, point out the shortcomings of the project of medieval Scholasticism, this criticism ought not become a reaction which fails to recognize that sooner or later an integral theology must face the analytical questions which preoccupied the Scholastics. Their answers to these questions have much that is of enduring worth.

16 See "The Origins of Christian Realism," *Theol. Digest*, 20 (1972):292-305. References which follow are to this article. See also F. Crowe, "Doctrines and Historicity in the Context of Lonergan's Method," *Theol. Studies*, 58 (1977):115-124.

17 "The Origins of Christian Realism," p. 293. We can relate Lonergan's distinction to that between history and story as *lived* and as *told* which has emerged as basic to our discussion of this point.

18 *Loc. cit.* In Lonergan's words: "In my opinion, the ambiguity of realism arises from the very simple and evident fact that infants do not speak. From this simple and evident fact it follows that infants, because they do not speak, do not live in a world mediated by language. Their world is a world of

immediacy, of sights and sounds, of tastes and smells, of touching and feeling, of joys and sorrows. But as infants learn to speak, they gradually move into a far larger world. It includes the past and the future as well as the present, the possible and the probable as well as the actual, rights and duties as well as fact. It is a world enriched by travellers' tales, by stories and legends, by literature, philosophy, science, by religion, theology, history" (p. 293).

19 *Loc. cit.*

20 *Loc. cit.* Lonergan's lasting contribution to contemporary thought was his analysis and definition of the processes called for in this exploration and his clarification of the criteria these processes should employ. See *Insight* (London, 1957); *Method in Theology* (London, 1972).

21 "The Origins of Christian Realism," p. 294.

22 *Ibid.,* pp. 293-294. "Naive realism" (according to which "knowing is a matter of taking a good look, objectivity is a matter of seeing what is there to be seen, reality is whatever is given in immediate experience") and its offspring "empiricism" attempted to collapse all acceptable meaning into the order of immediacy. The "critical idealism" of Kant, recognizing the distinction and exploring the realm of meaning, failed to maintain a satisfactory relationship with the world of immediacy. The "absolute idealism" of Fichte, Schelling and Hegel, maintaining the world of meaning, abandoned the world of immediacy as an illusion. Lonergan sees attempts to reestablish the relationship, through the mediation of practical reason and the existential option, made by Kant, Schopenhauer, Kierkegaard, Newman, Nietzsche, Blondel, Ricoeur, etc., as unsatisfactory.

23 *Ibid.,* p. 294. He continues: "In more traditional language, the objects intended are beings: what is to be known by intending *Quid sit?* (what this thing is) and *An sit?* (whether it is) and by finding correct answers."

24 For example, when we are given true answers to such questions as: Is that gold or copper? Is that a just price to demand or not? Is that load bigger than the other? Is that boy this man's son? Is my friend in Rome or New York?, we are grasping the reality of the objective world. In adopting this position, Lonergan situates himself within the tradition of

realism with which Aristotle and Aquinas were identified. Aristotle pointed out the fallacy of calling for a demonstration of *all* assertions. If one is to provide a basis for *any* demonstration, one must reject the infinite series which this fallacy would demand, and acknowledge that all demonstration is grounded, in the end, upon what is evident-in-itself. Of those things which are evident in themselves, our presence to reality itself in knowledge is primordial. If this is called into doubt, the basis of all truthful assertions is removed. The realism of Aquinas' expression of this tradition may be summarized as follows: 1) There are *categories of meaning* which may be identified and, within limits, defined (in the examples given above, these categories are *substance, quality, quantity, relation, place;* they are irreducible one to another); 2) The meaning grasped in these categories registers what is *essential* to reality itself: it is objective and not some subjective impression—found-by-us, not made-by-us; 3) These elements of meaning, while they have an enduring sameness, do not lock reality in an eternal immobility through this sameness, because their *manner of being* is not only actual but also *potential;* they may be in movement (passing from potentiality to actuality) without losing their essential sameness; 4) The determination registered in these categories of meaning is of the *essential* order, which of itself remains indifferent to *existential* status—that it does exist outside mere potentiality depends upon the determination bestowed by existence *(esse)* which is of an utterly different order of meaning and in no way affects the essential order in its essentiality; 5) The order existing in reality is established not only by the univocal categories of meaning of which we have been speaking in our examples, but also by the proportion, or *analogy*, which exists between various orders of being, to which reference has been made in speaking of Aquinas' "negative theology." Lonergan's presentation of "critical realism" has this advantage over Aquinas': that, whereas Aquinas' presentation is in terms of objective positions which one must accept if communication is not to break down, Lonergan's concentration upon the *processes* which all must use as they explore the world mediated by meaning, makes a much more fruitful dialogue possible. He writes: "It is only by objectification of such conscious operations, of our acts of understanding and formulating, of reflecting, weighing the evidence, and judging, of deliberating, evaluating, deciding, that we can reach any real apprehension of the mediation that meaning effects, of the broad and fine structures of the world that meaning mediates" (*ibid.*, p. 295).

25   *Loc. cit.*

26   *Ibid.*, pp. 295-296. Perhaps Lonergan may be criticized for not exploring more fully the "history" in which God's truth is embodied; but this criticism in no way touches the essentials of the argument with which we are concerned here.

27   *Ibid.*, p. 295.

28   *Ibid.*, pp. 296-298. See also *The Way to Nicaea* (London, 1976).

29   "The Origins of Christian Realism," pp. 296-297.

30   *Ibid.*, pp. 298-299. Lonergan adds: "It is this third view that finds expression in the Scholastic tag *Ens per verum innotescit*: reality becomes known through knowing what is true" (p. 299). It should be noted that, according to Lonergan's analysis, the meaning which mediates reality is to be found in the proposition in which the *essential* and the *existential* (cf. what was said concerning Aquinas' position, n. 24 above) are registered. Reflection will show that these two orders will be brought together in knowledge only if the "world of immediacy" and the "world mediated by meaning" are present to the knower.

31   *Ibid.*, p. 299.

32   *Ibid.*, pp. 299-300.

33   *Ibid.*, p. 300. Lonergan notes that, in our time, "linguistic analysts claim, rightly I believe, that one clarifies the meaning of a word, not by some universal definition, but by showing how the word is used appropriately" *(loc. cit.).*

34   *Loc. cit.*

35   *Loc. cit.*

36   Refer to what has been said about Aquinas' "negative theology" in n. 4 above.

37   For an official statement of the Catholic Church's position on this matter, see *Mysterium ecclesiae* of the Congregation of the Doctrine of the Faith, *Acta apostolicae sedis,* 65

(1973):386-408; English version in *Origins,* 3 (1973):97, 99-100, 110-112. See also Karl Rahner, "Open Questions in Dogma Considered by the Institutional Church as Definitively Closed," *Journal of Ecumenical Studies,* 15 (1978):211-226, for another aspect of this complex question; A. Keller, "Analytical Philosophy and the Magisterium's Claim to Infallible Authority," *Jour. Ecum. Studies* 19 (1982): 75-91.

CHAPTER EIGHT

1   See Peter Mann's *Martin Luther* (New York, 1982), p. 90 [52]. References are to this work, with references to a modified 1983 edition given in brackets.
2   *Ibid.,* p. 46 [58-59].
3   *Ibid.,* p. 124 [82].
4   *Ibid.,* p. 86 [50].
5   See Denzinger-Schönmetzer, no. 1501.
6   Pastoral Constitution on the Church in the Modern World, *Gaudium et spes,* no. 41.
7   Dogmatic Constitution on Divine Revelation, *Dei verbum,* no. 7.
8   Decree of the Church's Missionary Activity, *Ad gentes divinitus,* no. 8.
9   Puebla Address, 1979.
10 Louis Bouyer, *The Church of God* (Chicago, 1983), p. 146; see the conclusion of his *The Spirit and Forms of Protestantism* (London, 1963).
11 Dietrich Bonhoeffer describes this dialogic meeting with the "who" of the Lord: "The only real question which now remains is 'Who are you? Speak for yourself!' The question 'Who are you?' is the question of dethroned and distraught reason; but it is also the question of faith.... The question 'Who?' is the question about transcendence; the question 'How?' is the question about immanence. It is because the one questioned is the Son that the immanent question is not adequate. Not 'How are you possible?'; that is the godless question.... but 'Who are you?' The question 'Who' expresses the strangeness of the one encountered, and at the same time it is shown to be the question concerning the very existence of the questioner. He is asking about the being which is strange to his being, about the boundaries of his own existence" (*Lectures in Christology,* trans. by E. Robinson [London, 1978], pp. 10-11).
12 Stanislas Lyonnet writes: "I do not think that one can find a more perfect definition of 'evangelization': not only to

announce Christ or preach him, but to implant the evangelical economy, to bring about that men love each other as Christ loved us and that they become conscious that this love is given to them by the Other, freely, an Other who has loved them to the point of wishing to communicate to them his own love by dying and rising for them and by making himself their nourishment in the Eucharist."

13   *The Glory of God,* 2:11.

14   See J. Thornhill, *Sign and Promise,* pp. 75-76.

15   Decree on Ecumenism, *Unitatis redintegratio,* no. 11. For a survey of the literature discussing the "hierarchy of truths" in the twenty years after the Council, see W. Hann, "The Hierarchy of Truths Twenty Years Later," *Theological Studies,* 48 (1987):439-471; also A. Dulles, *The Resilient Church* (Dublin, 1978), pp. 56-57.

16   Dogmatic Constitution on Divine Revelation, *Dei verbum,* no. 11.

17   As Walter Kasper notes, the key to the unity of revealed truth must be found in Christ himself (*An Introduction to Christian Faith,* p. 109); see also Schillebeeckx, *Interim Report,* p. 39. Kasper notes, as we have done, that in providing this central point of reference, Christ is a *medium:* his whole mission was to make known who-God-is. The truth of who-God-is, as we have seen, is the central message of the gospel. All other truths of Christian faith will find their true meaning and order among themselves within the economy established by the gospel message.

CHAPTER NINE

1   On this question, see H. Urs von Balthasar, "Unity and Diversity in New Testament Theology," *Communio,* 10 (1983):106-116; E. Dussel, "Theologies of the 'Periphery' and the 'Center': Encounter or Confrontation?" in *Concilium,* (1984), pp. 87-97; P. Eicher, "Pluralism and the Dignity of Theology," *Concilium* (1984), pp. 3-12; V. Elizondo, "Conditions and Criteria for Authentic Inter-cultural Theological Dialogue," *Concilium* (1984), pp. 18-24; M. Fatula, "Dogmatic Pluralism and the Noetic Dimension of Unity of Faith," *Thomist,* 48 (1984):409-432; L. Gilkey, "Pluralism and Its Theological Implications," *East Asian Pastoral Review,* 22 (1985):326-339; M. Hegba, "From the Generalization of One Triumphant Particular to the Search for True Universality," *Concilium* (1984), pp. 46-51; International Theological Commission, "Unity of Faith and Theological Pluralism," *The Tablet,* July 7, 1973, pp. 646-647; B. Lonergan, *Doctrinal Pluralism* (Milwaukee, 1971); J. Macquarrie, *Principles of Christian Theology* (London, 1966), pp. 4-17; J.B. Metz, "Theology in the Modern Age and Before Its End," *Concilium* (1984), pp. 13-17; B. Mondin, "Legitimacy and Limits of Theological Pluralism," *L'Osservatore Romano,* English ed., April 6, 1978; V. Peter, "A Primer on Pluralism," *Communio,* 10 (1983):133-148; K. Rahner, "Pluralism in Theology and the Unity of the Creed in the Church," *Theological Investigations,* 11:3-23; J.M. Tillard, "Theological Pluralism and the Mystery of the Church," *Concilium* (1984), pp. 62-70.

2   See H. Urs von Balthasar, "Unity and Diversity in New Testament Theology," *Communio,* 10 (1983):106-116; E. Kaesemann, "The Canon of the New Testament and the Unity of the Church" in *Essays on New Testament Themes* (London, 1964), pp. 95-107; "Differences and Unity in the New Testament," *Concilium* (1984), pp. 55-61; J.-Y. Lacoste, "The Unfailing Witness: Notes on the Canon of Scripture," *Communio,* 10 (1983):167-184.

3   H. Urs von Balthasar, *Does Jesus Know Us? Do We Know Him?* p. 83.

4   Chenu, "The Need for a Theology of the World," p. 58.

5   "Unity of Faith and Theological Pluralism," as translated from *Civiltà Cattolica* (1973), p. 368; see the version in *The Tablet* (July 7, 1973), p. 647, which has an omission.

6   Newman's "idea" corresponds to Lonergan's "world mediated by meaning." See "An Interview with Bernard Lonergan," *Clergy Review,* 56 (1971):428, where Lonergan, after noting the Greek achievement of differentiating, within the universe of meaning, "the world of common sense and the world of theory," remarks: "Augustine is just in the world of common sense, a beautiful rhetorician; Newman, too. They're not technical people. They did tremendous work, but not technical in the way Thomas was and Aristotle was."

7   *An Essay on the Development of Christian Doctrine* (London, 1960; first ed. 1845), p. 21.

8   *Ibid.,* pp. 211-222; see also p. 28. The purpose of Newman's argument leads him to dwell upon the positive recognition of the abiding presence of the tradition, despite all appearances to the contrary. His analysis, however, also provides the basis for a critical examination of later developments. Not only will the milieu in which the message of Christian truth expresses itself call forth new and life-giving expressions of its import, it will also give rise to the limitations and imbalances which are characteristic of doctrinal development in particular periods.

9   *Ibid.,* p. 29. Newman continues: "From time to time it makes essays which fail, and are in consequence abandoned. It seems in suspense which way to go; it wavers, and at length strikes out in one definite direction. In time it enters upon strange territory; points of controversy alter its bearing; parties rise and fall around it; dangers and hopes appear in new relations; the old principles reappear under new form. It changes with them in order to remain the same. In a higher world it is otherwise, but here below to live is to change, and to be perfect is to have changed often."

10   *Ibid.,* pp. 41-42. Newman goes on to suggest criteria of genuine development; see pp. 124 and 149.

11   See J.B. Metz, "Theology in the Modern Age and Before Its End," *Concilium* (1984), p. 16: "I would...divide the history of the Church and of theology so far into three epochs: the epoch of Jewish Christianity, relatively short in terms of years but fundamental for the identity of the Church and of theology; then the very long epoch within a single culture, even if one with many different strands—in other words, the epoch of Hellenism and European culture and civilization up to our own days; and finally the epoch of a culturally polycentric, genuinely universal Church whose first hints and beginnings showed themselves at Vatican II."

12   See *La théologie au douzième siècle* (Paris, 1957), pp. 226-273—esp. p. 249.

13   See Etienne Gilson's Foreword to Augustine's *The City of God*, ed. by Vernon Bourke (New York, 1958).

14   See E. TeSelle, *Augustine the Theologian* (London, 1970), p. 183 ff.

15   See Peter Mann, *Martin Luther* (New York, 1982).

16   See J. Coulson, *Newman and the Common Tradition* (Oxford, 1970).

17   See Newman's *Apologia pro vita sua* (London, 1977; first ed. 1864).

18   "Dogmatic Reflections on the Knowledge and Self-consciousness of Christ," *Theological Investigations,* 5:200-201. It is illuminating to compare what Rahner says with Lonergan's "world mediated by meaning." Replying to a comment that he, Lonergan, laid emphasis on clarity in his writings, whereas Rahner's thought maintains a constant tension with the divine mystery, Lonergan replied: "But mystery remains. When you talk, you're not aiming at communicating a mystery. But you don't dispel it either. Rahner emphasizes mystery a lot. I have a few clear things to say" ("Interview," *Clergy Review,* 56 [1971]:430).

19   See Mondin's article "Legitimacy and Limits of Theological Pluralism," *L'Osservatore Romano,* English ed., April 6, 1978.

20   *Ibid.,* p. 6.

21   *Loc. cit.* Mondin illustrates this from the theologies of the Fathers: "Each one derives his distinctive structuring principle from Christ as the divine *Logos—Clement* takes Christ as

teacher; *Gregory of Nyssa*, Christ as the image of God; *Augustine*, the mystery of sin and grace; *Pseudo-Dionysius*, the goodness of God" (p. 7). He also suggests examples from contemporary theology: for *Teilhard de Chardin*, he suggests, the structuring principle is "Jesus Christ, the Omega point of everything"; for *Karl Rahner* it is "sanctifying grace"; for *Bultmann* it is "the Word of God"; for *Bonhoeffer* it is "God's love for one's neighbor"; for G. Gutierrez it is "liberation."

22 Puebla Address. This same theme is central to his encyclical *Redemptor hominis*, published the same year.

23 "Legitimacy and Limits of Theological Pluralism," p. 6.

24 *Loc. cit.*

25 *Ibid.*, p. 7.

26 *Loc. cit.*

27 See J. Thornhill, "Is Religion the Enemy of Faith?" in *Theological Studies*, 45 (1984):269-270.

28 See Hans Urs von Balthasar, *The Theology of Karl Barth* (New York, 1971).

CHAPTER TEN

1   Bonhoeffer's term, as we shall see when considering his theology.
2   "Towards a Fundamental Theological Interpretation of Vatican II," *Theological Studies,* 40 (1979):721. We have already quoted J.B. Metz as making a similar judgment. Concerning the first transition, Rahner continues: "This introduced a radically new period in Church history, a Christianity that was not the export of Jewish Christianity to the Diaspora but instead a Christianity which, for all its relationship to the historical Jesus, still grew on the soil of paganism.... It is not yet reflectively clear to us what Paul 'brought about' when he declared circumcision and everything connected with it superfluous for non-Jews" *(loc. cit.).*
3   *Ibid.,* p. 717.
4   Nicaea (325), Constantinople I (381), Ephesus (431), Chalcedon (451), Constantinople II (553).
5   *Medieval Essays* (New York, 1954), p. 99.
6   *La théologie au douzième siècle* (Paris, 1957), p. 232. In fact, the literary, dramatic, artistic and musical developments of Western culture all had their origins in this sacralized setting.
7   See M.-D. Chenu, *Toward Understanding St. Thomas* (Chicago, 1964); M. Colish, "Teaching and Learning Theology in Medieval Paris," ch. 8 of *Schools of Thought in the Christian Tradition,* ed. by P. Henry (Philadelphia, 1984).
8   We have already cited Chenu in this regard: see *La théologie au douzième siècle,* p. 249. See also J.C. Murray, *The Problem of God,* pp. 66-69; J. Thornhill, *The Person and the Group* (Milwaukee, 1967), pp. 8-9.
9   In Scholastic philosophy this name refers to the philosophical assumption that abstract terms do not convey a meaning which mediates reality itself. Reality is admitted only for actual physical particulars. Universal terms serve as useful ciphers for understanding to deal with real particulars. Lonergan calls this position "naive realism." He writes: "Its offspring is empiricism [which] proceeds to empty the world

mediated by meaning of everything that is not given to immediate experience" ("The Origins of Christian Realism," *Theological Digest*, 20 [1972]:293-294).

10   *The Methods of Dogmatic Theology* (New York, 1969), p. 14. Kasper notes that numerous attempts were made within Catholic theology to overcome this unfortunate isolation from the creative stream of Western culture and "to latch onto the reformatory notions of Humanism" (pp. 14-15, 19-20), but the pressures of historical circumstance, as he observes, doomed these efforts to failure.

11   *Ibid.,* p. 18.

12   Encyclical Letter *Aeterni Patris* (1879).

13   See J. Thornhill, *Sign and Promise,* pp. 4-9.

14   Foreword to H. Urs von Balthasar's *The God Question and Modern Man* (New York, 1967), p. xii. Macquarrie notes that, because Catholic theology has never been entirely negative to the "world," it is more easily able to maintain a critical attitude to secular reality and enter into a proper dialectic with that reality (p. xiii). We have noted already in earlier chapters the part played by the rhetoric derived from the scriptures in the shaping of this Protestant tradition.

15   Introduction to Schleiermacher's *The Christian Faith* (New York, 1963), p. ix. The course Schleiermacher adopted is not unrelated to Kant's influence upon Christian theology. Kant's criticism of metaphysical knowledge of God has posed a considerable problem for theology's task of interpreting the Christian faith.

16   Niebuhr, as cited, p. x. See K. Clements, *Friedrich Schleiermacher: Pioneer of Modern Theology* (London, 1987) for an introduction to Schleiermacher's thought and selected texts from his writings.

17   *Church Dogmatics,* I/2, p. 284.

18   *Ibid.,* p. 292.

19   *Ibid.,* p. 294.

20   See R. Johnson, *Rudolf Bultmann: Interpreting Faith for the Modern Era* (London, 1987) for an introduction to Bultmann's thought and selected texts from his writings.

21   See J. de Gruchy, *Dietrich Bonhoeffer: Witness to Jesus Christ* (London, 1987) for an introduction to Bonhoeffer's thought and selected texts from his writings.

22 *Modern Theology: Dietrich Bonhoeffer*, ed. by E. Tinsley (London, 1973), p. 78. Bonhoeffer writes of Barth that "in the non-religious interpretation of theological concepts he gave no concrete guidance, either in dogmatics or in ethics." Instead, in place of the religion of liberal Protestantism, he put "a positivistic doctrine of revelation which says in effect, 'Like it or lump it': Virgin birth, Trinity, or anything else" (*Letters and Papers from Prison*, ed. by E. Bethge [New York, 1972], pp. 328 and 285).

23 *Letters and Papers from Prison*, p. 285. The link between Bultmann's notion of "demythologization" and the desacralization essential to the process of secularization should not be overlooked.

24 *Ibid.*, p. 359.

25 *Modern Theology: Dietrich Bonhoeffer*, ed. by E. Tinsley, p. 79.

26 *Letters and Papers from Prison*, p. 381.

27 The Catholic theologian Louis Bouyer speaks of "the original, profound meaning of Protestantism" in the following terms: "To Catholics, lukewarm and unaware of their responsibilities, the Protestant movement, when rightly understood, recalls the existence of many of their own treasures which they overlook" (*The Spirit and Forms of Protestantism* [London, 1963], pp. 272-273). In a later work, Bouyer cites Archbishop Michael Ramsey's *The Gospel and the Church*, which he judged "may one day be acknowledged as marking the most decisive turning point in twentieth-century ecumenism" (*The Church of God* [Chicago, 1983], p. 146). According to Archbishop Ramsey, a viable ecumenism will seek a new and creative tension between the Church of Christ, fully conscious of the graces which constitute her existence, and the divine, transcendent Word, of which the Church is but recipient and steward. Bouyer argues that, because the Word cannot speak effectively to the world except in and through the Church, it is possible and necessary for Protestantism's essential concerns to be reconciled with the Catholic Church "as a prophetic movement of permanent significance and import." Outside the Church, on the other hand, "it loses its meaning, since the reformation to which it is directed, if it is not the reformation of the one

Church...must see its object, its reason or be vanished" *(loc. cit.)*.

28 See his *The Theology of Karl Barth* (New York, 1971).
29 See W. Nichols, *The Pelican Guide to Modern Theology,* 1:336.
30 Barth—and, to some extent, Bonhoeffer after him—identified the metaphysical approach to revealed truth as a turning to religion at the expense of faith (see Bonhoeffer's *Letters and Papers from Prison,* pp. 285-286 ff.). Schillebeeckx seems to have moved along the same path. This must be challenged, as Lonergan makes clear (see "The Origins of Christian Realism," *Theological Digest,* 20 [1972]:292).
31 See R. Haight, *The Alternative Vision* (New York, 1985).
32 Johann Baptist Metz's seminal work, *Faith in History and Society: Toward a Practical Fundamental Theology* (New York, 1980) touches upon many of the issues we have discussed in this text.

CHAPTER ELEVEN

1 See 1 Cor., chs. 1 and 2. "Christ did not send me to baptize but to preach the gospel...the word of the cross" (1:17); "We preach Christ crucified...the power of God and the wisdom of God" (1:23-24); "If anyone is preaching to you a gospel contrary to that which you received, let him be accursed" (Gal. 1:9).

2 See Mk. 1:1—"The beginning of the gospel of Jesus Christ, the Son of God."

3 See M. Colish, "Teaching and Learning Theology in Medieval Paris," in P. Henry, *Schools of Thought in the Christian Tradition* (Philadelphia, 1984), pp. 106-124; M.-D. Chenu, *Toward Understanding St. Thomas* (Chicago, 1964).

4 P. Benoit writes: [For] "St. Thomas—a child of his age and of the system in which he was brought up...speculative knowledge occupies pride of place in human activity, in which Truth is an Idea, an eternal concept mastered by the mind...the way to God is by meditation, contemplation and ecstasy" (*Aspects of Biblical Inspiration* [Chicago, 1965], p. 61).

5 London, n.d., edition prepared by English Dominicans.

6 *Summa theologiae,* I, q.43, art.1.

7 *Ibid.,* III, q.42, art.3.

8 See Chenu, *Introduction à l'étude de saint Thomas d'Aquin* (Paris, 1950), "Magister in sacra pagina," pp. 207-208.

9 These reflections remind one of Aquinas' seminal assertion: *Actus credentis terminatur, non ad enuntiabile, sed ad rem* (The act of belief [realized through Christian faith] attains, not a formulary of words, but the [divine] reality—*Summa theologiae,* II-II, q.1, art.2, response to objection 2)—a text in which the reader will recognize concerns similar to those of Lonergan. In fact, St. Thomas, following the format of the medieval schools, adopts an approach in his *Summa theologiae* which anticipates Lonergan's observation that reality is "intended by questions." Each article raises a clearly defined question. He then lists objections which seem to

point to a conclusion opposed to the response he will give. After arguing his conclusion in the body of the article—the texts selected belong to this section—he responds to the objections. Sometimes important elements in his exposition are to be found in these responses. In the article we have just considered, for example, he quotes as apposite Augustine's observation concerning the inspiration of the scriptures: "Christ is the head of all his disciples who are members of his body. Consequently, when they put into writing what he showed forth and said to them, by no means must we say that he wrote nothing"; he also quotes the words of Paul concerning the truth Christ brought to us: it is "the law of the Spirit of life" (Rom. 8:2); it is "written not with ink but with the Spirit of the living God, not on tablets of stone but on tablets of human hearts" (2 Cor. 3:3).

10   See B. Mondin, *Le teologie del nostro tempo* (Edizione Paolinc, 1976), pp. 35-36.

11   *Church Dogmatics,* I/2:506-508, 512-513.

12   "Fundamentalism" arose as a reaction to liberal theological views within North American Protestantism early in the present century, views which were related to the impact of historical criticism upon the understanding of the scriptures: the name came from this movement's call to get back to "fundamentals." Basic to the fundamentalist movement is a disregard for the historical and literary setting of the biblical text, and a failure to recognize that this must be identified if the text's genuine import is to be understood. We may note that this phenomenon finds parallels in all religious traditions today as they experience the pressures of modernity and secularization. See J. Barr, *Fundamentalism* (London, 1977); "The Fundamentalist Understanding of Scripture," *Concilium* (1980), pp. 70-74; S. Schneiders, "God's Word for God's People," *The Bible Today,* 22 (1984):100-106; A. Gilles, *Fundamentalism: What Every Catholic Needs to Know* (Cincinnati, 1984).

13   See his *The Theology of Karl Barth.*

14   See John Macquarrie's Foreword to von Balthasar's *The God Question and Modern Man* (New York, 1967), especially pp. xii-xiii.

15 See von Balthasar's *Love Alone: The Way of Revelation* (London, 1968). This theology thus redresses the inadequacy in Western theology criticized by Bulgakov.

16 See pp. 11-13. Citations which follow come from this passage.

17 Von Balthasar stresses that he is affirming something very different from "the simple radiance of the Platonic sun of the good; it is an act in which God utterly freely makes himself present."

18 See J. Fitzmyer, "Pauline Theology," *Jerome Biblical Commentary*, 79:71-73.

19 See T. McDonough, *The Law and the Gospel in Luther: A Study of Martin Luther's Confessional Writings* (Oxford, 1963).

20 See Luther's defense of his theses at Heidelberg, in M. Luther, *Early Theological Works*, Library of Christian Classics (London, 1962), 16:290-294; in the *Supplementary Texts*.

21 Thesis XX.

22 Thesis XXI.

23 This rhetorical emphasis and its ambiguity is becoming evident, for example, in his defense of Thesis XXV, where Luther declares: "Without any work of ours, grace and righteousness are infused.... Quite simply...works do absolutely nothing towards salvation." See. P. Mann: "In Luther's positive assessment of the role of good works under grace in justification there is not the theological clarity that characterizes his denial of works-righteousness. Instead, the relevant statements...are ambiguous, contradictory, in need of clarification, and therefore misleading." See "Absolute and Incarnate Faith—Luther in the Galatians Commentary of 1531-1535," in *Catholic Scholars Dialogue with Luther*, ed. by J. Wicks (Chicago, 1970), p. 125; in addition, see p. 121; see also J. Thornhill, "Is Religion the Enemy of Faith?" in *Theological Studies*, 45 (1984):256-257, where this issue is discussed.

24 C. Davis, Introduction to F.X. Durrwell's *The Resurrection* (London, 1965), pp. xvii-xviii. Davis sums up well the situation we have described.

25 See Durrwell's book cited in the previous note.

26   See *Gaudium et spes*, no. 22.
27   *The Crucified God* (London, 1974; German ed. 1973).
28   This is stated on p. 1.
29   He refers (p. 2) to the crushing of "socialism with a human face in Czechoslovakia," the setbacks of the civil-rights movement in the United States, and the slowing down of the movements of renewal and ecumenical endeavor within the Churches in the aftermath of the Second Vatican Council.
30   *Ibid.,* p. 2.
31   *Ibid.,* pp. 3-5.
32   Hans Urs von Balthasar is one Catholic theologian who has concerned himself with the theology of the cross. We may ask whether, as an admirer of Barth, he has made his interpretation too much in terms of God's anger, rather than his love (see *Does Jesus Know Us? Do We Know Him?* [San Francisco, 1983], pp. 30-37). In discussing the significance of the cross, Moltmann has pointed out that this significance cannot be found in a theoretical investigation; it must be found in probing the human situation (*The Crucified God,* pp. 68-69). Carlo Carretto gives expression to the Catholic emphasis upon the presence of divine love in the cross by situating himself within the depths of human experience: "To man in his blind alley of sin, the canons of justice and truth were unable to offer salvation.... Then Jesus came. And his own received him not.... All humanity surged round him to strike, spit and revile. And Jesus, the only truly innocent man, bent his head under the blows. He did not invoke justice, and with his flesh and spirit, he paid for the sins of the world.... After Calvary, peace was no longer to operate on the thin blade of truth or in the court of law, but in the torn heart of a God who had become man for us in Jesus Christ. The era of victimization had ended, and with Jesus the reign of the victim was to begin" ("The Revolt of the Good" in *Letters from the Desert*). Moltmann, in fact, opens up a similar perspective but does not follow out its immense potential as, at once, a source of gospel truth and a basis of reconciliation between the two approaches: "Love is the source and the basis of the possibility of the wrath of God. The opposite of love is not wrath, but indifference" (*op. cit.,* p. 272).

33   This name is known to us through the Greek form *Iesus*.

34   From the Greek *soteria*, salvation.

35   Translation from *The Incarnation of the Word of God*, cited in
      V. Zamoyta, *The Theology of Christ: Sources* (Milwaukee,
      1967), pp. 37-38.

36   See W. Nicholls, *The Pelican Guide to Modern Theology*,
      1:235-238, to whom what follows is indebted. See also M.K.
      Taylor, *Paul Tillich: Theologian of the Boundaries* (London,
      1987) for a survey of Tillich's thought and an anthology of
      representative texts.

37   *The Wounded Healer* (New York, 1972), p. 74.

38   Quoted, *loc. cit.*, from *On Becoming a Person* (London,
      1961), p. 26.

39   *The Wounded Healer*, pp. 84-85.

40   *Eruption to Hope* (Toronto, 1971), Preface.

41   *Followers of Jesus* (Guelph, 1973), p. 19.

42   See R. Haight, *The Alternative Vision* (New York, 1985); J.
      Mitterhoefer, "Liberation Theology: An Interim Report,"
      Theological Digest, 34 (1987):15-18.

43   See W. Brueggemann, *The Prophetic Imagination* (already
      cited in ch. 2), pp. 16-18.

44   Pp. 155-157.

45   It is customary to distinguish a theology of Christ "from
      above" and one "from below." The former, taking for granted
      the divine identity of Jesus, proceeds to consider his earthly
      life in the light of his divinity; the latter begins with the
      history of Jesus and follows the path followed by his first
      disciples—at first drawn by the mysterious greatness which
      they recognized in him, and finally led to acknowledge his
      divine identity. If the former has been taken for granted in
      Christian awareness since patristic times, the latter is
      reasserting its importance in the light of contemporary
      biblical scholarship, and in response to the exigencies of an
      age which needs to be evangelized anew. It has been pointed
      out that a Christology "from above" which is not built upon
      a Christology "from below" finds no justification in the New
      Testament: "The preexistence element in the pre-Pauline
      hymns is featured, not for its own sake, but in order to draw
      out the significance of the historical Jesus phenomenon....
      The movement of Johannine Christology was actually *from*

below *to* above, *from* the historical Jesus phenomenon *to* its prior background in eternity" (R. Fuller, *Who Is This Christ?* [Philadelphia, 1983], pp. 6-7).

46 See *A Catholic Dictionary of Theology,* ed. by H. Davis *et al.*, 1:57-60; R. Wilcken, "Alexandria: A School for Training in Virtue," *Schools of Thought in the Christian Tradition* (Philadelphia, 1984), pp. 15-30.

47 The Christological debates of the early centuries forced the Alexandrian tradition to recognize the ambiguity of the term "flesh" in their paradigm: it could refer to humanity or to the fleshly component of humanity.

48 *Adversus Nest.*, 4, 5, as translated in H. Bettenson, *The Later Christian Fathers* (Oxford, 1974), pp. 257-258.

49 "My Pathfindings in the Theology of Laity and Ministries," *Jurist,* 32 (1972):171-172, where further references will be found. Elsewhere Congar has pointed out the ambiguity of this notion of the life of the Church as a "continuing incarnation"; he suggests that if Paul's "body" theme is not balanced with the "espousal" theme—as it is in Paul's thought—it can give rise to a distorted understanding of the Church's identification with Christ: see "Constant Self-Renewal of the Church," *Theological Digest,* 10 (1962): 186; J. Thornhill, *Sign and Promise,* pp. 81-82.

50 Published in the United Kingdom (1957), this volume reproduced papers presented at a conference of Australian Catholic university students in 1955, as Vincent Buckley points out in his Introduction.

51 Bk. 10, chs. 26-29.

52 See E. TeSelle, *Augustine the Theologian* (London, 1970); H. Chadwick, *Augustine* (Oxford, 1986); J. Wilcken, "Augustine: Issues of Sin, Grace and Freedom," *Australasian Catholic Record,* 58 (1981):419-430; R. Haight, *The Experience and Language of Grace* (Dublin, 1978), ch. 2.

53 *Foundations of Christian Faith,* London, 1978, pp. 81-84.

54 See O. Muck, *The Transcendental Method,* translated by W. Seidensticker (New York, 1968).

55 See H. Vorgrimler, *Karl Rahner: His Life, Thought and Works* (New York, 1966); K.-H. Weger, *Karl Rahner: An Introduction to His Theology* (New York, 1980); R. Kress, *A*

Rahner Reader (Atlanta, 1987); G. McCool, *A Rahner Reader* (New York, 1975).

56 See Hosea 2-3; Is. 1:21-26; Jer. 2:2; 3:1, 6-12; Ez. 16 and 23; Is. 50:1; 54:6-8; 62:4-5; Song of Songs.

57 J.P. Burns, "The Concept of Satisfaction in Medieval Redemption Theory," *Theological Studies,* 36 (1975):285.

58 See G. Aulen, *Christus Victor: A Historical Study of the Three Main Types of the Idea of Atonement* (London, 1975).

59 See Burns, "The Concept of Satisfaction," pp. 298-301.

60 See *Justification by Faith,* a document of the United States Lutheran-Roman Catholic Dialogue, in *Origins,* 13 (1983):277-304; *Salvation and the Church,* an agreed statement by the second Anglican-Roman Catholic International Commission (1987).

61 *Justification by Faith,* no. 90.

62 *Loc. cit.* See no. 158: "Our common affirmation that it is God in Christ alone whom believers ultimately trust does not necessitate any one particular way of conceptualizing or picturing God's saving work. That work can be expressed in the imagery of God as judge who pronounces sinners innocent and righteous (cf. no. 90), and also in a transformist view which emphasizes the change wrought in sinners by infused grace."

63 The thought of Rudolf Bultmann belongs to this movement; see J. Macquarrie, *Twentieth-Century Religious Thought* (London, 1971), pp. 362-364.

64 See *Intelligent Theology* (London, 1967), 1:29-30.

65 See J. Thornhill, *Sign and Promise,* pp. 51-55.

66 *Ibid.,* pp. 56-64.

67 *Tradition and Traditions* (London, 1966), pp. 391-397. This text is also found in *Theologians Today: Yves M.-J. Congar,* ed. by M. Redfern (London, 1972), pp. 62-70.

68 *Catholicism: A Study of Dogma in Relation to the Corporate Destiny of Mankind* (London, 1950), pp. 93, 107, 117-118.

69 *Ibid.,* p. 93.

70 *Ibid.,* p. 118.

71 *La documentation catholique,* 45 (1963):1978.

72 *Acta apost. sedis,* 56 (1964):36-37.

73 See J. Thornhill, *Sign and Promise,* ch. 7.

74 *Our Lady and the Church* (London, 1961).

75 "Valiant woman" (Prov. 31:10).
76 *Our Lady and the Church*, p. 80.
77 *Ibid.*, p. 81.
78 *Ibid.*, p. 83.
79 *Ibid.*, p. 85.
80 *Ibid.*, p. 86.
81 *Ibid.*, p. 87.
82 On the nature of the apocalyptic literature, see C. Stuhlmueller, *Jerome Biblical Commentary*, 20:21-24.
83 See note in the *Jerusalem Bible* on the last of these texts.
84 B. Vawter, *Jerome Biblical Commentary*, 63:24.
85 *Jerusalem Bible*, note on Jn. 19:34.
86 *Serm. 227*, P.L. 38:1247.
87 See B. Piault, *What Is a Sacrament?* Faith and Fact Books: 49 (London, 1963), pp. 45-53; P.-Th. Camelot, " 'Sacramentum': Notes de théologie Augustinienne," *Revue Thomiste*, 57 (1957):429-449.
88 *Apologia pro vita sua* (London, 1977; first ed. 1864).
89 Some pages earlier than the passage which has been given, Newman described the adolescent experience to which he makes reference at the end of our passage—how, for the first time, he was challenged to take up a doctrinal position in the interpretation of the Christian mystery: "When I was fifteen (in the autumn of 1816) a great change of thought took place in me. I fell under the influences of a definite Creed, and received in my intellect impressions of Dogma, which, through God's mercy, have never been effaced or obscured.... Above and beyond the conversations and sermons of the excellent man, long dead, who was the human beginnings of divine faith in me, was the effect of books which he put in my hands, all of the school of Calvin.... I was elected to eternal glory.... This belief...I retained...till the age of twenty-two, when it gradually faded away; but I believe that it had some influence on my opinions, in the direction of those childish imaginations which I have already mentioned, viz. in insolating me from the objects which surrounded me, in confirming me in my mistrust of the reality of material phenomena, and making me rest in the thought of two and two only supreme and luminously self-evident beings, myself and my Creator" (pp. 97-98).

90   See J. Thornhill, "Newman's Stature as a Theologian," *Shadows and Images: The Newman Centenary Symposium,* ed. by B.J.L. Cross (Sydney, 1979), pp. 19-41, and especially 28-31.

91   Philip Murnion, "A Sacramental Church," *America,* March 26, 1983.

92   J. Ratzinger, *Introduction to Christianity* (New York, 1970), p. 174; cf. J. Thornhill, *Sign and Promise,* pp. 35-47.

93   See E. Bethge, *Dietrich Bonhoeffer: Theologian, Christian, Contemporary* (London, 1970); J. de Gruchy, *Dietrich Bonhoeffer: Witness to Jesus Christ* (London, 1987), giving a representative selection of texts.

94   See *Letters and Papers from Prison,* ed. by E. Bethge (London, 1971), p. 327. In Bonhoeffer's words: "The weakness of liberal theology was that it conceded to the world the right to determine Christ's place in the world; in conflict between the Church and the world, it accepted the comparatively easy terms of peace that the world dictated. Its strength was that it did not try to put the clock back, and that it genuinely accepted the battle (Troelsch), even though this ended with its defeat" (cited in de Gruchy, pp. 37-38).

95   *Modern Theology: Dietrich Bonhoeffer,* ed. by E. Tinsley (London, 1973), pp. 77-80.

96   See A. Dulles, *Models of the Church* (New York, 1974), pp. 83 and 85.

97   By identification with the figure of the "suffering servant," Jesus entered into one of the most profound expressions of Old Testament faith. See Is. 42:1-4; 49:1-6; 50:4-11; 52:13 to 53:12.

98   See S. Schneiders, "The Foot Washing (Jn. 13:1-20): An Experiment in Hermeneutics," *Catholic Biblical Quarterly,* 43 (1981):80-88.

99   See also H. Urs von Balthasar, *A von Balthasar Reader,* ed. by M. Kehl and W. Loeser (New York, 1982), pp. 285-288; K. O'Shea, *The Christ-Life* (Homebush, 1970), pp. 32-39.

100   See "Eschatology," *Theology Today: Renewal in Dogma,* ed. by J. Feiner (Milwaukee, 1965), p. 222.

101   *Ibid.,* p.223.

102   *Loc. cit.*

103   "The Church: The People of God," *Concilium* (1965), p. 10.

104 *Theology of Hope* (London, 1969).
105 *Ibid.,* p. 11.
106 *Basic Questions in Theology* (Philadelphia, 1971), 2:241-244.
107 See W. Nicholls, *The Pelican Guide to Modern Theology* (1969), 1:338-344.
108 *Basic Questions in Theology,* 1:xv.
109 What has been said about the "negative theology" of Aquinas should be recalled here. The problem which Pannenberg raises is not new. Medieval Scholasticism appealed to *analogy* in its response, affirming that after creation there existed "not more *being* but more *beings*" (Cajetan). For a contemporary formulation of this response, see H. McCabe, *The Honest to God Debate,* ed. by J.A.T. Robinson and D. Edwards (London, 1963), pp. 167-168.
110 See N.M. Wilders, *An Introduction to Teilhard de Chardin* (London, 1968); E. Rideau, *Teilhard de Chardin: A Guide to His Thought* (London, 1967); for a critical assessment, see E. Benz, *Evolution and Christian Hope* (New York, 1966), chs. 12-13.
111 *The Future of Man* (London, 1964), pp. 304-305.

CHAPTER TWELVE

1 *Gaudium et spes,* no. 22.
2 See J. Weisheipl, *Friar Thomas d'Aquino: His Life, Thought and Work* (New York, 1974), pp. 333-334.
3 See "Moines, clercs, laics: Au carrefour de la vie évangélique," in *La théologie au douzième siècle* (Paris, 1957), pp. 225-273.
4 Aristotle distinguished between universal *discourse* (made possible by the intellect's grasp of what is formal in reality) and a universal *mode of existence* (such as postulated by Plato). He wrote: "...some things can be spoken of universally, whereas others cannot. The proximate principles of everything are the proximate particular thing which exists in actuality, and something else which exists potentially. The universals, then, to which we referred, do not exist; for the cause of an individual is an individual; man is the cause of man universally, but there is no such thing as universal man" (*Metaphysics,* bk. 12, ch. 5, 1071a17). The relationship to Lonergan's "world mediated by meaning" should be noted.
5 See R. J. Henley, *St. Thomas and Platonism* (The Hague, 1956). Aquinas transcended the achievement of Aristotle most notably in his emphasis upon the act of existence *(esse)* as the central point of reference in his metaphysical system. For Aristotle, *actuality* (as distinct from *potentiality*) constituted this central point of reference; Aquinas appreciated the absolute uniqueness of *esse* in the order of actuality: for him, it constituted "the actuality of all actualities and the perfection of all perfections" in the metaphysical order.
6 On ideology, see J. Thornhill, *Sign and Promise,* pp. 4-6.
7 See W. Nicholls, *The Pelican Guide to Modern Theology,* vol. 1 (1969); J. Macquarrie, *Twentieth-Century Religious Thought* (London, 1971); A. Dondeyne, *Contemporary European Thought and Christian Faith* (Louvain, 1958).
8 See Lonergan, "The Origins of Christian Realism," *Theological Digest,* 20 (1972): 296-297.

9   See J. Coulson, *Newman and the Common Tradition*
     (Oxford, 1970); J. Thornhill, *Shadows and Images,* ed. by
     B.J.L. Cross (Melbourne, 1981), pp. 24-25.
10   As distinct from the two other established traditions, that of
     "behaviorism" and that deriving from the pioneering work of
     Sigmund Freud concerning the "unconscious."